JOURNEY TO JOBS
Techniques for Successful Recruitment and Retention

edited by

Maury Forman

*Washington State Department of Community,
Trade and Economic Development*

and

Audrey Taylor

Chabin Concepts, Inc.

Foreword by

Martha Choe

*Director
Washington State Department of Community,
Trade and Economic Development*

KENDALL/HUNT PUBLISHING COMPANY
4050 Westmark Drive   Dubuque, Iowa 52002

CONTENTS

FOREWORD v

PREFACE vii

ABOUT THE EDITORS xi

1 WORKING WITH A LOCATION CONSULTANT 1
   Kate McEnroe

2 COMMUNITY ASSESSMENT 9
   Audrey Taylor and *Fawn McLaughlin*

3 BUSINESS SITE DEVELOPMENT 40
   Leland F. Smith

4 TARGETING THE RIGHT AUDIENCE 53
   Dean Whittaker, CED, and *Maury Forman, Ph.D.*

5 EXISTING BUSINESS PROGRAMS 66
   Eric P. Canada

6 MARKETING TECHNIQUES 95
   Lindy Hoppough and *Roger Brooks*

7 DUE DILIGENCE 119
   David Wingate, CEcD

8 ECONOMIC IMPACT ANALYSIS 139
   Jim Mooney, CED

9 THE HOST COMMITTEE AND TEAM 153
   Jack Wimer

10 CLOSING THE DEAL 161
    Leslie Parks and *Jim Mooney, CED*

11 PROJECT REVIEW 173
    Rick L. Weddle

CHECKLISTS

✓ PROSPECT'S PROJECT 8

✓ COMMUNITY ASSESSMENT 20-39

✓ BUSINESS SITE DEVELOPMENT 52

✓ TARGET MARKETING 64-65

✓ EXECUTIVE CONTACT PLANNING 89-94

✓ MARKETING 110

✓ WEBSITE DESIGN 111-115

✓ WEB DATA 116-118

✓ DUE DILIGENCE 131-137

✓ DEAL OR DOG 138

✓ ECONOMIC IMPACT ANALYSIS 151

✓ EIA WORKSHEET 152

✓ TALENT IDENTIFICATION 160

✓ CLOSING THE DEAL 171-172

✓ PROJECT REVIEW QUESTIONNAIRE 183-184

<u>FOREWORD</u> — *The "Magic" of Economic Development*

Reading *Harry Potter and the Goblin of Fire* as a 40+-year-old, I have sometimes felt I should invent fictitious nephews and nieces so I can justify reading about Harry's adventures to other adults. But, I found there are plenty of us reading about Harry on airplanes, in city parks, and elsewhere. There must be something that captures us, young and old, about the magic incantations that might make someone disappear or something else explode.

In the minds of some people, economic development is a mystery that could easily be solved with a wave of the wand or the chant of a magic spell. Presto, chango, 1,000 jobs appear—instantaneously, where you want them and when you want them, all without lifting a finger.

This isn't a manual for a magic incantation, because that version of economic development just doesn't exist. *Journey to Jobs* takes the smoke, mirrors, and mystery away from what economic development is. This book is filled clear, proven, and practical advice from the best minds in the country who explain the various and challenging elements of growing an economy. They bring actual experience in siting a company or marketing a community and know that it takes time, research, skills, and a strategy. They tell us that this business of economic development is hard and sometimes tedious work. They tell us it's not magic but that it requires a long-term and informed commitment to knowing our own communities in the same way we know our own families—with all the good, the bad, and the ugly that comes with them.

Journey to Jobs is also about shaking us out of living in the good old days and what used to be. It used to be all the glamour and focus was on business recruitment—on landing the big one. But as we've learned over the years, sometimes painfully so, keeping and growing our own companies is the best formula for attracting new ones with the kinds of jobs we'd want our kids to angle for some day.

We used to be focused on what our neighboring states did, and we still are. However, now we know that the competition is no longer limited to just that neighboring state or one on the other coast. The competition is also Dublin, Singapore, or China. And the competition is fierce, unforgiving, and hungry. We can no longer rest on past successes or the luck of living in a beautiful place. Our success will be decided by whether or not we are smarter, better prepared, more strategic, and more persistent than our competitors. *Journey to Jobs* isn't the magic manual, but rather a road map to success on that journey.

When taking that journey, it is always good to have people with you that share a common goal. *Journey to Jobs* is an educational partnership between the Washington State Community, Trade and Economic Development and Bonneville Power Administration. I would like to express my sincere thanks to Bonneville for their continual interest in providing tools and resources for community success. They have been a wonderful partner, and we hope that this book will help communities achieve economic development with a lot of preparation and just a little magic.

Martha Choe
Director
Washington State Department of Community, Trade and Economic Development

PREFACE

If you are one of the diligent few who found your way to this page, I feel obligated to reward you with some profound nugget of wisdom that will make it worth your while. Something with the staying power of, say, "location, location, location," or, "If you build it they will come" or at the very least, an updated version of that timeless bit of advice offered to young Benjamin Braddock in *The Graduate*: "Bio-tech." However, economic development is not about cute phrases; it's about long, hard work on the part of the practitioners. Anyway, the economic development wisdom seems to stay around well beyond its useful time.

In these times you need to stay on top of your craft. *Journey to Jobs* is a complete revision of the earlier book, *Race to Recruit*, edited by Jim Mooney and myself. In the period that it took to write this book, we moved from a booming economy that made "available labor" the flavor of the month, to a battered economy that shifted the pitch to cost savings. By the time you read this, we will have likely moved on to yet another stage. But those are surface changes. You may need to hone your skills more sharply as the competition intensifies during an economic downturn, but peaks and valleys in the economic landscape don't change the underlying process of creating jobs.

Every chapter in this book focuses on specific activities that a practitioner needs to do in order to be successful in the journey to create high-quality jobs. All contributors to this book are either site selectors or economic development professionals, and their emphasis is on real-world solutions. Therefore, they not only provide you with a step-by-step look at how to create jobs by attracting a business, they also provide checklists at the end of each chapter to help you maintain the right course as you find your way in that real world.

That said, we have noticed some new trends in economic development that are independent from the shifting economy. Therefore, we have changed the focus away from some of the issues presented in *Race to Recruit*. For example, there is greater demand now for data—blame it on the Information Age. A few years ago, CUED and AEDC (now combined into the International Economic Development Council) settled on data standards guidelines identifying the data points most important to site selectors. Tools are available to compile and present this information more efficiently. Audrey Taylor, one of the most results-oriented consultants in the profession, along with Fawn McLaughlin, describe not only why data collecting is so important but also which data catches the attention of different industries. This may be tedious for many practitioners, but it is the primary way of getting on a short list.

Related to the quest for information is the increasing prominence of websites. Many site selectors use community websites as an essential source for initial information about a community. The inclusion of websites in the marketing mix should be a given, not an afterthought. Roger Brooks and Lindy Hoppough go into great detail about how to do a marketing plan and provide information on which tools work best, as well as how to create a website that emphasizes substance over style. This information, which is based on site selector input, will go a long way towards achieving a community's goal in being prepared.

There is less emphasis on incentives in *Journey to Jobs*. In *Race to Recruit*, a whole chapter was devoted to the subject. And while Kate McEnroe's chapter in *Race to Recruit* is considered a classic on the subject and incentives are still a part of the recruitment package, we don't believe they should drive the process. Instead, Jim Mooney writes a chapter on the importance of an economic impact analysis and then gives us a step-by-step example. This behind-the-scenes tool can help determine just how far to go with incentives and can save a community a great deal of time and money. Jim does an incredible job of explaining an EIA in simple terms and laying out how to undertake such a process so that a community can understand the impact of an economic development decision. Most consultants would charge thousands of dollars to provide this analysis for your community. By doing your homework on the true value of a company, you can more accurately gauge how much to offer—and justify this amount to skeptical public officials.

And finally, we have included a chapter on business retention. Note the shift in emphasis in the title of the book from *Race to Recruit* to *Journey to Jobs*. Ultimately, economic development is about *jobs,* and while it may be flashier to tout the location of a brand new company, the majority of new jobs will be created right in your own backyard. Consequently, one chapter in this book is an excellent comprehensive chapter devoted to business retention by Eric P. Canada, one of the gurus in the expansion and retention of jobs. You may ask what's a chapter like that doing in a book about recruitment? It's simple. Without business retention, you will have no business recruitment. Don't even bother reading the rest of the book because it will do you no good. Businesses want to feel a part of the community before they relocate as well as after they settle. Remember the first commandment of economic development: Thou shalt retain before thou shalt recruit.

That's it: the best we can offer in the way of sage observations about the changing world of economic development. For the truly useful information, we recommend turning to the eleven chapters prepared by our wonderful authors. And to those authors who were willing to reveal their trade secrets in this book for little more than a big thank you, what can we say but *THANK YOU.*

There is one other major change that has made this book an important and practical tool for practitioners. Audrey Taylor, president of Chabin Concepts, located in Chico, California, has been my co-editor in producing *Journey to Jobs.* Audrey has provided an incredible amount of knowledge and insight into this economic development manual. It has been said that she "probably knows more than anyone in the country about the nuts and bolts of economic development." I think few people who know her would dispute that. It is no surprise that she was the recent winner of the Golden Bear Award from the California Association for Local Economic Development (CALED) at their annual conference on April 4, 2002, in San Diego. Her attention to detail and her never-ending supply of checklists has improved the quality of this book for all practitioners.

In addition to the authors, there are a number of people who deserve a special mention for their support of our activities and the influence they have had on our work. First and most importantly are two people who allow me the time, opportunity, and resources to produce educational material for practitioners. Martha Choe, Director of the Washington State Department of Community, Trade and Economic Development (CTED), and Robin Pollard, Assistant Director for Economic Development, CTED, believe that educated practitioners are an essential part of the process. They recognize that economic development is not seasonal and continue to fight hard to provide the right tools for all communities in their quest to create jobs,whether they are urban or rural, rich or poor. What separates them from other administrators is their passion and vision. In today's economic development environment, it is not enough to be a skilled administrator or world-class manager. To be a true leader, we need the passion of our dreams and a vision of how to make them real. Washington state is fortunate to have these people who are able to fuse them into one powerful source for change.

Secondly is Jim Mooney, the co-editor/author of mine for two of the most popular books that we have produced, *Race to Recruit* and *Learning to Lead*. Though Jim was not able to co-edit *Journey to Jobs,* he played an essential role in reviewing and editing many of the chapters in this book. Jim's approach to economic development is very simple: It should create societal wealth. That means creating jobs, respecting the environment, and developing wealth-creating businesses that benefit the community. His economic impact analysis software is a practitioner-friendly tool that should be used by every community wanting to create societal wealth. Jim has been a mentor to me since I entered this field and deserves more attention than this book allows.

This book is an educational partnership between the Washington Department of Community Trade and Economic Development and the Bonneville Power Administration. Successful economic development requires a long-term commitment to the education of practitioners. These two agencies have a history of providing training and resources necessary to make sure that practitioners maintain professional standards and are kept abreast of state-of-the-art tools. Tom Von Muller, Economic Director for Bonneville, deserves a special mention for his work and constant support for rural communities so that they may compete equally and successfully in this competitive environment. The Northwest has become a better place to live because of his recognition that an educated practitioner is as important in economic development as a well-trained workforce or a well-maintained community infrastructure.

We all have mentors in this field, and Audrey has time and time again mentioned the incredible work done by Don Schjeldahl with the Austin Company. He has shared his wisdom gleaned from more than 20 years in corporate site selection; without his knowledge, this book would not have been as valuable to those people practicing economic development in the real world.

There are also a number of people who have provided technical support for this book. Without their assistance, our words would never make it to print. Therefore, our appreciation and thanks go to Sally Ledgerwood, Jack Wimer, and Jim Mooney as our readers; Cathy Swirlbul, our editor; Evelyn Roehl, for layout and design; Neal van Deventer and Jennifer Pirak, for computer assistance; and David Horsey, for his creative cover artwork.

Finally, let's appreciate the people out there who are actually doing economic development 60 or 80 hours a week to create jobs for their communities. Writing about economic development is easy when compared to the work done by these individuals.

Maury Forman
Director of Education and Training
Washington State Department of Community, Trade and Economic Development

ABOUT THE EDITORS

Maury Forman, Ph.D., is the Director of Education and Training for the Washington State Department of Community, Trade and Economic Development. He was the winner of the American Economic Development Council's Preston Award in 1998 for outstanding contributions in educational advancement, the U.S. Small Business Administration's 1998 Vision 2000 Award, and the ROI Research Institute Award for Innovation in Adult Education. He is a popular speaker across the country and known as an educator and humorist. Dr. Forman is the author and editor of numerous books on economic development, including *Race To Recruit, Learning to Lead, Washington Entrepreneurs Guide, Community Wisdom,* and *How to Create Jobs Now and Beyond 2000.*

Audrey Taylor has prepared marketing and industrial recruitment plans, strategic plans, and enterprise zone applications for more than 100 clients, ranging from small communities to the State of Oregon. She is president of Chabin Concepts, a private economic development consulting firm. She is the author of *So You Want to Make a Company's Short List, Huh?,* a data collection manual for economic development, published by Expansion Management. Her firm also produces DataFast and DataFast Online, a computer application for compiling and reporting community data.

CHAPTER 1

WORKING WITH A LOCATION CONSULTANT
Advice from a Site Selector

Kate McEnroe
Proprietor, Kate McEnroe Consulting

———— ◆ ————

Sometime during the process of creating a competitive community, targeting attractive companies, and creating effective marketing programs, most economic developers meet a site selector or location consultant. These intermediaries are hired by companies to advise them or to supplement their own staff.

Usually, receiving a call from a location consultant is good news, because it means that there is an opportunity to bring new jobs to the community. It can also be the start of a frustrating and confusing process, because consultants often work under conditions of confidentiality and use processes that are not always fully revealed to the community. This chapter will offer some insights into who these consultants are, what they do for the client, and how they work with and through economic developers.

DEFINITIONS

The following definitions describe the various individuals and organizations involved in the site-selection process:

Site-selection consultant, location consultant, and **intermediary**—Individuals and firms that are hired to represent companies in their site selections. The terms are used interchangeably in this chapter.

Economic development organization, development organization, and **developer**—The individuals and for-profit or not-for-profit companies that recruit new companies to an area. They may represent a state, region, county, municipality, or any other

geographic area, and interface with consultants.

Client—The company or corporation that hires a consultant to conduct site-selection projects.

Prospect—A company that may wish to locate a facility or expand its present facility in the community.

In most cases, a client chooses from a menu of services that location consultants offer, which can include:

- Helping to identify key criteria that should guide the location search
- Identifying a short list of candidates by evaluating all possible candidates against the key criteria
- Further researching the short list of candidates and providing a final recommendation
- Negotiating the real estate transaction
- Negotiating public incentives
- Organizing client tours
- Managing the construction process, and
- Managing staff relocation

CONSULTANTS

During the past ten years, the ranks of location consultants have expanded considerably, and the experience these companies bring to the profession has also changed.

Consultants vary according to their services and types. Some consultants serve corporate clients, others serve economic development clients, and some do both. Some consultants limit their practice to working only for entities that engage them in site selection and related projects. Others offer their services to economic development organizations in putting together organizations, strategic plans, and marketing programs, among other services, but do not do corporate site-selection projects. Several consultants serve a number of corporate clients, but also rely on that personal experience to help development organizations make their programs more effective.

Among the consultants who serve corporate clients, a few specialize in certain types of industries, projects, or geographic areas, or work exclusively for a single client, but most will work on a variety of projects through the world over the course of several years. Many of the most active consultants in North America are based in the United States, with major clusters in the New York area, Atlanta, Chicago, and Los Angeles. They fall into four major categories:

▶ *Location consulting companies,* which tend to derive most or all of their income from the site selection and economic development projects, or from allied services such as incentive negotiation or planning and managing personnel relocation. They tend to be compensated by clients on a fixed-fee basis, though some may offer clients the option of variable fees. Examples of this type of company are Moran Stahl and Boyer, Mullis and Associates, and Semradek and Associates. My company, Kate McEnroe Consulting, comes under this category as well.

▶ *Real estate companies,* especially those that specialize in tenant representation services, often have groups that offer site-selection services in addition to their expertise in the transaction itself. Many of these companies are compensated on the real estate transaction but may also receive a fixed consulting fee if no transaction ensues. These firms include Jones Lang LaSalle, Staubach, CB Richard Ellis, Arledge Power and Wadley-Donovan (a Grubb & Ellis company).

▶ *Accounting/consulting firms,* which also represent site-selection projects. While these companies all have hundreds of employees throughout the world, frequently the location-consulting practices are centered in a few cities. They too may work on a fixed fee or some type of more flexible compensation. These firms include Andersen Consulting, Deloitte Touche Fantus (the location consulting practice within Deloitte & Touche), KPMG's Business Incentive Practice, Pricewaterhouse-Coopers LLP, and Ernst & Young.

▶ *Construction/engineering firms,* which offer site-selection services either separate from or as part of a package of services that include design, construction, and project management. Fluor Daniel and Lockwood Green are two such firms.

The firms listed here are by no means the only ones that will approach economic development organizations requesting information for client projects. Unfortunately, there is no single source that tracks who is in the business, and there is ongoing change in the industry. No definitive list of consultants is commercially available. The best resource is the state or provincial economic development agency, which can provide lists of consultants active in or around a community. The most frequently attended conferences by the broadest range of consultants are IDRC/NACORE (recently merged as CoreNet Global).

The best resource for lists of consultants is the state or provincial economic development agency.

Although no fixed numbers are available, many state economic development agencies in the United States have found that approximately 30 percent of their prospects come to them through consultants. The remaining 70 percent are handled internally by company staff. Consultants may not represent the majority of projects, but they do represent multiple projects. If a consultant considers an area for a project and ultimately does not recommend it, there will be many other projects they handle that may be more suitable. Even a sole proprietor within the consulting industry may handle 30 or more projects per year. For better or worse, when an area builds a reputation within the consultant community, it spreads. Also, although the number of consultants is growing, it is still a relatively small group to target, and many consultants know one another, so news travels quickly.

HOW LOCATION CONSULTANTS WORK WITH CLIENTS

Despite all of these differences among consulting firms, when they contact economic developers they have one thing in common: they need specific information and they almost always need answers quickly.

In many cases, consultants will not reveal the name of their client company, and they are often required by clients to sign confidentiality agreements. While this is a source of frustration to developers, the clients have several reasons to prefer anonymity. In other situations, the project has a low profile because companies do not want competitors to be aware of their plans until they can control the timing of public announcements. They also often do not want to deal with the potential disruption of employees being distracted by speculating on what decisions are being made and how it may impact them. Even though many projects deal with expansion rather than relocation, employees sometimes take any news of this type of project as being potentially threatening to their own location. Finally, in many cases the corporate staff is simply not able or willing to deal with being inundated by economic developers once the word is out that they are looking for a new location.

There is some comfort in the fact, however, that if a company has hired a consultant, they likely are seriously considering the project, and that the consultant has enough confidence in the company to believe their fees will be paid. Even if an economic developer somehow uncovers the identity of the company, remember that companies request confidentiality and rarely reward a community for breaching it. Also, only about half of a consultant's clients are ready to announce an investment within 12 to 18 months.

The process of conducting a site-selection study is fairly standard, although each consulting organization customizes the methods of evaluation and data collection. Consultants can be called upon at any phase of the process, but a site-selection project typically has three phases before it reaches the final recommendation stage:

PHASE ONE: **Developing the Criteria**
PHASE TWO: **The Screening Process**
PHASE THREE: **Field Work**

PHASE ONE: DEVELOPING THE CRITERIA

The first phase starts by working with a client to determine what the key criteria are that will make the project successful. This part of the process can be very straightforward in cases where the client is simply looking for another location similar to those already in operation. In other cases, the issues may be more complex and may require the consultants to conduct a series of internal interviews in order to better define the project's scope and parameters. Less frequently, rather than setting criteria, the client may simply provide the consultant with an initial list of cities determined internally in some fashion, and the analysis focuses only on those areas.

PHASE TWO: THE SCREENING PROCESS

Once the criteria are set, the screening process involves measuring how well the entire universe of possible contenders satisfies those criteria. The initial list of possibilities is created by considering which areas—whether they are provinces, states or communities—minimally satisfy the least restrictive criteria. For example, the list may consist of all areas within a certain time zone or zones, may comprise all areas within two hours of an airport with international air service, or may include all areas free from nonattainment status.

The objectives of the screening analysis are to eliminate areas that fail to satisfy the criteria and to identify those that require the fewest compromises. One method is to create benchmarks for each of the major location criteria and eliminate areas that fail to meet one or more of those benchmarks. For example, a benchmark for labor supply may be a minimum population size, and a benchmark for labor cost may be an average wage less than a fixed amount. Then, in a second round of screening, those areas that remain are compared to one another, and only the best of the best are recommended for further analysis.

PHASE THREE: FIELD WORK

The third phase, also called field investigations, is the part of the analysis when consultants usually visit the community. The purpose of the field work is to verify secondary source information with primary research, usually by meeting with major employers, educators, and utility companies and by personally inspecting site and building options. At the conclusion of this phase, a recommendation of the best location is delivered, including an estimate of operating costs and an initial estimate of the value of incentives.

After completing these stages of the analysis comes all of the negotiation and implementation tasks that take place in the final one or two candidate locations. Some consultants refer to this state as part of Phase Two or Three, while others will define these tasks as Phase Four and/or Phase Five. When a consultant is involved, it is also at this point that the clients may visit the community.

HOW LOCATION CONSULTANTS WORK WITH THE ECONOMIC DEVELOPER

From the viewpoint of the economic developer, the process often appears far less structured. Depending on the level of internal resources the client has, the consultants can develop criteria and do a screening analysis without any contact being made with an economic developer. At the other end of the spectrum, some consultants submit extensive questionnaires to the community with a very short deadline for response. Most commonly, consultants use their internal resources and databases first, then check the state or provincial and community websites for information to complete their data gathering. At the end of the screening phase, they will e-mail or telephone the appropriate state or local development organization to get the remaining information required to make a recommendation of the short list. At that point, time is very short and responses are required immediately.

When a great deal of research has taken place before the development organization is contacted, consultants are usually interested only in exact facts or figures. Sometimes, however, economic developers inundate people with every piece of information available on the community, burying the answers to specific questions in an avalanche of paper, video, and on-screen material. Or they may misinterpret what issues are most critical to a project. If the first phone call or e-mail from a consultant asks questions about incentives, for example, that may be the only information that can't be found elsewhere—not the most important factor to a client.

The consultant's commitment to client confidentiality is often at odds with the developer's desire to understand who is looking at the community and what they are looking for. The consultant may or may not offer information about the client, but is usually able to answer the following questions, if asked:

❖ What general industry group is the project part of?
❖ How many employees would be hired by the project?
❖ What skill levels or job types would be required?
❖ How large will the site or building need to be?
❖ Does the client prefer to lease or buy?
❖ Does the timeline require an existing building, or is a build to suit possible?
❖ What are the general transportation requirements (i.e., rail, port, etc.)?
❖ What utility services are required?

On the other hand, there are data that economic developers may feel should be available from a client, but frequently are not:

• **Pay rates:** There are some cases in which a client has predetermined the wages offered regardless of the community that is chosen, but in most cases part of the consultant's responsibility is to determine what the competitive pay rates would be in any given community.

- **Utility usage:** Although the consultant usually knows what utilities are required, often the use rates aren't known at the time of the site search. This is especially common in manufacturing environments, because new plants often have new technology installed and are not cookie-cutter copies of other plants.

- **Project deadlines:** Consultants are very focused on the deadline for their own deliverables to their clients. They can also communicate what they have been told about the date that a plant or an office should open, but those dates are estimates that often slip as the project progresses. Deadlines also impact the existing building/build-to-suit issue. Many clients indicate they must have an existing building, but if the process eliminates areas that fail to satisfy their criteria, it may wind up extending the deadline to the point where building a new facility would have been possible.

The focus of the site-selection process is usually on finding reasons to eliminate an area, not on finding reasons to recommend it. (One exception can be projects for which the consultant is asked to simply evaluate a single community and highlight any red flags.) It is very important for economic developers to correct any misperceptions that community data or reputation may foster as part of a proactive marketing program, and to include these explanations in brochures and websites.

Some communities withhold data, thinking they can force prospects to contact their economic development organization directly. In this way, they feel they can better track prospects and can provide mitigating explanations for any information that would paint the community in a negative light. This strategy may be locally satisfying but is not very effective in the long run.

VISITS

During the field investigations when consultants are visiting the community, remember the most basic rule: Listen to the location consultant. Visits by consultants are usually frustratingly short, and economic developers may have to choose between meetings that are important to the consultant and meetings that are important for local considerations.

Remember who the client is. Depending on the project, consultants are likely to want to spend the majority of time meeting with employers, seeing sites and buildings, and perhaps attending a presentation and discussion of available incentives. Traveling throughout the community will help them gain a sense of the neighborhoods and their proximity to sites. Although a meeting with some public officials may be in order, particularly to discuss incentives, it is usually not wise to devote much time to meetings where the sole purpose is to have public officials express their interest in the project. Also, once prospects do visit the community, keep the amount of time spent in the office viewing presentations to a minimum. This type of activity could take place anywhere and should not take the place of experiences that people can have only in the community itself.

The focus of the site-selection process is on finding reasons to eliminate an area, not on finding reasons to recommend it.

A economic developer is ready for a consultant's visit if he or she can:

1. Recommend the most convenient way for them to travel to their community, even if it means using an airport outside the area.

2. Conduct site and building tours, since consultants rarely want to be handed off to real estate brokers. If the consultant is not a broker, meeting with one can create an obligation they don't want for their client.

3. Convince the human resource representatives of major employers to meet for 30 to 60 minutes to discuss their experiences in the labor market. The developer must be able to schedule four or five of these interviews within a week of being asked by the consultant.

4. Protect prospects from the local media.

5. Plan a tour by driving it ahead of time.

DEADLINES

Projects with consultants put a lot of pressure on economic developers to respond to requests for information and for visits. Often, the developer must wait patiently to learn the community's status among contenders. In the past 15 years, the typical deadline for a consultant to deliver a recommendation to a client has been cut in half. The first two phases of a project used to take up to three months each to complete, and now an entire project may have to be completed in as little as six to eight weeks. While there are exceptions, those deadlines represent the time that elapses between the consultant being hired and the delivery date of the consultant's report.

For the economic developer, deadlines are even shorter. Much of a consultant's preliminary work now involves using internal databases, third-party sources of information, and Internet resources, so calls to the state, province, or local communities often don't take place until these other resources are exhausted. The purpose of the first call is often to fill in the last pieces of information required before a screening report is delivered. Therefore, information requested by consultants must be readily available. Typically, a consultant will be looking for a response to a voice mail or e-mail

within one business day. If the call is to schedule a visit, it is also not unusual to have little notice.

Following this flurry of activity, there is often a frustrating lack of feedback or action, leading many economic developers to suspect that the deadlines were arbitrary and the project may not be serious. In fact, after consultants deliver their reports to the clients, an entirely new level of internal analysis can take place, comparing the proposed investment to other potential uses of corporate capital. In other cases, location searches take place as part of the planning process based on expectations of production-capacity requirements. Sales projections for either manufactured products or services often lead companies to conclude that their current facilities will not be able to keep up with demand. The location search takes place to provide an option that can be acted on quickly, but in some cases the need for the capacity is overestimated or will be delayed.

EXPENSES

Although many economic development organizations dedicate at least part of their marketing budgets to raising their visibility with consultants, the cost of actually working an individual project with a consultant is no higher than working with most corporate prospects. Most consultants are compensated on a fee-plus-expenses basis, although location consultants sometimes work on a fixed-fee basis for a defined scope of services, or on a time-and-materials basis up to an agreed upon maximum amount. States and communities rarely charge consultants for materials that may be sold to others, such as manufacturers' directories, and typically send requested material by express delivery at their own cost if it is not available on the Internet. Also, when a consultant visits a community, it is common for the local area to pick up the cost of meals and hotels.

FINAL THOUGHTS

Successful business recruitment depends on strong community development programs, effective marketing initiatives, and outstanding facilitation of the site-selection process. Consultants can be valuable but demanding customers, and lessons learned from working on projects with them can make a community more aware of its strengths and weaknesses and more competitive. Follow these tips to satisfy those customers and increase the chances of recruiting the projects they represent:

- *Respect the confidentiality* of the process. Remember, the company brought the consultant into the project.
- *Do the homework.* By the time the developer is contacted by a client, there is often little time to research local information.

- *Cooperate regionally* in providing information and arranging the logistics of visits. If the consultant is focusing on a metropolitan area, cooperate with other counties. If the focus is on the county, cooperate with other municipalities.
- *Use technology* to help track prospect activity, rather than forcing prospects to funnel through the community's tracking process.
- *Don't withhold important data* from the community's website or from other materials as a means of controlling the consultant's or company's process.
- *Follow up* at regular intervals, and notify a consultant of any major project announcements or legislative changes that occur during the course of the research for a given project.

About the Author . . .

Kate McEnroe Consulting is a nine-year-old sole proprietorship that focuses on site selection and economic development consulting. Ms. McEnroe was previously a vice president and principal with PHH Fantus (now part of Deloitte Touche), and worked on divestiture-related site-selection projects and in marketing and back office management positions for AT&T. Some of the practice's more notable corporate clients include Bertlesmann, Sprint, UnitedHealth Group, Anderson Financial, and RR Donnelley. In addition to this corporate site selection experience, Ms. McEnroe brings to assignments a network of contacts in economic development and human resources throughout North America. The practices economic development clients include the City of Nashville, the Southeastern North Carolina Regional Economic Development Commission, and the Ontario Ministry of Economic Development, Trade, and Tourism. She frequently leads seminars and delivers presentations to economic development, corporate, and real estate audiences on topics such as labor market analysis and incentives. She has written for *Site Selection* and *Expansion* magazines, the *Journal of Corporate Real Estate,* and the *Canadian Journal of Economic Development.* She was a contributing author in *Race to Recruit,* a learning guide for economic development practitioners, as well as the author of *Web Sites: the Economic Development Solutions Series.* Ms. McEnroe can be reached at *kmcenroe@mindspring.com.*

PROSPECT'S PROJECT CHECKLIST

PROJECT TITLE _____ PROJECT NUMBER _____

A community being considered for a new manufacturing plant, logistics facility, or office operation is expected to provide requested information to site location consultants and corporate managers. It is also reasonable for development officials to expect a project description from a prospect that will help guide data assembly. The consultant or corporation should provide the following information to the community:

Project Description—Functional description that would include description of distribution, manufacturing, research and development, headquarters, "office" operations (i.e., inbound/outbound calls, processing, billing, collections), etc.   ____

Project Schedule—Expected start-up date for the facility and expected date full employment will be reached.   ____

Workforce—Characteristics of workers to be hired locally including approximate number of full-time and part-time hourly and salaried workers and description of skill requirements.   ____

Transferred Employees—Number of workers/families to be transferred to the community.   ____

Operating Schedule—Facility operating schedule including hours/shifts per day and days per week.   ____

Local Purchases—Expectations with regard to the local purchase of raw materials and specialized business services.   ____

Inbound Transportation—Modes of transport used (e.g., air, water, contract hauler, commercial carriers, courier services), expected number and frequency of inbound shipments of raw materials.   ____

Outbound Transportation—Modes of transport used (e.g., air, water, contract hauler, commercial carriers, courier services), expected number and frequency of outbound shipments of finished products.   ____

Employee/Visitor Access—Expected vehicle movements for employees and visitors.   ____

Building Requirements—Proposed building size, configuration and dimensions.   ____

Site Requirements—Site size requirements including acreage needed for future expansion.   ____

Water Requirements—Estimated water use including gallons per day, maximum flow rates, water quality expectations, and seasonal variations in use.   ____

Wastewater Discharge—Estimated wastewater discharge, characteristics of effluent, and seasonal variation in discharge levels.   ____

Natural Gas Requirements—Annual and monthly natural gas requirements for process equipment and space heating; expectations regarding firm or interruptible supply.   ____

Telecommunication Requirements—Inbound or outbound calls.   ____

Investment Estimate—Expected value of land and building, machinery and equipment, and inventories.   ____

Environmental Impact—Expected air emission discharge and solid waste disposal requirement.   ____

The following information is often not known by the client or consultant in the early stages of the project and may evolve as the project goes forward:

Wages and Fringe Benefits—Expectations regarding wage and fringe benefits to be offered employees.   ____

Electric Power Requirements—Expected electric power demand (KW), consumption (KWh) per month, power factor, time of day and time of week use patterns, and preference relative to ownership of transformers.   ____

CHAPTER 2

COMMUNITY ASSESSMENT
Meeting the Expectations of Business

Audrey Taylor
President, Chabin Concepts

Fawn McLaughlin
Principal, FJMcLaughlin & Associates

——— ◆ ———

Think about it: Why do most communities initiate an economic development program? Often, it's because of a crisis or because they want to attract new businesses. But do they want to take the time to do their homework to ensure their investment in economic development will bring a return?

SUCCESSFUL BUSINESS ATTRACTION: THE FIRST STEP

The community assessment is the first step toward a community's planned economic growth. Communities entering the economic development game for the first time definitely need to conduct community assessments. But established economic development organizations should also do assessments every five years to chart the progress their community has made toward its vision.

In simple terms, a community assessment identifies what needs improvement in order to maintain the existing business and job base *and* determines what is needed to expand into new market opportunities to maintain a sustainable and healthy economy.

The community assessment helps a community evaluate its *preparedness* for economic growth. The assessment takes into account a community's key socioeconomic indicators (industry base, infrastructure, labor pool, education, leadership, etc.) to see how they are performing. For example, if a community wants to attract high-tech industries, the community assessment would determine if there are available research facilities, engineering talent pool, community amenities to attract the needed labor pool, professional management, etc. A community assessment can also be used to identify what might best fit with the community based on what it already has.

The community assessment has five purposes:

1. To assist in the compilation of data needed by prospects
2. To assist in defining the product and benefit to be used in a strategic positioning and marketing plan
3. To assist in identifying strengths, weaknesses, opportunities and threats for community action planning
4. To serve as a source document for compiling analytical data and research data needed for planning and marketing, and
5. To highlight the facts necessary to prepare competitive proposals for prospective clients

Before embarking on a community assessment, identify how the community's vision and economic development goals fit the bigger community and economic picture. This chapter assumes consensus of the community vision has been developed. Community leaders should determine where it should be in ten years and what goals—such as creating jobs, lowering the unemployment rate, or raising the average income—must be achieved to get there.

The questions a community assessment should answer include:

1. Is the community prepared to develop its economy?
2. What are the community's weaknesses?
3. Can those weaknesses be mitigated?
4. Will the weaknesses constrain the community from being successful in reaching its goals?
5. Are there hidden weaknesses?
6. How is the community's economy currently structured?
7. Does the community's economy have strong prospects for growth?
8. Are there opportunities that have not been addressed?
9. Are businesses in the community happy?
10. Are these businesses growing?
11. What kind of life cycles has the community experienced?
12. Is the community positioned to move into the new economy?
13. Can the community meet the needs of its businesses?
14. Is everyone working as a team?
15. What kind of labor force does the community have?
16. Is the community looking for new businesses?

COMMUNITY CHARACTERISTICS

Quality of Life	Human Resources	Economy
Housing Housing Affordability Standard of Living Recreational/Cultural Ease of Commute Low Crime Rate School System Environmental and Social Health Business-Friendly Healthy Community	Availability of High-Quality Labor Force Entry-level, Skilled, and Professional Employees Educational Opportunities Essential and Basic Skills Training Industry-Specific Skills Training Labor Relations Cost Effectiveness Underemployment/ Unemployment Educational Involvement— all levels	Diverse Economic Base Industry and Employment Mix Jobs and Population Growth Personal Per Capita Income Local Revenue Generation Real Estate Demand Market Accessibility Average Manufacturing Wage Economic Self-Sufficiency Economic Stability Business Competitiveness
Physical Environment	**Political Effectiveness**	**Public Finance**
Real Estate Demand Real Estate Availability Physical Infrastructure Energy, Sewer, and Water Telecommunications Transportation Natural Resources Environmental Protection	Leadership Business Attitude Community Identity Consistency and Stability Vision	Revenue Base Service Delivery Infrastructure Delivery Taxes Impact Fees Cost of Doing Business Business Incentives

---

A community assessment identifies a community's competitiveness within a regional, national, or international marketplace.

Information gathered from a community assessment is used to develop a strategic action plan for mitigating the community's weaknesses and capitalizing on its strengths. It is the foundation for *strategic* action plans and ultimately job creation and capital investment through expansion of existing business and recruitment of new businesses and industries. This is true for every economic development program's small business creation, existing business retention and expansion, business attraction and recruitment, and tourism.

An important reason to conduct a community assessment is to compile the information that national and international corporate executives and site-selection consultants need to evaluate your community as a potential location for a new facility. The site-selection game today is not just about being considered—it's about not being eliminated by the site selectors. Communities that do not have the right information available on their website or within a four-hour response time will be quickly dropped from a search process. While having the information available does not guarantee that your community will acquire a new facility, you will be armed with a more competitive tool than most communities.

The community assessment process is more than just a data collection exercise; it's a means to an end and can easily be presented to a board or council as something that must be done to meet the expectations of new business.

GUIDELINES FOR SUCCESSFUL COMMUNITY ASSESSMENT

1. Make assessment the first phase of your economic development strategic planning. It provides the information needed to successfully evaluate, define strengths, weaknesses, opportunities, and threats and to initiate strategic initiatives.

2. Form a strong, proactive leadership team to guide the assessment process. Assessing the community is a team effort, which includes local government, businesses, neighborhood and faith-based organizations, workforce development groups, educational institutions, and other key stakeholders.

3. Be inclusive. Invite all interested groups to the table.

4. Define the "Vision for the Future": *What would success look like?*

5. Start with clearly defined objectives, milestones, and timelines.

6. Define economic development goals and measure the assessment against your goals. Can you get there based on your assessment, or will other actions need to happen first? Economic development should always have a "reality check." Do you have the natural and human resources and physical infrastructure to actually be successful?

7. Focus on creating strategic initiatives that meet the needs of existing businesses with opportunity to create jobs and to take advantage of opportunities that will bring wealth to the community.

THE SIX TYPES OF ANALYSES

To perform a community assessment, you will need to conduct six analyses:

1. **Economic and Business Base**
2. **Product**
3. **Cost of Doing Business/Competitiveness**
4. **Quality of Life**
5. **Political Attitude and Business Service Delivery**
6. **Market Opportunity**

Each analysis includes a multitude of factors. For each analysis, you will collect data and assess your community's strengths, weaknesses, opportunities, and threats (SWOT), and its performance.

1 — Economic and Business Base

- Business/employment diversification
- Business and job growth trends
- Job growth potential of existing businesses
- Public revenue generation
- Location quotients
- Demographics—population, growth estimates, median age, population by age, median household income—defined by time and trend information

2 — Product

- Community image—what it looks like from an outsider's view
- Logistics analysis:
  - Regional, national, and international context
  - Proximity to a major metropolitan area
  - Distance to major markets
  - Transportation
- Workforce analysis:
  - Occupational availability
  - Starting and median wages for major manufacturing and office occupations
  - Skill sets
  - Labor force size (defined by time rather than geography, such as a 30-minute commute)
  - Labor force participation and unemployment rate histories, underemployment
  - Education—K-12 and secondary
  - Training and vocational education
- Real estate analysis:
  - History of development—central business district, office complexes, campus settings, industrial parks
  - New developments started and ready to start—current year; including housing developments
  - Planned developments—with timelines
  - Inventory of buildings for sales or lease—commercial, professional, industrial (include office buildings and retail or other spaces that may be appropriate for adaptive reuse).
  - Inventory of sites for sale or lease—commercial, professional, industrial
  - Capital improvements plan—recent expenditures and future expenditures in three years and five years.
- Infrastructure analysis:
  - Contacts who can discuss rates and availability of service
  - Electric power: provider(s), status of deregulation, typical rates, capacity, grids
  - Gas service: provider(s), status of deregulation, capacity, maps of lines
  - Water and sewer: provider(s), capacity, excess capacity, expansion plan
  - Telecommunications—local and long distance providers, cellular providers, long-distance points of presence, fiber availability, central-office switch locations, digital switching
  - Air and water quality

3 — Cost of Doing Business/ Competitiveness

- Sample proforma operating costs for different types of business operations
- Labor costs:
  - Unemployment insurance rate for new companies (i.e., X% for the first $X of payroll)
  - Workers' compensation rates
- Business amenities and support services
- Tax rates:
  - State personal and corporate income tax
  - City income tax, if any
  - Sales and use tax: state and local-option
  - Property tax, assessment ratios for major jurisdictions

- State telecommunications tax
- Local assessments and fees

4 — Quality of Life

- Education—public and private K-12 schools, test scores, teacher/student ratios, etc.
- Climate—typical temperatures, rainfall, snowfall, days of airport and school closure due to weather
- Crime—FBI statistics, if available
- Culture and recreation—golf courses, museums, theaters, etc.
- Cost of living
- Aesthetics—scenery, cleanliness, character

5 — Political Attitude and Business Service Delivery

- Support for economic development
- General attitude—business friendliness
- Regulatory environment
- Incentives—case examples, program criteria
- Business assistance programs:
  - Delivery system
  - Existing business evaluation of services
- Private programs

6 — Market Opportunity

- Attributes
- Business benefits
- Uniqueness
- Image

Remember, an assessment is useful only if it leads to a plan of action. Without action, the community will get frustrated, and the ability to recruit support will be difficult. Success will depend on public participation and involving citizens in the effort of economic development.

An assessment is useful only if it leads to a plan of action.

The checklist at the end of this chapter is a good place to start to assess your community's preparedness for economic growth. It includes questions within each of the six assessment areas and is a guide to the information needed by corporate real estate executives and site selection consultants to evaluate a community for a facility location.

ASSESSING FROM THE BUSINESS POINT OF VIEW

To help facilitate the assessment process, it is good to understand what different business sectors are looking for. The table on page 14 outlines the typical factors companies consider for site selection.

METHODS AND TECHNIQUES

Community leaders usually have a general idea of their problems and needs, but a community survey and assessment will help to better define the issues of development and growth opportunity. The methods and techniques you can use to identify your community's strengths and weaknesses include:

- Surveying businesses through written questionnaires or personal interviews
- Soliciting citizen groups about opportunities and barriers
- Creating focus groups with concerned and interested citizens
- Interviewing seniors who understand the history of the community
- Sending out a community questionnaire
- Conducting public hearings
- Involving the local media
- Using university research, and
- Conducting a third-party evaluation

All of these techniques will generate a host of ideas that can stimulate discussion about the strengths and weaknesses of your community.

The easiest approach is to appoint a steering committee, with members from public and private sectors, and a champion or co-champions who believe in the process. The champions will coordinate the various efforts and to ensure that everyone is on an agreed-upon schedule to keep the project on track.

All economic and community development entities should be involved in the process. Each analysis of the assessment could be assigned to a subcommittee that either performs the analysis or arranges for the analysis to be completed within a set timeframe and reported back to the steering committee. The members can use any of the techniques to perform their analysis and should recruit others to assist them. In their analysis process,

LOCATION REQUIREMENTS—A COMPARATIVE ANALYSIS

TYPE OF OPERATION	ACCESS TO MARKETS	FINANCIAL CAPITAL	INTELLECTUAL CAPITAL	INFRA-STRUCTURE	SUPPORT SERVICES	QUALITY OF LIFE
Research and Development	Critical—product life cycles getting shorter	Venture capital Angel investors Coffee bars Tax incentives	Depth of engineering talent Highly skilled workforce Coffee bars	High-speed data connection First-class offices	Incubators Special interest groups (SIGs) Research institutes Coffee bars	Recreation Urban lifestyle 24/7 work/live
High-tech Manufacturing	Transpor-tation is critical Time-to-market important	Less important	Workers must have technical skills—math and science Training support	Protected industrial parks Good telecom-munications and data connections Redundancy Favorable operating costs	Driven by Just-in-Time	Affordable housing Family-oriented
Call Centers/ Back Office	Depends if it is inbound or outbound center	Not important	Training im-portant Skills bars getting higher for hard and soft skills	High-speed data connections Low-cost office space	Computer systems support	Affordable housing and amenities
Corporate Headquarters	Major airport	Venture capital Financial institutions	Good-quality higher education, executive clubs, and other corporate headquarters	High-speed data commu-nications Class A office space	Legal, marketing, and advertising	Expensive homes, amenities
High-tech Suppliers/ Services	Need to be close to customers Transporta-tion access is critical	Less important	Productive, educated workforce	Properly zoned industrial parks with good infrastructure	Less important	Affordable housing

they need to do outreach to residents and business in the community. A fund should be available to each committee to help them complete their analysis. The economic and business base analysis should be completed by an entity with research capabilities; volunteers can only do so much.

DATA THAT DOES NOT LIE

The real challenge will be to analyze the information and determine what kinds of strategies you need to adopt. A good method to motivate people to act is to analyze your community trends and compare them to other communities or the state's average. Is your community doing better or worse than it was ten years ago? Consider—

Population—Has it grown or declined in the past five and ten years? What are the changes in age distribution, median age, average household size?

Financial Assistance—What were and are the unemployment rates, percentage of people in poverty, and number of persons on welfare programs?

Education—What were and are the enrollments, teacher-student ratios, SAT scores, educational attainment, and drop-out rates?

Economic Indicators—How has the economic base shifted by industry sector and occupation, retails sales, number of building permits, farm receipts, or municipal revenue?

Quality of Life—Have there been changes in median household income and family income, average wage earned per job, average manufacturing wage per job, median price of a home, median sales value of a home, and cost of living?

The results can uncover interesting facts about your community, which may be used to attract targeted industries and retain existing ones. The results might also reveal emerging industries or trends and barriers that have hindered your community's efforts to attract and retain businesses. Conducting an assessment may also lead to a collaboration among entities with common goals, such as workforce development and economic development.

TIPS FOR INITIATING A SUCCESSFUL COMMUNITY ASSESSMENT

1. There must be commitment from the local government to conduct an assessment. As a motivator, use the tactic of "Are we competitive?"
2. There must be champion(s) from the private sector to lead the process.
3. The economic development professional must be involved and engaged in the process.
4. Sell the process as preparation for new business, meeting the needs of corporate executives and site selectors.
5. Use existing issues as a catalyst to do assessment, i.e., does the existing issue have deeper root? Does it affect other issues in the community? If nothing is done, what would happen?
6. Appeal to the desires of residents to have their children and grandchildren have the ability to have a job in the community.
7. Involve students in the process.
8. Phase the analyses—they don't all have to be done at one time.
9. Spread the news via local newspapers, radio/television, and local organizations to generate enthusiasm and support.
10. Understand the motivations, interests, concerns, and commitment levels of the leadership group. Learn what each needs to see happen in order to feel satisfied with the time and energy they have invested in the process.

GOOD ASSESSMENTS TAKE TIME

The time it takes to complete a community assessment depends on the preparedness of the community, its size, and the commitment of leaders and volunteers. What will also be critical are your community service providers' expertise and knowledge of existing conditions in the community and their availability to participate. Generally, allow three to six months to complete the assessment. The table below shows a workable schedule for most assessments.

TIMELINE

ANALYSES	MONTH 1	MONTH 2	MONTH 3	MONTH 4	MONTH 5	MONTH 6
Economic and Business Base Analysis	▓					
Product Analysis Cost of Doing Business or Competitiveness Analysis	▓	▓	▓	▓		
Quality of Life Analysis			▓	▓	▓	
Political Attitude and Business Service Delivery Analysis				▓	▓	
Market Opportunity Analysis					▓	
Review and Prioritize						▓
Strategic Plan						Start Strategic Action Initiatives

FROM ANALYSIS TO ADOPTION

When all of the analyses are completed, the steering committee should meet to review each of the analyses to identify all the SWOTs. These should be prioritized based on your community's vision, and the economic goals can then be presented to the governing body for action.

In order for the assessment to be valuable, both the public and private sector must be part of the process. The assessment will include an evaluation of both private (land, building, financing) and public (sewer, water, safety) sector interests and infrastructure. These interests must be at the table to commit to change and investment once the assessment is completed. Both have a vested interest in the community. The public sector seeks ways to enhance its ability to provide and expand high-quality services to residents and businesses. The private sector is motivated by profit and improving local services. Understanding each other's needs is essential for coming together with strategic initiatives to address the SWOTs.

THE GOOD, THE BAD, AND THE UGLY
Following are examples of positive and negative findings that could come from an assessment:

Positive	Negative
+ Favorable cost profile	− Adults without high school education
+ Attractive labor market	− Average public education system
+ Permitting speed	− High workers' compensation
+ Surplus, reliable electric power	− Lack of commercial air service
+ Sophisticated telecommunications	− Confusing incentives
+ Impressive corporate roster	− Weak image

The community assessment will typically provide valuable information, which will be needed to:

- Select or narrow industry targets to diversify the economic base
- Identify infrastructure needs
- Identify demographic and business trends
- Determine the adequacy of real estate availability and cost
- Determine the adequacy of utility availability, reliability and cost
- Determine the adequacy of telecommunications
- Assess the tax and regulatory structure
- Assess labor, education and training programs, and
- Assess the community's quality of life

The community assessment will supply the data site selection consultants seek to evaluate communities. Make this data readily available to prepare customized packages for prospective new businesses and, if possible, put it on your community's website for easy access by prospects.

CERTIFICATION

Several states have developed a certification program with the goal of preserving existing employment, creating new employment opportunities, and developing a strong leadership base. The programs may vary to some extent, yet all of them require a community to complete an assessment and develop a strategic plan in order to be certified.

After a community is certified, the state or community can try to attract public attention and recognition. They can use the certification program as a marketing tool to site selectors and industries interested in relocating. Companies planning to move know they will have readily accessible information when working with a certified community, which will help them make an informed decision quickly.

Washington State's Office of Trade and Economic Development provides a template to its practitioners seeking certification. The template allows a community to collect hundreds of pieces of data that can be reviewed for decision-making and strategic planning.

OTHER STATE CERTIFICATION PROGRAMS

State	Program	Website
GEORGIA	Regional Economic Advancement and Development Initiative	*http://www.georgiareadi.org/*
IDAHO	Gem Communities	*http://www.idoc.state.id.us/ comdev/pdfs/GCI2001Handbook.pdf*
IOWA	Community Economic Preparedness Program	*http://www.state.ia.us/ided/crd/ consultants/industrial.html*
KENTUCKY	Certified Community Partnership Program	*http://www.kychamber.com/ issue_central/econ_dev/ccpp.htm*
OREGON	Community and Economic Development Readiness Assessment	*http://www.econ.state.or.us/ readintro.htm*
TENNESSEE	Three Star Program	*http://www.state.tn.us/ecd/3star.htm*
WEST VIRGINIA	Certified Development Community Program	*http://www.wvdo.org/index.cfm? main=/search*

ASSESSMENT EQUALS INVESTMENT

A community assessment is an investment rather than an expense. The community will pay far more by not conducting the assessment than the cost of doing the work. Using templates and guidebooks, a community can prepare its own assessment at relatively moderate costs. One of the most comprehensive guidebooks, *So You Want to Make a Company's Short List, Huh?*, was written by Audrey Taylor and published in conjunction with the American Economic Development Council (now the International Development Council).

For communities that want to conduct their own assessment, the primary expense may come in the time-consuming process of collecting the data. Since data interpretation is a skill, a community may also want to hire a professional to assist in the analysis. Many communities hire a consultant to conduct the entire assessment process at a cost that may range between $15,000 and $50,000, depending on the depth of information and size of the community.

AFTER THE ASSESSMENT IS COMPLETED

Once the community assessment and analysis are completed, use the data and information gathered to develop strategic initiatives for the community that:

- Promote economic growth to specific target audiences
- Capture opportunities
- Mitigate weaknesses, and
- Eliminate threats

With the completion of the community assessment, community leaders can make informed and intelligent decisions and investments based on facts.

For example, the assessment may show that the community has an attractive labor market: high skill levels, multiple training programs, a good educational system a fit for high-tech businesses. Assuming the other factors for high-tech businesses are also ready, the strategic initiative may be a recruitment plan.

Some strategic initiatives may be focused on correcting weaknesses. For example, the community could develop strategies to increase the community's sites and buildings, and to upgrade the skill level of the labor pool.

At a minimum, the assessment will reveal what businesses best fit in the short term and what strengths can be marketed to those businesses, whether existing or new. The marketing plan can be adjusted to begin taking advantage of those opportunities.

The next step is to prioritize the strategic initiatives (action steps for strengths and weaknesses) as part of the vision and economic goals. Then add timelines, funding commitments, and roles and responsibilities for action. These initiatives then become the strategic plan.

THE EXPERTS CONCLUDE . . .

Several years ago, the Site Selection Data Taskforce of the International Economic Development Council and the Economic Developers Association of Canada convened a panel of distinguished site-selection consultants, public sector/community representatives, utilities, and others to review the site-selection process. They concluded that communities that are prepared have a major advantage over those that are not. They defined preparation as "extensive data collection." They determined that the community assessment and data collection process accomplishes several things:

— It benchmarks existing economic development against neighbors and competitors
— It weighs the strengths and weaknesses of the economic environment
— It determines needed community improvements and the right mix of program strategies
— It provides the core information that site selectors are seeking for evaluation
— It shows that the community is prepared for growth, and
— It attracts repeat business by successfully meeting client needs.

If economic development means giving the customers what they want, communities would do well to start collecting data and information so that they start appearing on the short lists of businesses that are looking to relocate. Only then will preparation be another word for success.

About the Authors . . .

Audrey Taylor has prepared marketing and industrial recruitment plans, strategic plans, and enterprise zone applications for more than 100 clients, ranging from small communities to the State of Oregon. She is president of Chabin Concepts, a private economic development consulting firm. She is the author of *So You Want to Make a Company's Short List, Huh?*, a data collection manual for economic development, published by Expansion Management. Her firm also produces DataFast and DataFast Online, a computer application for compiling and reporting community data. Ms. Taylor can be reached at *chabininc@aol.com*.

As principal of FJMcLaughlin & Associates, **Fawn McLaughlin** has provided technical assistance, community assessments, and strategic planning to more than 40 communities. She also has extensive experience in workforce development, project evaluation, and grant writing. Prior to founding her company, she was program manager with the San Francisco EDC and executive director with the Stanislaus County Economic Development Corporation. She holds a master's degree in urban and regional planning. Ms. McLaughlin can be reached at *fjmclaughlin@attbi.com*.

COMMUNITY ASSESSMENT CHECKLIST

PROJECT TITLE _____ PROJECT NUMBER _____

A. ECONOMIC FOUNDATION —
ECONOMIC INDICATORS . . . .

ECONOMIC INDICATORS	1990	1998	2003	% Growth '90-'98
Population				
Region				
Labor Force				
Region				
Unemployed				
Underemployed				
Unemployment Rate				
Average Wage Per Job				
Average Manufacturing Wage				
Median Household Income				
Per Capita Income (1989)				
SAT Scores				
% of Degreed Graduates				
# of Persons in Poverty				
% of Population Below Poverty				

Describe Strengths: _____
_____
_____
_____
_____

Describe Weaknesses: _____
_____
_____
_____
_____

COMMUNITY ASSESSMENT CHECKLIST page 2 ✓

PROJECT TITLE _____ PROJECT NUMBER _____

NEW BUSINESS ACTIVITY ....

**Locations/Leads and
Inquiries in Past Year**   **Current Economic Activity**

Current Business Activity	Expansion	Locating From/ Lead From	Comments/What's Driving Activity?
Manufacturing			
Distribution			
Administrative Offices			
Information Services			
Business and Professional Services			
Agribusiness			

Describe Strengths: _____
_____
_____

Describe Weaknesses: _____
_____
_____

COMMUNITY ASSESSMENT CHECKLIST page 3 ✓

PROJECT TITLE _____   PROJECT NUMBER _____

BUSINESS ACTIVITY . . . .

Closures/Reductions in Employees
—Last 3 Years   Current Economic Activity

	# of Employees Laid Off	Comments/ What's Driving Declines/Closures?
Manufacturing		
Distribution		
Administrative Offices		
Information Services		
Business and Professional Services		
Agribusiness		

Describe Strengths: _____
_____
_____

Describe Weaknesses: _____
_____
_____

PROJECT TITLE _____   PROJECT NUMBER _____

BASE ECONOMY . . . .

Describe the base economy (e.g., lumber, agriculture, manufacturing): _____

List the top 5 businesses in each of the following categories:

BUSINESS	Inc. Date	SIC	Product	# of Employees	Locally-Owned/ Corp.
Manufacturers					
1.					
2.					
3.					
4.					
5.					
Suppliers					
1.					
2.					
3.					
4.					
5.					
Service Businesses					
1.					
2.					
3.					
4.					
5.					
Agribusiness					
1.					
2.					
3.					
4.					
5.					
Emerging Industries					
1.					
2.					
3.					
4.					
5.					

PROJECT TITLE _____   PROJECT NUMBER _____

BASE ECONOMY (continued) . . . .

List the top 5 businesses in each of the following categories:

BUSINESS	Inc. Date	SIC	Product	# of Employees	Locally-Owned/ Corp.
Highest Number of Employees					
1.					
2.					
3.					
4.					
5.					
Largest Revenue Contributors					
1.					
2.					
3.					
4.					
5.					
Regional Market Strengths (list)					
1.					
2.					
3.					
4.					
5.					

Crops (list)	Acreage	Production	Processed	Locally? (describe)
1.				
2.				
3.				
4.				
5.				

Describe Strengths: _____

_____

Describe Weaknesses: _____

_____

COMMUNITY ASSESSMENT CHECKLIST   page 6 ✓

PROJECT TITLE _____   PROJECT NUMBER _____

B. ADVANCED PHYSICAL INFRASTRUCTURE — PRODUCT (REAL ESTATE) ....

BUSINESS PARK/ SITE LOCATION	Zoning	Total Acres	Lot Sizes		Improvements			Line Sizes Sewer/Water	Distance From Highway	Rail Availability
			Min.	Max.	Raw	Semi	Full			

Total Zoned Industrial Land Available: _____.0 acres

Existing Tenants: _____

_____

☐ *Overall map with Business Park and sites identified available upon request.*

Describe Strengths: _____

_____

_____

Describe Weaknesses: _____

_____

_____

PROJECT TITLE _____　　PROJECT NUMBER _____

PRODUCT (REAL ESTATE) (continued) . . . .

Vacant Buildings

	Location	Sq. Ft/ Lot Size	Zoning	Listing Broker	Price	Former Use
Industrial:						
Commercial:						
Professional:						

PROJECT TITLE _____   PROJECT NUMBER _____

PRODUCT (REAL ESTATE) (continued) . . . .

Special Facilities:

Spec Buildings: _____

_____

Incubators: ☐ Yes   ☐ No   ☐ Future Plans _____

R & D Facilities: ☐ Yes   ☐ No   _____

Meeting and Training
Facilities: ☐ Yes   ☐ No   _____

Preapproved Building Plans ☐ Yes   ☐ No   _____

Amenities for Employees (at business centers—downtown, industrial or business parks, buildings):

_____

_____

Case Scenario: (City should create a typical project scenario to develop cost scenarios. Insert typical case here.)

_____

_____

Impact Fees: _____

_____

_____

Average Time to Permit: _____

Describe Strengths: _____

_____

_____

Describe Weaknesses: _____

_____

_____

PROJECT TITLE _____ PROJECT NUMBER _____

INFRASTRUCTURE ....

A. Water Supply
Server: _____
Total Capacity: _____
Current Peak Demand: _____
Available Capacity: _____
Additional Capacity: _____
Source of Water: _____

B. Sanitary Sewer/Treatment Plant
Server: _____
Area Served: _____
Age of Plant: _____
Total Capacity: _____
Current Peak Demand: _____
Available Capacity: _____

C. Utilities
Electric Supplier: _____
Gas Supplier: _____

D. Telecommunications
Local Providers: _____
Long Distance Providers: _____
ISDN (Digital Switching): _____
Fiber Optic Cabling to buildings and business parks: ___
Point of Presence (POP) Accessibility: _____
Alternate Routing/Disaster Recovery: _____
Power Protection System: _____
Video Conferencing: _____

E. Air Quality Control
☐ Attainment Area: _____
☐ Nonattainment Area: _____
☐ Describe: _____

Describe Strengths: _____
_____

Describe Weaknesses: _____

PROJECT TITLE _____   PROJECT NUMBER _____

TRANSPORTATION . . . .

Nearest Interstate (name): _____

Miles—Direction: _____

Other Major Highways: _____

Miles—Direction: _____

Nearest Rail Yard/Unloading: _____

Railroad Company: _____

Miles—Direction: _____

Shipping: UPS   FedEx   DHL   Other

   Drop Time Night: _____

   Delivery Morning: _____

Amenities:

   Child Care Facilities: _____

   _____

   _____

   Public Transportation: _____

   International Airport: _____   Distance: _____

   General Aviation: _____   Distance: _____

   _____   Distance: _____

   Other: _____

   _____

Physical Attraction of the Community for the First-Timer: _____

_____

_____

_____

Describe Strengths: _____

_____

Describe Weaknesses: _____

_____

PROJECT TITLE _____   PROJECT NUMBER _____

C. ADEQUACY OF FINANCIAL CAPITAL — BUSINESS ASSISTANCE ....

PROGRAMS

Financing	Adequate		Potential Actions
	Yes	No	
SBA 7A			
SBA 504			
Industrial Revenue Bonds			
Tax Increment Financing			
CDBG Loans			
Revolving Loan Fund			
Loan Guarantees			
Loan Subsidies			
Micro-Enterprise Loans			
Venture Capital			

Technical Assistance			
Export Assistance			
Technology			
Small Business Consulting			
Market Analysis			

Local Lenders (identify loan characteristics preferred by each lender):

Describe Strengths:_____

_____

Describe Weaknesses:_____

_____

PROJECT TITLE _____   PROJECT NUMBER _____

D. AVAILABILITY OF SKILLED WORKFORCE —
LABOR AVAILABILITY AND SKILLS ....

	CITY	1990	1998	SMSA	1990	1998
Total Employed Labor Force						
# of Persons Employed in: Manufacturing						
Wholesale/Retail Trade						
Services						

| | # CURRENTLY | AVAILABILITY RANK | | NEED TO | | |
OCCUPATIONS—RATINGS	EMPLOYED	EXCELLENT	GOOD	RECRUIT	WAGE RANGE	
Professional Manager						
Accountant						
Engineer						
Supervisor						
Computer Programmer						
Computer Operator						
Supervisor						
Skilled Manufacturing Worker						
Semiskilled Worker						
Unskilled Worker						
Client Services Rep.						
RANK AVAILABILITY OF 2ND LANGUAGE EMPLOYEES	EXCELLENT	GOOD	FAIR	POOR		

Educational Levels: _____% with 2-year degree _____% with 4-year degree

Local College Enrollment: _____ Location: _____

Describe Strengths: _____

_____

Describe Weaknesses: _____

_____

COMMUNITY ASSESSMENT CHECKLIST page 13 ✓

PROJECT TITLE _____   PROJECT NUMBER _____

E. INCENTIVES —
BUSINESS ASSISTANCE . . . .

PROGRAMS

Incentives	Description
Redevelopment Agency	
Development Incentives	
Land Write-Down	
Land or Building Donations or Sales	
Land or Building Leases	
Sales Tax Sharing	
Sales/Lease-Back Arrangements	
Public Investor Capital (shared equity position)	
Subsidies	
Fee Deferrals or Waivers	
Development Cost Financed	
Relocation Assistance	
Tax Abatement/Deferrals	
Enterprise Zone	

Describe Strengths: _____

_____

Describe Weaknesses: _____

_____

PROJECT TITLE _____   **PROJECT NUMBER** _____

F. ACCESS TO TECHNOLOGY —
EDUCATION/TRAINING ASSISTANCE ....

	# ENROLLED	LOCATION/DISTANCE	UNIQUE PROGRAMS
Universities			
Community Colleges			
Vocational/Technical Schools			
Training Programs			
Technology Centers			
High School Vocational Training			

Describe Strengths: _____

_____

Describe Weaknesses: _____

_____

PROJECT TITLE _____ PROJECT NUMBER _____

G. TAX AND REGULATORY ENVIRONMENT —
TAXES ....

TYPE OF TAX	RATE
Corporate Income Tax	
Franchise Tax Rate	
Unemployment Compensation Rate (maximum)	
Disability Compensation Rate	
Workers' Compensation Rate	
Personal Income Tax Rate (maximum)	

Sales & Use Tax:
    Machinery
    Inventory	

Real Property Tax	
Local Utility:	

Describe Strengths: _____

_____

Describe Weaknesses: _____

_____

PROJECT TITLE _____ PROJECT NUMBER _____

REGULATORY . . . .

	BASE/MEASUREMENT	AVERAGE RAGE	ADMINISTERING AGENCY
IMPACT FEES			
Water			
Sewer			
Traffic			
Drainage			
Public Facilities			
AIR QUALITY			
Attainment		Contact:	
Nonattainment			
PERMIT PROCESS REQUIREMENTS (please describe)			
Environmental Impact Reports			
Specific Plans			
Discretionary			
Average Time to Permit (assume 50,000 sq. ft. metal fabrication facility w/80 employees)			
Review Agencies			

Describe Strengths: _____

_____

Describe Weaknesses: _____

_____

PROJECT TITLE _____   PROJECT NUMBER _____

REGULATORY . . . .

Development Permit Process (please describe preapplication, entitlement, construction, and final occupancy):

_____
_____
_____
_____
_____
_____
_____
_____

Describe when EIRs or Specific Plans will be required: _____

_____
_____
_____
_____
_____

Permit Timing—based on project scenario, please provide average time to permit.
(Project Scenario: Metal fabrication facility, 80 employees, no major *water or disposal*.)

Permitted Use—Average time to permit: _____

_____
_____
_____

Conditional Use—Average time to permit: _____

_____
_____
_____

Zoning Change—Average time to permit: _____

_____
_____
_____

Please list all agencies reviewing applications: _____

_____
_____
_____
_____

PROJECT TITLE _____   PROJECT NUMBER _____

H. QUALITY OF LIFE —
QOL . . . .

CATEGORY	CITY	SMSA
Cost of Living Ranking Source: *Places Rated*		
Housing		
Single Family Home Sales (Yr.) Base: 3 bdrm, 2 bath, 2,000 sq. ft.		
New Home		
Resale		
Middle Management Residential		
New Home		
Resale		
2-Bedroom Apartment Rental		
Education		
K–12		
Number of Schools		
Pupil/Teacher Ratio		
SAT/ACT Scores		
Special Programs		
Continuing Education		
Universities		
Community Colleges		
Vocational and Technical Schools		

COMMUNITY ASSESSMENT CHECKLIST ✓

PROJECT TITLE _____   PROJECT NUMBER _____

QOL (continued) . . . .

CATEGORY	CITY	SMSA
Child Care		
Number of Facilities		
24-Hour Care Facilities		
Health Care		
Hospitals		
Local HMOs		
Outpatient Clinics		
Emergency Services		
Business-Oriented Services (wellness, industrial medicine)		
Hotels		
Name		
Number of Rooms		
Meeting Rooms		
Name		
Number of Rooms		
Meeting Rooms		
Name		
Number of Rooms		
Meeting Rooms		

COMMUNITY ASSESSMENT CHECKLIST

PROJECT TITLE _____   PROJECT NUMBER _____

QOL (continued) . . . .

CATEGORY	CITY	SMSA
Conference Facilities		
Name		
Maximum Floor Space		
Name		
Maximum Floor Space		
Name		
Maximum Floor Space		
Social and Cultural Amenities		
Sports and Recreation Amenities		
Public Safety		
Crime Rate		
Describe Source		
Climate		

CHAPTER 3

BUSINESS SITE DEVELOPMENT
The Community's Product

Leland F. Smith
President, Elesco, Ltd.

——— ◆ ———

Business site development is one of the most important factors for being prepared for business—it is the community's product. It includes a range of options, from planning and zoning tracts of land in advance of development to the construction of buildings for lease or sale. Site and facility development ensures that "shovel-ready" land and existing facilities will be available to prospective businesses and/or existing expanding businesses. In large cities and metropolitan areas, private-sector developers perform this function. In small communities, the economic development organization may function as the site developer.

Business site development:

- Is a major commitment
- Involves risk, and
- Should not be undertaken without assessing the probability of success.

This chapter provides tips for reducing risks while creating products that can be competitive.

HOW SITE DEVELOPMENT HELPS RECRUITING

When companies make a decision to locate to a new facility, they usually want to start operations as quickly as possible. Some may want to buy or lease existing buildings, while others want a new building constructed to their specifications. Most companies don't want to get into the land development business. They want ready-to-build (also referred to as "shovel-ready") sites that enable them to start construction as quickly as possible.

Communities that want to recruit businesses from outside the area or want local companies to expand must have suitable land and/or buildings available for these operations. If you offer better sites and buildings in better locations and at better prices than economic development professionals in other communities, you will increase the chances of winning a location decision by almost twofold.

> **CASE IN POINT—**
> A software company in a Western state was nurtured by a university incubator until it outgrew its start-up facility. The firm searched for a local site to construct its own building but found no suitable properties in the community. It ended up moving its business and 42 employees to another state.

GUIDELINES FOR SUCCESSFUL BUSINESS SITE DEVELOPMENT

Each business site development project is different and must be evaluated in terms of community needs and resources. The following guidelines generally apply to most projects, however, and can be adapted to specific situations.

A MULTIDISCIPLINARY ACTIVITY

Business site development requires the application of several disciplines:

Step	Discipline
1. Determine the need	*Market research*
2. Determine the demand	*Market analysis*
3. Identify a suitable site for development	*Real estate analysis*
4. Determine development capabilities	*Engineering*
5. Decide who will own/develop the site	*Organizational management*
6. Master plan the site	*Land planning*
7. Analyze financial feasibility	*Financial analysis and planning*
8. Arrange the financing	*Grant writing/negotiating skills*
9. Plan/prepare off-site infrastructure	*Utilities/road extensions*
10. Develop the site	*Construction contractors*
11. Market the site	*Marketing and sales*
12. Arrange for building construction and management	*Building contractors*

Several steps can be accomplished simultaneously, such as master planning the site at the same time off-site development issues are being addressed. Business site development should not be undertaken unless all of these disciplines are available and can be combined to make the project work.

Step 1:
DETERMINE THE NEED

A community must match its business site requirements with its economic development goals and market demand. For example, a goal of tourism enhancement may not require developing business sites. However, if the goals include recruiting or expanding industrial operations, some simple formulas can be used to determine the amount of land required.

THINGS TO WATCH FOR

Unsuccessful efforts to develop business sites usually fall prey to one or more of these deficiencies:

A mismatch between the site and the market.	The site may be in the wrong location or it may be the wrong product. If designed for high-value tenants, it may be too expensive for companies that want low-cost operating space. Conversion of older industrial sites may reveal inadequate infrastructure for the needs of modern businesses.
Inability to complete the process.	Communities sometimes zone raw land for business sites without providing the resources to complete the development, expecting to find tenant companies that will develop the site for them. This usually involves a lack of understanding of both the development process and the needs of businesses looking for new sites.
Insufficient financial staying power to make the process succeed.	Developing a business site requires substantial amounts of capital that may not produce financial returns for several months or years or ever, depending on the site development costs and purchase/ lease price comparable to competitive areas. Business site development must have adequate "patient" capital backed by a long-term commitment.

According to this formula, the five-year objective of creating 1,500 new light-industrial jobs can be accommodated on 77 acres of land with 28 percent coverage of the gross acreage. Not all businesses want to be in the same location, of course, so a better strategy would be to have smaller sites in several locations to meet this total requirement.

The types of businesses being recruited or expanded will determine the types and amounts of land and/or buildings required. Data show that the space-per-employee figures range from a high of 2,746 square feet per employee in warehousing districts to 347 square feet in general office buildings.

The Institute of Traffic Engineers shows employment densities per acre in eight different categories of use. The building square-footage-per-employee and building/site-coverage ratios are typical for new developments in major West Coast markets and will vary by

specific locations.

- Based on their average of 19.0 employees per acre for an industrial park, it would take about 79 acres to accommodate 1,500 workers.
- However, a business park with a density of 34.8 employees per acre would require only 43 acres.
- An office park with 55.9 employees per acre would require only 27 acres of land.
- The type of product targeted will determine the amount of land needed.

Step 2:
DETERMINE THE DEMAND

Setting target goals for a business site needs to be realistic in terms of what the market can support. One method to determine goals is to use business land absorption trends. Land absorption can be identified by tracking sales and lease activities with real estate brokers and title companies. Local planning agencies can also identify trends using building permits for industrial and commercial activities. A good source for overall trends by industry sectors is the annual data published by state employment agencies, especially changes in numbers of establishments. If trend data show there is a steady market for business sites in the community, then this information can be used to forecast future needs and provide a rationale for developing business sites that will meet those needs.

On the other hand, if business sites are being developed as an inducement to recruit unknown prospects to the community, then the types of companies targeted for the region

Type of Business	Building Square Feet per Employee	Building/site Coverage Ratio	Average Employees per Acre
General light industrial	1,000	40%	17.4
General heavy industrial	1,433	25%	7.6
Industrial park	688	30%	19.0
Manufacturing	758	35%	20.1
Warehousing and distribution	1,462	47%	14.0
Office park	327	42%	55.9
Research center	575	35%	26.5
Business park	476	38%	34.8

needs to be known along with their typical site/building requirements. A survey of state, provincial, or regional agencies will reveal patterns of what typical prospects are looking for in their area. The table below shows a survey conducted for a project in Northeast Oregon. The Oregon Economic and Community Development Department provided a list of the site requirements of prospects over a two-year period.

An essential part of determining the need is to take an inventory of what land and space is vacant and available. Vacated land or buildings could be redeveloped instead of developing new sites and facilities. These may include brownfield sites where redevelopment achieves an additional objective of remediating environmental contamination issues. The difference between need and existing inventory will be the net additional land and buildings required to meet the goals.

Step 3:
IDENTIFY A SUITABLE SITE

If the market demand review indicates there is opportunity for development of business sites, the next step is to select the optimum site. Too many communities promote a vacant piece of land that has marginal development potential. When selecting a business site, look for property that already has the appropriate planning and zoning designations (to avoid complications and delays) and other features that match the needs of the businesses selected as targets, such as proximity to highway.

Methods for identifying potential sites:

✓ Commercial real estate brokers and agents will know of land currently on the market.
✓ Planning and zoning maps will identify general locations.
✓ Specific parcels can be researched through county assessor's records.

OECDD-ASSISTED PROSPECTS FOR NORTHEAST OREGON							
INDUSTRY	LAND	REQUIRE EXISTING BUILDING	WATER	SEWER	RAIL	FREEWAY VISIBILITY/ ACCESS	AIR
RV Manufacturer	10 acres	No	Minimal	Minimal	No	Yes	No
Composite Trailer Manufacturer	5-10 acres	Yes	Yes	Yes	No	Yes	No
Call Center	No	Yes 10,000 sq. ft.	Minimal	Minimal	No	No	No
Food Processor	4-5 acres	Preferred	Yes	Yes	Yes	Yes	Yes
Call Center	Yes	Yes 20,000 sq. ft.	Yes	Yes	No	No	Yes
Fiberboard Manufacturer	40 acres	Yes	Yes	Yes	No	Yes	Yes
High Technology	30-50 acres	No	Yes	Yes	No	Yes	Yes
Food Processor	10-15 acres	No	Yes	Yes	No	Yes	No
Call Center	No	Yes 40,000 sq. ft.	Yes	Yes	No	No	Near

✓ Aerial photographs are a good source of information, often available from agencies such as the Natural Resources Conservation Service, the U.S. Army Corps of Engineers, the U.S. Forest Service, or the Bureau of Land Management.

✓ Railroads often have information about sites along their rights-of-way.

✓ Vacant land may be available at commercial or general aviation airports.

✓ Large corporations may have surplus land that could be developed into business sites.

If redevelopment of a former plant site is to be considered (brownfield sites), that site must be investigated for potential environmental problems that could require expensive remediation. A Level 1 environmental assessment will indicate whether the costs of remediation will make the site cost effective in comparison to a greenfield site (a site where a plant has not been located). Communities that develop business sites must evaluate properties the same way potential users would evaluate them and choose the best alternatives.

Step 4:
DETERMINE DEVELOPMENT CAPABILITIES

Development of a new business site usually requires off-site developments to extend or improve road access, drainage, water and sewer lines, electricity and gas, and communication lines. Municipalities, special districts, or private companies may be responsible for infrastructure improvements. In remote areas, the business park developer may have to provide water and sewer with wells and septic systems. An engineering firm will investigate

service capacities and requirements to extend these services to the site. Line sizes and capacities may be significantly greater for business park uses than for other municipal uses. The engineer will recommend solutions and quantify the costs. Permitting requirements will also be identified, especially for issues such as water rights and discharge permits. Utility easements and road right-of-ways may need to be negotiated with adjacent property owners.

Step 5:
DECIDE WHO WILL DEVELOP/OWN THE SITE

Developing a business park requires extensive technical knowledge and expertise. Decide early in the process how the various tasks will be organized and who will perform them. Typically at this point an engineer or planner is involved in the process, and he or she could prepare a Critical Path Chart or PERT Chart.

• A Critical Path Chart shows all the required steps sequentially and assigns target completion dates,
_OR_
• A Project Review and Evaluation Technique (PERT) allows the developer to keep apprised of the project's progress at all times.

(See example below.) Descriptions of these tools are available in libraries.

Some consulting engineers or land planners will act as project managers who will oversee the process from start to finish, leaving the economic development organization with the primary responsibilities for funding and marketing the project. It may be wise to hire an individual with development experience who can oversee the process.

Example — Critical Path Chart with PERT decision points:

▶ = Proceed to next step   • = Decision point to proceed or stop

Determine Site Needs	Identify Site and Option	Determine Off-Site Development Capabilities and Costs	Master Plan Site	Determine Development Costs	Financial Analysis	Develop Site

Site Developer

Decide who will acquire and own the site. Some communities develop business sites through a nonprofit or for-profit development organization organized for that purpose, redirecting all revenues from sales and leases back into new development. There are also advantages of public agencies owning and developing sites. They can often obtain grants or low-cost financing that are not available to private developers, even nonprofits. An industrial park in Colorado, developed by a nonprofit foundation created by a consortium of banks, had the advantage of being able to roll over the financing when revenues were insufficient to meet payment schedules. In Washington, the state's Constitution prohibits the lending of public credit. This effectively bars cities and counties from financing development of business sites for private industries, so port districts have become major developers of industrial sites. Ports of Tacoma, Longview, Vancouver, and others have industrial parks to support both water-side and inland business development. The Port of Moses Lake is the primary developer of business sites at the Grant County International Airport. In Oregon and Idaho, urban renewal districts often perform the industrial site development functions.

Step 6:
MASTER PLAN THE SITE

Master planning the site can be done at the same time the off-site development issues are addressed. The master plan will show:

- The site layout
- Individual lot sizes and locations
- The street grid
- Where the utility lines will go, and
- Where the connections will be made to off-site services and streets.

The master plan has two purposes:

1. It is used by the developer to guide the development process and will show prospective tenants what the full-use capability of the site is when it is built out. The market absorption projections developed earlier can be used to decide whether the site should be developed in phases instead of all at once.

TYPE OF ORGANIZATION	ADVANTAGES	DISADVANTAGES
PUBLIC	1. Access to lower costs of financing or general fund revenues. 2. May be able to bundle federal, state, and local funding. 3. Ability to manage the permitting and regulatory processes. 4. May have greater "staying power" because of lack of need to earn a profit. 5. Ability to assign support staff and allocate costs within the larger organization.	1. May have higher costs because of "prevailing wage" requirements. 2. Inability to "make deals" in private because of open meeting laws. 3. Competition for funding of other public needs. 4. Restrictions on selling land, such as at airports, making leases the only option. 5. Perception of being bureaucratic and subject to politics. 6. Competition with the private sector.
PRIVATE	1. Ability to negotiate and make deals with prospects. 2. Ability to provide confidentiality in negotiations. 3. Usually a dedicated effort, not part of a larger operation. 4. Focus on bottom line aims at efficiency and low costs. 5. May have greater access to equity capital and joint venture financing.	1. Costs of capital generally higher. 2. Return on investment factor increases prices of product. 3. Need to work through the permit and regulatory process from the outside.

2. It is filed with the local regulatory agencies to obtain permits and approvals. Final plan approval will require that the locations of all streets, curbs, sidewalks, and utility easements are shown, as well as any special restrictions, such as building setback lines. Final plan approval may also establish a set of conditions that the developer must meet in the construction of the project.

Drafting covenants, conditions, and restrictions (CC&Rs) should be part of the master planning process. CC&Rs describe allowable uses, lot coverage, landscaping requirements, and a wide range of other considerations designed to protect the integrity of the business site and its property values. These recorded documents are attached to a deed or lease agreement. The developer or a tenants' association enforces compliance.

The architectural firm or land planning company that creates the master plan will design it for the types of industries specified in the project goals. These may include mixed uses, such as light industrial, warehousing and distribution, multi-tenant flex space, and offices for research and development or information technology companies.

THE MASTER PLAN WILL ADDRESS:

→ **Off-street parking**

→ → **Traffic flows**

→ → → **Pedestrian patterns,** and

→ → → → **Common area amenities.**

Step 7:
ANALYZE FEASIBILITY

A standard development feasibility study usually begins with an all-cash analysis, showing the schedule of costs as determined by the engineering and planning analyses matched to the *pro forma* revenues. A simple model is shown below, based on the following assumptions:

1. Total size = 25 acres
2. Acquisition cost = $10,000 per acre
3. Costs of development = $10,000 per acre
4. Five acres developed and sold each year, with sales beginning in year two
5. Sales prices are $30,000 per acre

	Year 1	Year 2	Year 3	Year 4	Year 5	Year 6
Costs						
Site acquisition	$250,000	0	0	0	0	0
Development costs	$50,000	$50,000	$50,000	$50,000	$50,000	0
Total costs	$300,000	$50,000	$50,000	$50,000	$50,000	0
Revenues						
Sales	0	$150,000	$150,000	$150,000	$150,000	$150,000
Annual profit/loss	($300,000)	$100,000	$100,000	$100,000	$100,000	$150,000
Cumulative profit/loss	($300,000)	($200,000)	($100,000)	-0-	$100,000	$250,000

This highly simplified cash-flow schedule shows that there needs to be $300,000 worth of equity to buy the land and finance the first year's development costs. Negative cash flow needs to be carried to the fourth year, which is the break-even point. Cash flows are positive in years five and six.

Financing the land acquisition and development costs will change the model. In that case, the up-front costs are replaced by a debt-service amortization schedule. This will reduce the negative cash flows during the initial years, but it will also reduce the positive cash flows until the debt is fully amortized. In any case, this kind of model shows the gap between costs and revenues that needs to be financed either by debt or equity. Preferably, it will be covered by grants.

Step 8:
ARRANGE FINANCING

How the business site is purchased and the development is funded depends upon what kind of organizational structure is used.

- A private development company will usually form a limited partnership and syndicate the financing or borrow capital from insurance companies, pension funds, commercial banks, savings and loan institutions, or real estate investment trusts.

- A community economic development corporation may have access to lower-cost financing and subsidies in the form of grants and low-interest loans, especially for infrastructure development.

- The land may be donated, and some of the site development work may be performed with contributions of labor and materials from local utilities, public works departments, or local contractors supporting the site development program.

Step 9:
PLAN/PREPARE OFF-SITE INFRASTRUCTURE

The developer of a business site usually relies on municipal agencies to extend water, sewer, and roads to the site and often participates in the funding of those improvements. When the site is chosen, an investigation is made to determine that there is sufficient capacity in the municipal utility systems to serve the requirements of the project at full build-out. That investigation also considers the capacity and expansion requirements for road access, extensions of electric, gas and telephone lines, and any other special needs. The developer will need to work with the agencies or companies providing these infrastructure systems and ensure a development process that meets the requirements of the project as well as its time schedule. The developer's contribution to the costs will also need to be quantified so that those costs can be factored into the feasibility analysis.

Step 10:
DEVELOP THE SITE

With all of the predevelopment planning completed, the next step is to develop the site at least to a standard where it can be marketed to prospective tenants. This step requires several important decisions:

A. *Should the off-site infrastructure be constructed in advance of finding a tenant?*

CASE IN POINT—
A 327-acre industrial park in central Oregon is owned by the county, so no land acquisition costs are charged to the project. Development and marketing are contracted to a nonprofit organization, whose members include the local electric utility, several contractors, and construction suppliers. Funding is obtained from grants and low-cost loans, plus revenues from sales and leases that are reinvested in the project for additional development. Members of the organization contribute their labor and charge minimum rates for construction equipment and materials. This enables them to offer developed sites at below-market costs.

CHARACTERISTICS OF GOOD BUSINESS SITES

Checklists for site selection can be very detailed,
but the primary selection criteria are summarized as follows:

General Location Factors

1. A business environment that offers access to other firms that provide support products or services, facilitates business interaction, and minimizes potential conflicts with other land uses.
2. Accessible to the area's labor force—especially if companies are expected to draw from a regional labor pool. Companies usually prefer to be in the center of a labor pool rather than on the periphery.
3. On or near major highways with direct routes that avoid commercial traffic through residential areas. Some companies prefer an interstate highway interchange or a site within 5 minutes of one.
4. For some target industries, access to air, rail, or water transportation. Business sites at airports may offer advantages for firms that have requirements for frequent airline travel.
5. Industrial-grade utilities available to the site. Examining potential sites for the locations and capacities of water and sewer systems along with electric and gas services. Areas served by 10-inch or 12-inch water lines will have much more capacity for development than those served by 4-inch or 6-inch lines.
6. Access to municipal services, such as fire and police protection, without impediment by traffic or trains.
7. Development capability—companies usually want clean sites without constraints such as wetlands, flood plains, or easements.

Site-Specific Location Factors

1. Reasonably level land with not more than 5 degrees of slope, capable of being graded without undue expense.
2. Size and configuration that allows maximum site development and use.
3. Good soils throughout, without pockets of expandable clay or other soils that would affect construction.
4. Good drainage without upstream or downstream impacts.
5. Commercial highway frontage, preferably with multiple ingress and egress routes.
6. Environmentally clean or capable of remediation without excessive costs.
7. Minimum requirements for extension of off-site utilities and roads.
8. Appropriate zoning and regulatory processes in place or easily obtained.
9. Capable of being developed at reasonable costs.

The answer is usually "yes," in order to assure prospective tenants that the site is in a ready-to-build condition.

B. *Should the interior streets and on-site utilities be constructed prior to finding a tenant?* If the master plan provides flexibility to meet different tenants' needs, then it may be desirable to develop a first phase according to the master plan with the assurance that special needs can be met by shifting to undeveloped areas of the business site. This creates an opportunity to offer ready-to-build sites, as well as sites that can be custom designed to individual specifications.

C. *Who will develop the site, and how will it be done?* Usually, this process can be completed by using a consulting engineer to design the project specifications as part of a bid package and issuing a request for proposals (RFP). Every qualified contractor who bids will be required to perform according to the specifications. The low bidder may base the bid on greater efficiencies in the use of labor and equipment, lower prices and/or markups on materials, or the ability to cost-share with other projects in the same area. Overhead costs play a major role in bid estimates.

WHO IS INVOLVED IN THE PROCESS?

Business site development is a team process.
The professional disciplines required for successful development
and management of business sites include:

| + Property owners | + Land developers | + Building contractors | + Financial agencies |
| + Public and regulatory agencies | + Utilities, public or private | + Highway agencies | + Realtors |

As noted above, there may be opportunities to use donated labor and equipment for a bootstrap project. However, it is difficult to be competitive in recruiting companies if the business site is not professionally developed. The worst case is to ask the tenant to do the site development work.

Step 11:
MARKET THE SITE

The cash-flow analysis shown previously assumed that five acres of land would be sold each year. If this objective is not met, then the cash flow projections will also not be met. Marketing the site and generating revenue is essential to the success of the project. Marketing should begin while the site is being developed so that buyers are ready to close as soon as sites become available.

The most essential requirements in marketing are to:

1. Have control over the sale and deliverability of the property
2. Be able to offer the site at a firm price and terms, and to offer the ability to use the site according to the buyer's needs.

If the site has been developed to the needs of the market and is priced competitively, then the project has met the criteria for success.

The only thing left is to inform potential tenants about the business site. Economic development agencies usually promote their communities by advertising, direct mail, telemarketing, and trade shows. Brochures can be developed with pictures of the site and details of its services. These efforts can be effective, but they are often aimed at long-term results. Selling a business park requires short-term

sales. An effective strategy is to combine marketing and selling.

While business sites can be marketed through promotional media, plan to use the services of real estate agents and brokers to achieve sales, especially among local companies that are expanding. Real estate brokers tend to focus on local opportunities instead of relying on new companies moving into the area. The key to enlisting their support is to pay commissions on lot sales or leases. A commission of 5 percent is typical for land sales if it does not have to be split with a cooperating broker. In exchange, a real estate broker will not only promote the property in the local market, it will also negotiate terms and conditions, prepare the purchase and sale agreements, open escrow accounts with title companies, and monitor the process through closing. If any problems arise, the real estate broker is usually the one to negotiate solutions.

Step 12:
ARRANGE FOR
BUILDING CONSTRUCTION
AND MANAGEMENT

Developers gain a significant competitive advantage when they can offer build-to-suit construction for sale or leaseback to their tenants. This saves the tenant the time and expense of having to shift resources away from its primary business to manage the construction of the facilities. It is wise for the development agency to establish relationships with architects, contractors, and financial agencies in order to offer a construction package to qualified companies.

BUSINESS SITE DEVELOPMENT OPTIONS

Virtual Sites

For communities without the financial ability to develop business sites, an alternative may be to develop a "virtual" site. This is usually a master plan, often with architectural renderings of buildings, that shows all the details of a development plan but is not actually constructed. This technique is increasingly being used to create virtual buildings that have the appearance of already being constructed on the site. It is a ready-to-build business site, with all the details in place and all the decisions made to implement development as soon as a user is identified. It is marketed as if it actually exists, but with a provision that delivery is available within 180 days or whatever time frame is required for completion.

Pre-Permitting

Another effective way to develop and market a business site is to carry the process through to pre-permitting for construction of a tenant's building. This requires close cooperation with the regulatory agencies to complete all the work required for a building permit. The development agency plans a building, meets the permitting requirement for its construction, and obtains preliminary permit approval, but waits until a user is found before actually filing the permit application. Any user-defined changes are included in the final application. This moves beyond the popular one-stop permitting process by assuring that the permits will be readily available as soon as the application is filed.

Build-to-Suit Construction

Most companies do not want to be in the site development business, but many also do not want to be in the construction business. More than 85 percent of all new business locations are in leased facilities. The business site developer who can construct build-to-suit facilities for tenants, either for sale or lease, will have a substantial competitive advantage. This requires making arrangements with financing agencies or institutions, as well as qualified builders who would construct buildings for tenants that meet standard credit criteria and who are willing to enter into either a purchase agreement or a long-term lease.

After the business site is developed, implement a management strategy to maintain the site. A large, multi-tenant site may benefit from a tenants' association that assesses property owners in order to pay for maintenance of streets, common areas, signs, and other shared facilities. In a smaller business site, the developer may need to perform these functions. Many business parks appear unkempt because the developer did not plan ahead for the maintenance and management of the overall property.

HOW EXPENSIVE IS BUSINESS SITE DEVELOPMENT?

Costs for land vary by location and can range from free to many thousands of dollars per acre. In most smaller or rural communities that do not have private developers building product, experience has shown that undeveloped land can usually be found for less than $10,000 per acre (though some areas have indicated a higher range). However, development costs may actually be higher in smaller communities, especially if it is necessary to increase capacity for water and wastewater systems. Generally, the cost of land and development should not exceed two-thirds of the projected price of ready-to-build lots.

In the example used earlier, the combined cost of land and development was $20,000 per acre, while the price of the finished lots was $30,000 per acre. Plan to allow for the additional expenses of financing, marketing, and management. Operating on a thin margin is an easy way to get into financial trouble.

Generally, the cost of land and development should not exceed two-thirds of the projected price of ready-to-build lots.

TIME FOR COMPLETING
BUSINESS SITE DEVELOPMENT

The time it takes to complete site development varies by location and project size. In some locations, construction shuts down for several months during the winter because of frozen ground and snow cover. Types of soils will also affect the timing of development. Soft alluvial soil may allow utility lines to be installed with a trencher, while areas with hard rock may require excavating trenches with dynamite.

In general, a site can be developed, after purchase and analysis, over a period of eight months or less if all conditions are favorable. This includes:

- ✓ **The engineering analysis** . . . . 45 days or 1.5 months
- ✓ **Master planning** . . . . 30 days or 1.0 month
- ✓ **Bid processes** . . . . 15 days or 0.5 month (may be longer for public agencies)
- ✓ **Financing** . . . . 30 days or 1.0 month
- ✓ **Construction** . . . . 120 days or 4.0 months

FINAL THOUGHTS

Business site development is not easy and not without risk. Properly done, however, it can offer an economic development agency an important resource for recruiting new companies or retaining and expanding existing ones.

About the Author . . .

Leland F. Smith is President of Elesco, Ltd., an Oregon corporation that provides land use consulting and development services to public and private clients throughout the Pacific Northwest and western Canada. Elesco specializes in identifying revenue enhancement opportunities for underutilized or surplus real property assets and develops strategies for their implementation. Mr. Smith can be reached at *elesco@teleport.com.*

BUSINESS SITE DEVELOPMENT CHECKLIST ✓

PROJECT TITLE _____ PROJECT NUMBER _____

TASK	OPTIONS	ANALYSIS DONE	DECISIONS MADE	TASKS DONE
1. Decide on the type of site to be developed	a. Industrial sites vs. business park b. Developed sites for sale or lease. c. Buildings for lease d. Build-to-suit or turnkey construction			
2. Market analysis: For whom is the site being developed and what do they want?	a. Manufacturing, warehousing b. High-tech, research, engineering c. Industrial service center d. Office flex uses			
3. Determine size, location requirements	a. High amenity area or industrial district b. Transportation (rail, highway, air, water) c. Size based on market analysis			
4. Select site and hold it for evaluation	a. General location factors b. Site development capabilities c. Cost/availability			
5. Engineer and master plan site and off-site infrastructure	a. Off-site roads and utilities b. On-site development c. Net product			
6. Feasibility analysis	a. Acquisition costs b. Cash outflow from development c. Revenue stream from net product d. Pro forma feasibility analysis			
7. Financial structuring	a. Acquisition strategy, e.g., joint venture? b. Grants, equity, other non-debt c. Debt financing d. Sources and debt service schedules			
8. Regulatory issues	a. Regulatory issues and permits b. Zoning and CC&Rs c. Pre-permitting strategies			
9. Site development	a. Off-site infrastructure development b. Site development c. Construction packaging d. Leaseback and management strategies			
10. Marketing the site	a. Who are the likely buyers/lessees? b. What are the best ways to reach them? c. Develop marketing strategies d. Develop marketing materials e. Professional marketing support?			

CHAPTER 4

TARGETING THE RIGHT AUDIENCE
Fishing for Companies

Dean Whittaker, CED
President, Whittaker Associates, Inc.

Maury Forman, Ph.D.
Director of Education and Training
Washington State Department of Community, Trade and Economic Development

———— ◆ ————

Targeting is the process of identifying an audience that has a need and high probability of responding positively to the promotion of a region, community, neighborhood or other location. Successful businesses identify potential customers who will most likely buy their product or service, using many factors to target their market, such as gender, age, and annual income. In economic development terms, target marketing is a process by which an economic development organization focuses its time and money on those companies most likely to have needs that the community can fill and will respond to the marketing and recruitment efforts. This chapter will provide steps that will allow a community to target an industry that is right for them.

The purpose of targeting is to reduce the inefficiencies in the marketing process. By focusing your limited resources of time, talent, and money through a targeted marketing process, your organization will be more effective in maximizing its return on its investment. Additionally, your organization is more likely to achieve its goals.

STEPS IN THE TARGETING PROCESS

There are six steps to targeting:

1. Review results of community assessment and SWOT analysis.
2. Identify industries that reflect the community's assets and strengths and match its products.
3. Select desirable companies within feasible industries.
4. Find company data sources.
5. Compile database of best-fit companies.
6. Qualify leads and narrow the field.

Step One:
REVIEW RESULTS OF COMMUNITY ASSESSMENT AND SWOT ANALYSIS

The old saying that information is power is as true in economic development as it is with any other business. The right data is usually the basis of all location decisions, so collecting that data is important. The community assessment may seem like a senseless and thankless process. Conducting a strengths, weaknesses, opportunities, and threats (SWOT) analysis may cause conflicts, but that preliminary work is the basis of a strategic direction that will help create a focused plan.

As discussed in Chapter 2, the goal of the community assessment is to identify your community's assets and strengths—and its *products*. To determine what industries and companies are a good fit with your community, you must know what products your community has to market. At a minimum, to begin identifying targeted audiences, the assessment data must answer the following questions:

1. *Does your community have available work-force with specific skills?*

2. *Are there appropriate buildings and/or developed sites for build-to-suit options?*

3. *Does your community possess adequate utility infrastructure including water, sewer, electricity, and telecommunications?*

4. *Is there an adequate transportation system for movement of raw materials, finished products, customers/clients, and staff?*

Any other data collected will help you make a more informed decision as to who to target and what products are true benefits for the companies being targeted. The community assessment and the SWOT analysis will reveal:

► The industries that your community can support

► The industries that your community desires

The industries that meet these two criteria are the ones which your community has the best chance of recruiting to its area.

Step 2:
IDENTIFY INDUSTRIES THAT REFLECT THE COMMUNITY'S ASSETS AND STRENGTHS

All industries have basic requirements for facility expansion or new facility location. If the community does not have the products to meet the needs of an industry, it will never be considered, much less selected. The table below will give you some idea of the products, programs, and services that must be in place to attract different industry sectors to your community.

Using a matrix of basic requirements of different industry sectors, create the community's matrix of how well the area fits the needs of industry sectors. The weight given to each is somewhat subjective, but the relative ranking is what is important. The matrix is merely a tool to help think through the process of which industries are feasible based upon your community's resources. Remember, these are *basic* requirements of these industry sectors. There are many types of manufacturers who may have other requirements for them to operate efficiently and cost-effectively in the community.

ESSENTIAL RULES TO SUCCESS

Some people say that economic development is a game. Like most games, the industries with the highest scores of matching the resources and assets of the community are the ones on which a community should focus its efforts. Games also have rules and, like economic development, your community can score high if you understand the rules.

SECTOR	TYPE OF SITE/BUILDING	UTILITY NEEDS	TAXES	INCENTIVES	WORK-FORCE	OUTSIDE CONNECTIONS	TRANSPOR-TATION	FINANCE
Manufacturing	Usually single facility w/1000 sq.ft./emp.	Electricity, water, natural gas, telecommuni-	Large tax payer	Occasionally required	Mixed between high- and low-skilled	Many	Close to highway; easy access to airport	May take low-cost financing assistance
Distribution	Large site w/ easy access to major highways	Electricity, water, natural gas, telecommuni-	Medium level of tax revenue	Moderate requirement	Mostly low to moderate skill level	Usually few	Close to highway; often with rail	Often have their own financing capability
Back-Office	Centralized in labor market	May require excellent telecommu-nications	Personal property tax revenue often greater than real estate tax	Moderate requirement	Mostly low to moderate skill level	Many due to labor-intensive nature of busi-ness	Not a major factor	May take low-cost financing assistance
Research & Development	Natural setting/scenic view; business	Good telecommu-nications	Proportionate to size of facility	Frequently do not qualify	High-skilled with administra-	Often university or other educa-tional institutions	Air transpor-tation can be a factor	Often have their own financing

INDUSTRY SELECTION SAMPLE MATRIX
FEASIBILITY FACTORS: DOES IT FIT HERE?

TARGET INDUSTRY	WORKFORCE 1 — Low 2 — High	BUILDINGS 1 — Low 2 — High	INFRASTRUCTURE 1 — Low 2 — High	TRANSPORTATION 1 — Low 2 — High
Call Center	1	5	3	3
Headquarters	4	3	4	4
Manufacturing	4	4	5	5
Research	5	3	4	4
Technology	5	3	4	4

1. Objective self-assessment is critical to success.

Most community leaders feel that their community is the ideal place to be since they have chosen to be there. An outside observer can often draw attention to issues that go unnoticed by locals. An often sited example is the entrance to the community. Local residents become unaware of the appearance since they pass through it daily. A fresh perspective is needed. Take visiting relatives on a tour and ask them to comment on what they see.

2. Put time into building a consensus to determine which industries to target.

The temptation is to bypass this step through an autocratic decision-making process. The risk of this approach is that there will be a lack of focused energy, and perhaps divisiveness and counter-productive efforts. Also, if this rule is ignored, important commitment of resources of time, money, and people will be missing when they are most necessary. Consistent effort in the same direction is important to successful achievement of milestones.

3. Target industries that support the community's existing businesses.

Overlooking existing companies in pursuit of the new firm is a common mistake resulting in poor relationships with existing employers and an inability to have them serve as part of the host team. Recognize those existing industries in a strategic plan. They may be the community's best recruiting agents when a company comes to town.

4. Select appropriate industries based upon current and future resources.

This step is necessary in order not to squander efforts on industries for which the community is ill suited, although it may be politically expedient to do so. Again, an objective perspective may be helpful.

5. Identify the targeted industries first.

This approach quickly reduces the total number of companies from hundreds of thousands of potential companies to tens of thousands of targeted companies.

FISH FOR THE FISH THAT ARE BITING

The universe of prospects can be narrowed further by focusing efforts on industries that are compatible and feasible within an area and that exhibit the most activity in terms of expansion and new locations. While the order of industries has changed over the past five years, those in the top 10 have remained the same. (See table on next page.)

TIP: Many communities attempt to recruit the big fish. Yet 80 percent of companies have fewer than 20 employees. To reduce the ocean of potential targeted companies, identify small firms that have growth potential. It's better to have several goldfish in the community's pool than one shark.

PRO- JECTS	PRODUCT/SERVICE	NAICS CODE	SIC CODE	AVERAGE INVEST- MENT (millions)	AVERAGE EMPLOY- MENT	AVERAGE SQ. FT. (thousands)	# U.S. COMPA- NIES IN INDUSTRY	PERCENT OF PROJECTS OF TOTAL COMPANIES
778	Transportation Equipment	336	37	$27.7	134	108	20,945	3.7%
632	Professional, Scientific and Technical Services	541	738, 87	$15.4	205	92	912,086	0.1%
471	Plastics and Rubber Products	326	30	$6.3	64	84	22,282	2.1%
454	Chemical	325	28	$30.0	141	88	27,988	1.6%
431	Computer and Electronic Product	334	36	$81.8	262	150	36,672	1.2%
428	Fabricated Metal Product	332	34	$4.2	72	64	55,566	0.8%
424	Machinery	333	35	$6.3	107	69	93,858	0.5%
364	Food	311	20	$11.8	130	102	36,403	1.0%
355	Information and Data Processing	514	737	$19.6	246	95	213,023	0.2%
328	Broadcasting and Telecommunications	513	48	$27.2	277	98	86,177	0.4%

This approach also allows you to focus on companies within industries whose characteristics best fit the area's attributes and will help meet its economic development objectives. In other words, fish for the fish that are biting. Note that each industry is cyclical in its expansion and location activity. Knowing where the industry is in its cycle can help determine if it is becoming more active or less so.

The table above is an analysis of those industries that had the most announcements in 2000, the total number of companies within the industry, and total number of companies with 100 or more employees. The number of companies within each industry drops dramatically as the employment level rises.

Step Three:
SELECT DESIRABLE COMPANIES WITHIN FEASIBLE INDUSTRIES

The next step is identifying targeted companies within the selected industries. Screening those companies that fit the profile of the ideal company requires a well-defined sense of what the ideal candidate companies look like. Companies can be selected using many factors, perhaps the most obvious being size of sales and employment.

Out of the 10 million companies in the universe, which firms will relocate, expand, or consolidate in the next 12 to 18 months? This, obviously, is the key question. In order to answer that question, you must understand why companies relocate or expand.

A company expands or relocates for several reasons; the overriding influence, however, is that of *change*. Something has changed within the company or its business environment to cause it to need to relocate, expand, or consolidate. The following table shows examples of internal and external events that would impact a company's facility requirements. Understanding the impact that change has on the characteristics of these firms is vital.

TIP: Observing a company's environment can help you target companies that have a need to relocate or expand.

INTERNAL CHANGES

1. *Processes* (re-engineering)
2. *Products* (new products)
3. *Strategies* (competing in time)
4. *Demand for the company's products or services* (sales)
5. *Ownership* (sale, merger, or acquisition)
6. *Leadership* (new chief executive officer)

EXTERNAL EVENTS

1. *Industry trends* (outsourcing)
2. *Consumer trends* (recycling)
3. *Technology* (information management)
4. *Business trends* (market shifts)
5. *Government regulations* (environmental)
6. *Relationships with customers/suppliers* (just-in-time delivery)

EXTERNAL EVENTS:

INDUSTRY TRENDS

TECHNOLOGY

INTERNAL CHANGES:
Processes
Products
Strategies
Demand
Ownership
Leadership

CONSUMER TRENDS

CUSTOMER/SUPPLIER RELATIONSHIPS

GOVERNMENT REGULATIONS

DESIRABILITY FACTORS —
DO WE WANT IT HERE?

During the most recent years of economic expansion, communities have become more selective in the companies that they would like to have relocated to their area. Some communities have turned down companies that have wanted to relocate because they did not offer desirable factors. Communities have to ask themselves, "Do we want this company here?" In order to answer that, your community must make sure that the company has:

1. **Positive benefit/cost ratio:** Just as the company has to make sure that the cost of doing business will be financially satisfying, your community has to make sure that the benefits it offers will be a financial asset to your community. This is why an economic impact analysis is necessary before any commitment is made.

2. **Good-quality jobs:** Your community should not pursue just any jobs, but rather the right jobs.

3. **Company values that match with those of the community:** Community values are important. Your community's uniqueness should not be sacrificed for a company that may alter one of its strengths.

4. **Strong company leadership—both local and national/international:** Strong leaders put communities on the map. Other companies will often follow leaders, which will result in strengthening the local economy.

5. **Financial health:** Communities look for businesses that have a future in their community. A community that does not conduct a due diligence on a company that is relocating will suffer long after the company fails.

6. **A fit with the existing economic base:** Support of existing businesses should be the first priority for targeting companies. Assure existing firms that they will have an opportunity to help identify companies that will help them compete in the global economy, not in your own community.

7. **Community wage objectives:** Communities that have lost a major employer should look for industries and companies that pay comparable wages. Though this is not always possible, the goal is not to reduce the standard of living for the community. Knowing the average wage by industry can help guide you towards those firms more likely to help achieve this economic development wage objective, and it will further narrow the universe of possible companies to target.

Step Four:
FIND COMPANY DATA SOURCES

There are two types of information: **primary data,** which is collected directly through firsthand observation, such as a survey or an on-site visit; and **secondary data,** which is obtained through another party, such as a publishers of directories or online databases. Secondary data is usually less expensive than primary data because the cost of collection is shared by many users, but it may not be as current nor as focused as primary data. Other the other hand, primary data is often more costly and time-consuming to collect, but is likely to be more up to date and answers targeting questions.

Type of Data	Advantages	Disadvantages
PRIMARY	Timely Accurate Exclusive	Expensive to collect Time-consuming Focused
SECONDARY	Less expensive Readily available	Not as focused May not be current Nonexclusive

Using drive-by observation, aerial photography, and/or satellite images, you can determine operating capacity of a specific facility by checking the number of cars in the parking lot during one period compared to another point in time. Also, by estimating the square footage of the facility and number of employees, you can determine relative employee density and compare that to their industry norm to determine the degree to which new space is needed. Several websites now offer digital imagery at 3-meter resolution, and a more accurate system is coming online soon.

Also, by observing the facility, you can determine if it is feasible for a company to expand at the current location or if a new site would likely be needed.

Primary Sources:

Other methods for gathering primary information include focus groups and surveys. By interviewing industry leaders, trends as well as critical site-location factors can be determined. Telephone surveys can be used to quickly screen a large number of firms within a specific industry to determine the level of interest in relocating or expanding.

Referrals from existing companies and other community supporters are another primary source. People in the community have an enormous amount of information about business relocation. Many travel often in their work and meet hundreds of people in a year. Having a system in place to collect this valuable information and acknowledge those who provide it will encourage more leads. Some communities have an official reward system for leads resulting in locations or expansion. Others have a less formal system of recognition.

Secondary Sources:

CD-ROM Company Directories

A number of CD-ROM databases are now available. *iMarket* (recently acquired by Dun & Bradstreet) is one of the more useful, because it allows the user to filter information by a large number of variables and perform detailed analysis of targeted company lists. The final selections can be downloaded into a spreadsheet or prospect-tracking software. Financial details of publicly traded companies are available on Moody's CD-ROM, as well as on their website.

Internet Websites

One of the most useful search engines for researching company information is *www.*

google.com. This search engine has the ability to accurately determine the most relevant websites in response to an inquiry based on the number of links to a site.

Hoover's *www.hoovers.com* is also a useful site for company-specific data. It enables the user to obtain a list of company profiles that give a brief history of the firm, officers, detailed financial information, recent company news, and more. A list of the company's competitors is available, as are biographies of officers. Two levels of service are available: a free summary of companies, and a more in-depth company profile, available for $15 per month or $1,500 per year for multiple access corporate users. Hoover's continues to improve. Review the advanced-search features frequently to stay current—easily worth the $15 monthly fee.

Use *www.zapdata.com* to get a targeted list of companies. Companies can be selected based upon industry, size, type of ownership, geography (city, state, zipcode, telephone prefix), and other parameters. This service can quickly generate a downloadable list of targeted companies.

SOURCES OF COMPANY INFORMATION

DATA SOURCE	COST	CONTENT	COMMENTS
CD-ROMs			
iMarket	$600/year subscription	Dun & Bradstreet information	Useful for industry analysis; company data 6-12 months old
Moody's	$1,000/year	Limited to publicly traded companies	Financial screening tool.
Websites			
www.ceoexpress.com	Free	Directory of business links	Comprehensive guide to business-related websites
www.findarticles.com	Free	Periodicals	Key word search articles appearing in periodicals
www.google.com	Free	Internet search engine	Provides prioritized results
www.hoovers.com	$1,500/year	Large companies	Comprehensive company information in an easy-to-use format
www.Insitepro2.com	$800/month	Full-text articles searchable by event	Detailed company data
www.Onesource.com	$3,600/month	Multiple sources of detailed company information	Very comprehensive source of articles and related company information
www.whittakerassociates.com	Free	Directory of economic development–related websites	Economic development websites categorized by topic
www.wsj.com	$59/year	Electronic *Wall Street Journal*	Search archive for corporate events; news alert service
www.zapdata.com	$2.66/ company	Company profile	Data 6-12 months old; similar to *iMarket*

Monitoring corporate events is another important part of the targeted company database marketing work. *www.wsj.com* offers a great deal of information in its archive, and its online subscription *Who's News* section lists leadership changes. Some professional sales organizations use *www.findarticles.com* to research companies prior to sending a sales person to call on the leadership there.

Two relatively expensive Internet accessible resources are *www.Insitepro2.com* and *www.Onesource.com.* Both of these websites contain detailed company data and are available by subscription. *www.Insitepro2.com* contains full-text articles searchable by event. The fee for a single user is $800 per month. Onesource, an aggregator of company-specific data vendors, has a great deal of information at the international level. Onesource charges $3,600 per month per user.

A broader directory of web links for researching companies and industries can be found at *www.ceoexpress.com.* Also, *www.whittakerassociates.com* has links to search engines and various websites that are helpful to economic development activities.

Other sources to consider are local business journals, newspapers, and magazines covering the targeted geographic areas, as well as targeted industry journals and newsletters. Last but not least, obtain or review the annual reports of publicly traded companies.

Step Five:
COMPILE A DATABASE OF BEST-FIT COMPANIES

Creating a company target profile consists of selecting the industry, determining the minimum employment and sales, choosing the geographic area of focus, and any other factors that would help match the company characteristics to the strengths of the community.

Once the targeted-company profile has been constructed, the next step is to filter company data sources with this profile to select those companies that are a best fit. Depending on the source, the names of these targeted companies can be downloaded electronically or entered into a client-tracking program, such as Outlook, ACT, or Goldmine, or into a custom-designed database using Access software. Regardless of which client-management tool is selected, you should have a good method for tracking results and follow-up appointments with promising prospects.

You can use *www.zapdata.com* to select a group of companies to target by choosing the location, industry by Standard Industrial Classification (SIC), employment, and the sales size of the company. For example, by selecting zipcode 49422-4, SIC 3089, 50 or more employees, and sales of $50 million, you can review a list of firms that meet these conditions. Each profile will contain the company's address, telephone number, chief executive officer, product, sales, and employment.

By searching *www.hoovers.com,* a comprehensive company profile can be obtained that includes recent articles about the firm in addition to the standard contact information. Hoover's also offers a competitive analysis that lists the firm's major competitors.

CREATING A COMPANY TARGET PROFILE

Factors to consider:

- Sales range
- Employment range
- Privately held or publicly traded
- If publicly traded—market valuation,
  - 3- to 5-year earnings growth rate
  - earning per share
- Beta (volatility of stock price with market fluctuations)
- Sales growth range
- Employment growth range
- Geographic location
- Headquarters or branch/division
- Years at current location
- Recent change in leadership
- Recent change in ownership
- New product announcements
- Recent initial public offering
- Product market—local, regional, national, international
- Years at current location

Step Six:
QUALIFY LEADS

Once the database of prospect companies has been compiled, the process of further qualifying these leads begins. Again, the purpose is to carefully select those companies most likely to relocate or expand in the area and that fit the economic development organization's objectives.

Qualification of leads using a website has become another popular method of determining a company's level of interest. Your community should be able to understand its competitive position relative to other communities as it relates to the cost of operating a business. <www.opcost.com> by Whittaker Associates is a website geared to the needs of the chief financial officers of a company by providing them an opportunity to compare the cost of operating their business in one geographic location versus another. The following example shows the operating-cost comparison for a call center for Los Angeles, Portland, and Seattle. Knowing a company's competitive position relative to other communities as it relates to the cost of operating a business is important information to have for targeting.

A number of economic development organizations provide detailed site and building data as a method to attract prospective companies in their area. Comprehensive websites, such as <www.loopnet.com>, are fast becoming a portal for commercial and industrial property. Loopnet will provide lists of companies looking for specific types of property. Listing vacant buildings on Loopnet will provide a broad exposure to a large audience of potential users of these facilities. Loopnet sells access to the names and contacts of companies who have searched their website.

The table on page 62 provides a method for rating prospective companies in order to focus on those firms most likely to have a need that the community can meet.

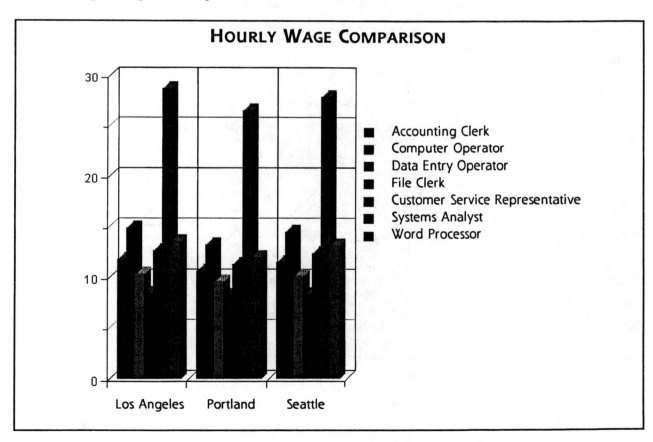

HOURLY WAGE COMPARISON

Legend:
- Accounting Clerk
- Computer Operator
- Data Entry Operator
- File Clerk
- Customer Service Representative
- Systems Analyst
- Word Processor

Los Angeles   Portland   Seattle

COMPANY SELECTION INDEX

Category	Criteria	Score
Is a Project being Considered?	• Not yet, but indications are good there will be	10
	• Yes, but not announced yet	8
	• Yes, just announced	7
Relationship with Prospect	• Have a champion at the CEO level	15
	• Have a relationship with CEO level or VP level	8
	• Unknown/Just Starting/Adversarial/No interest	3
Presence of Similar Companies	• Yes, same city or county	10
	• Yes, within 50 miles	7
	• No similar company now or in the past	3
Prospect's Perception of Area	• Admittedly partial to your area	10
	• Neutral/uninformed/never heard of it	5
	• Admittedly not interested	0
Raw Material and/or Labor Availability	• Yes, good match, slam dunk	10
	• We can make a reasonable case	5
	• It would be a stretch	Minus 5
Technology Match	• Our level of technology matches their needs	10
	• Near-match, or will match within 18 months	5
	• We don't have/can't get what they need	Minus 5
Infrastructure Match	• Close match on utilities, transportation, etc.	10
	• Near-match, not more than one problem area	5
	• No match, or missing more than two areas	Minus 5
Business Requirements	• Clear, defined business objectives understood	10
	• Vague requirements, or economic development organization doesn't know yet	3 / Minus 5
Level of Contact for Day-to-day Operations	• Executive sponsor in communication loop	10
	• Midmanagement sponsor assigned by top	8
	• Midmanagement acting on their own	5
	• Dealing with gatekeepers and nonleaders	Minus 10
Perception of Value of Place	• Demonstrable return on investment (ROI) in writing	10
	• ROI generally perceived but not in writing	5
	• No ROI or operating cost comparison	0
Understanding of Hot Buttons	• Understand needs and wants of key contacts	5
	• Understand some	2
	• None	0
Prospect Expectations	• Reasonable, businesslike	10
	• Overly aggressive, or slightly illogical	5
	• Questionable	Minus 10
Relocation/ Mobility Culture	• Aggressively seeking expansion/relocation benefits	10
	• Prospect thinks expansion/relocation might help	5
	• Prospect does not understand value	0
Quality of Life (QOL) Match	• Prospect has defined QOL needs you match	10
	• Prospect has vague QOL requirements	5
	• No match on QOL	0
Competition	• No competition yet	10
	• There is some competition, and it is localized	5
	• General media accounts of who's in the running	Minus 5

TOTAL SCORE: Below 100 = more work to do.   **150 pts.**
Below 75 = caution.   **max.**
Below 50 = drop.

FINAL RULES FOR SUCCESS

Targeting is an essential activity that requires a great deal of work prior to marketing your community. This chapter has provided some tools, tips, and ideas that will allow you to become more focused in the search using limited resources more effectively. Follow these guidelines for all activities to increase your chances of successful recruitment:

Communicate benefits. As this chapter has shown, companies move because it will benefit them first. They want to know, "What's in it for me?" The community's message must be concise and must list the advantages a company will receive by moving there. One of the most successful efforts consists of sending an introductory letter or other attention-getting device followed within a few days by a telephone call. Periodic contact with a simple postcard can be important to building and maintaining a relationship.

Follow up—be persistent but not a pest. Persistent and consistent effort leads to success. Many objectives are achieved when extra effort is put in. There is always a way — it is just a matter of being tenacious over a long enough period of time to achieve the desired outcome.

Maintain a clear vision. Having a clear vision is vital for focusing on those opportunities that will lead to the desired result stated in the business plan. Companies like to see a flexible, straightforward plan that has their mission complementing the community's mission. Staying focused and not getting lost in a sea of information along the way is difficult to do but rewarding.

Follow through. You must keep your word in order to build the trust necessary for a long-term mutually beneficial relationship.

Be patient—all things come to those who wait (but not too long). If it's too good to be true, it probably is. This statement applies to offers made by prospective companies soliciting community support in exchange for their commitment of jobs and tax base. Reasonable expectations are the rule. The objective is for both parties to achieve a mutually beneficial long-term relationship. Companies are able to relocate faster than ever before, but it still takes time.

So let's go fishing!

About the Authors . . .

Dean Whittaker, CED, is President and founder of Whittaker Associates, Inc., a business-to-business market research firm specializing in meeting the business intelligence and targeted-market information needs of economic development, commercial and industrial real estate firms, and corporate site-selection clients. Mr. Whittaker was formerly the managing director of the Illinois Office of Industrial Development. He served as the director of the Center for Entrepreneurial Resources and Applied Research at Ball State University and as director of the Indiana Economic Development Academy prior to forming Whittaker Associates, Inc. in 1987. He is a frequent lecturer, teacher, and author on the use of information technology in economic development. He can be reached at *dean.whittaker@whittakerassociates.com.*

Maury Forman, Ph.D., is the Director of Education and Training for the Washington State Department of Community, Trade and Economic Development. He was the winner of the American Economic Development Council's Preston Award in 1998 for outstanding contributions in educational advancement, the U.S. Small Business Administration's 1998 Vision 2000 Award, and the ROI Research Institute Award for Innovation in Adult Education. He is a popular speaker across the country and known as an educator and humorist. Dr. Forman is the author and editor of numerous books on economic development, including *Race To Recruit, Learning to Lead, Washington Entrepreneurs Guide, Community Wisdom,* and *How to Create Jobs Now and Beyond 2000.* He may be reached at *mauryf@cted.wa.gov.*

TARGET MARKETING CHECKLIST

PROJECT TITLE _____ PROJECT NUMBER _____

Community Assessment

List five major strengths that the community has to offer to prospective companies.

1. _____
2. _____
3. _____
4. _____
5. _____

What industries would benefit most from the community's strengths?

1. _____
2. _____
3. _____
4. _____
5. _____

List five challenges the community faces in attracting prospective firms.

1. _____
2. _____
3. _____
4. _____
5. _____

How can these challenges be overcome? _____

_____
_____
_____
_____
_____
_____
_____
_____
_____
_____

TARGET MARKETING CHECKLIST

PROJECT TITLE _____ PROJECT NUMBER _____

Industry Feasibility

Are the target industries feasible based upon the community's resources?

_____

_____

_____

_____

Industry	Work-force	Building or Site	Utilities	Transportation	Raw Material	Finance

Industry Desirability

Are the target industries desirable based upon the community's economic development objectives?

_____

_____

_____

_____

_____

Industry	Wage Scale	Training Opportunities	Long-Term Growth	Environmentally Conscious	Sound Management	Safety

CHAPTER 5

EXISTING BUSINESS PROGRAMS
Retention in a Recruitment World

Eric P. Canada
Partner, Blane, Canada, Ltd.

———— ◆ ————

Why include business retention in a book about business recruitment? Because . . .

Your community's best companies are a competitor's best prospects!

Dozens of other economic development organizations may be communicating with your community's best employers right now. If your community is not helping them achieve their dreams, they will turn to another community that they believe will. Your competitors regularly invite even small companies to consider leaving the community they are in and locating or expanding in the competitor's community.

In business, every satisfied client will tell one other potential client about a good service or product. On the other hand, every dissatisfied client will tell 10 to 15 potential clients about the poor service or product they received. The same holds true for a community. Business executives talk to colleagues within their company, outside suppliers, executives within their industry, and others within the community. No growth-oriented community can afford the risk of not knowing what employers think about doing business in the community.

Without an existing business program, business attraction is a high-risk proposition, and economic development opportunities <u>will</u> be lost.

WHY BUSINESS RETENTION IS IMPERATIVE

Business retention programs have emerged in an attempt to slow business defections and the negative impacts those defections have on a community's economy. Today, these programs have increased in importance as communities recognize that real job growth over time comes from the expansion of businesses already in the community.

Formal business retention programs provide a systematic approach to working with existing employers to:

- Identify problems that could cause employers to leave a community
- Identify opportunities to help companies expand their presence in the community
- Build relationships with individual employers

Historically, the typical business retention program involves a process of executive interviews or an employer survey. The process, well documented in economic development literature, has been around for years with little significant change. Most economic development professionals begin with "the process" in mind (see Figure 1). Focused on the "visit/survey" process, the steps fall into place, action unfolds, interview/survey forms roll in, results are tabulated, a report filled with pie charts, graphs, and quotes is prepared. The end is celebrated. Only then, at the end of the process, does it become painfully clear that no companies on the verge of pulling out of the community were identified.

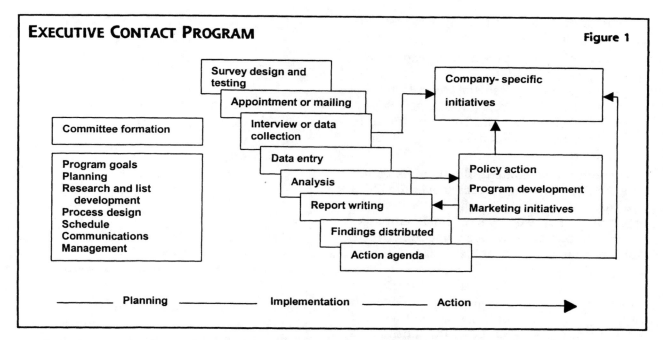

EXECUTIVE CONTACT PROGRAM   Figure 1

Survey design and testing

Appointment or mailing

Committee formation

Interview or data collection

Company- specific initiatives

Data entry

Program goals
Planning
Research and list
    development
Process design
Schedule
Communications
Management

Analysis

Policy action
Program development
Marketing initiatives

Report writing

Findings distributed

Action agenda

————— Planning ————————— Implementation ————————— Action —————▶

Community leaders also recognize the economic development organization's role in helping companies expand is limited to physical and emotional support and networking, which are valuable but seldom make deals. Also, little new information was gained from the superficial interview questions. Finally, pie charts and bar graphs don't help leaders understand what will drive the community's economy forward. Reports don't help leaders anticipate which companies will be the center of the community's economy in the future.

The approach recommended here views business retention as an element of a comprehensive existing business program. It encourages community leaders to engage in business retention and use contact with executives to build a meaningful existing business program around business development. This approach:

▶ Helps existing companies draw new sales dollars from outside the area
▶ Builds the economic base, adding new jobs and cash flow to support other business and government
▶ Supports the resource needs of existing businesses, rather than competing with their needs as business attraction can
▶ Creates a self-sufficient attitude within the community or region

EXISTING BUSINESS STRATEGY— A NEW FRAME OF REFERENCE

Movement away from the process-driven style of retention and expansion program begins with understanding what an existing program is and is not.

AN EXISTING BUSINESS PROGRAM

Is	*Is NOT*
• It *is* an executive contact program.	• It *is not* an R & E program.
• It *is* about gathering strategic intelligence about the companies that will drive the community's economic future.	• The purpose *is not* to save companies and help companies expand. That will be a by-product of the bigger picture.
• It *is* about the policies and programs that form the environment where existing companies thrive—the same environment any new investors must find compelling before they choose to invest in a community.	• It *is not* about existing companies.

The premise behind existing business programs is simple:

- New clients are hard (read "expensive") to get
- Increasing the value of current clients is where it is at (read "less expensive")
- New clients are drawn to communities that provide good service to existing clients.

In economic development, the "lifetime value" (the economic benefit generated over the life of the business) of even a small employer can be substantial. For example, a small employer with 15 employees (average wage $13.75) will put an annual payroll of $430,000 into the community every year. That same employer will pay property taxes and contribute to various charitable and community initiatives as shown. The direct financial benefit of that single employer is $490,000. If that business is in the community ten years, it will pump a total of more than $4.9 million (direct dollars, no estimated increases, no growth, no multiplier) into the community. In 20 years, that business will pump in excess of $9.8 million into the community. Give that same company modest growth (5 percent) that allows for pay increases, and the direct contribution to the community balloons to over $16.2 million in 20 years.

Yet, as with any annuity, an existing business is easily taken for granted.

Is it possible to make a business retention program pay the same kind of dividends as a successful business attraction program?

Yes! It is all perception management. How the economic development practitioner manages the perception of a community's business and political leadership will determine how the existing business program is viewed. Most business retention programs are built on the "business service model" in which the economic development organization is there to respond to the needs of a specific company related to doing business in the community.

The most advanced existing business programs, however, are built on a "portfolio management model." In this model, the first objective is to gain a deeper understanding of each company to determine how it will fit in

---

**LIFETIME VALUE
OF A SMALL EMPLOYER**
15 employees
⇓
$430,000 payroll
$ 45,000 property tax
$ 15,000 charitable contributions
$490,000 annual
⇓
$4.9 million over 10 years
⇓
*$9.8 million (20 yr.)
Lifetime Value*

---

the community's economic future. The company's needs are not ignored. The top priority is to prepare to actively manage the community's economic portfolio. To do this requires information similar to that which an investor would look at to evaluate the investment potential of a company's stock value, information that will allow the user to evaluate every company on five critical factors:

- Value to the community
- Growth potential
- Technological adaptation and leadership
- Risk of downsizing and/or leaving
- Satisfaction with the community

This information goes beyond the typical investigation of community problems and business concerns needed to provide direct services.

BUILDING THE ULTIMATE EXISTING BUSINESS PROGRAM

Business retention/expansion is seen by many as equivalent to an existing business program. This is not the case. There are four elements to a comprehensive existing business program. Business retention and expansion is only one of these elements. Each element is associated with a progressively higher level of commitment of time and money, as shown in Figure 2. The reward in each case is commensurate with the investment.

- *Responsive Retention*
  - Respond to the problems/needs of individual companies.
- *Attention Retention*
  - Create opportunities to shower attention on existing employers.
- *Executive Contact*
  - Conduct personal interviews or surveys to identify company and community issues.
  - Collect company-specific strategic information.

- *Business Development*
  - Provide support and services to help individual and groups of companies increase sales and grow.

Each of the components is important to the long-term vitality of the community's economy. Any of the elements can be undertaken independently, but collectively, they contribute to a growing community with an entrepreneurial spirit that is attractive to new employers.

RESPONSIVE RETENTION

Responsive retention is being available to provide support and assistance when the company calls. Every economic development organization will respond to the needs of their business executives. However, not all organizations have the same level of expertise to solve problems or the network of contacts to tap into resources provided by the state, utilities, and others.

Responsive retention is the lowest possible commitment. It requires no office, no staff, no program, or any official activity. The only requirement for responsive retention is a contact person who is willing to listen and provide support. The contact could be a volunteer, a public official, a staff member, or anyone with a telephone number, a sympathetic ear and a desire to serve.

The supplement to a successful responsive retention approach is a passive network— people in the community who interact with business executives and know who to call when a company needs help. The people involved in a passive network include the individuals shown in Figure 2A.

Benefits of responsive retention approach are company-specific. However, there can be powerful media opportunities for the company and the organization when assistance is delivered with positive results.

EXISTING BUSINESS ELEMENTS   Figure 2

Business Development

Executive Contact

Attention Retention

Responsive Retention

Level of Benefit

Level of Effort

Figure 2A
PASSIVE NETWORK CONTACTS

- **Accountants**
- **Bankers**
- **Business associations**
- **Business executives**
- **City/county officials**
- **Lawyers**
- **Real estate brokers**
- **Utility representatives**

ATTENTION RETENTION

The next step up on the ladder of existing business programs is attention retention, which provides recognition to executives and companies in the community. Recognition can come in many forms. For example, the states of Kansas, Oklahoma, and Virginia each have industry week programs that focus on the importance of existing companies in their states. Press releases, a governor's breakfast, 100- or 50-year certificates, and other recognition devices are used to spotlight existing employers. Each state also encourages community-based organizations to sponsor special events to recognize and honor area companies during industry week.

RECOGNITION METHODS　　　　**Figure 2B**

- Awards, e.g., years in business
- Ambassadors to attend ribbon cuttings or other official business events
- Industry appreciation week
- Industry of the week/month
- Business appreciation breakfast
- Newsletter recognition
- Media coverage
- Recognition in front of peers

At the regional level, the Partnership of Southeast Texas circulates a monthly newsletter to area companies called *Bragin' Rights*. It highlights area company success stories. The Partnership also moves its existing business committee meetings from company to company. The privilege of hosting a committee meeting brings additional recognition with peers in the community.

Attention retention stimulates goodwill, increases awareness of the businesses in the community and helps build relationships with business executives. Beyond this, the practice has little value for actually encouraging companies to stay or expand in a community. In fact, there is a higher value for the organization than for the business community through the visibility created for the organization.

Attention retention only requires a slightly higher level of commitment than a responsive retention approach. Yet, it requires an ongoing commitment. A single award or recognition event has little impact. Only through repetition is the value of a recognition program established.

EXECUTIVE CONTACT
(Business Retention and Expansion)

The days of being paid to wait for the phone to ring from an executive asking for help are long past. Not many boards are willing to sponsor a staff person to "stand by" just in case an area company calls for help or bounce from meeting to meeting.

Boards and political leadership want to see action. Business attraction is viewed positively by boards and political leaders because it is proactive. It is a symbol of the organization taking charge of the community's economic destiny. Regardless of the odds for success, the emphasis is on action. To win real respect, existing business programs must foster the same action orientation. The structure of a typical business retention program is shown in Figure 1. Many choices must be made in planning an executive contact program. The checklist found at the end of this chapter lists options to consider when planning the executive contact program.

Contact Form

The first assumption in planning a retention and expansion program is that executive contact means a personal visit. While that is often the case, it is not the only option. Executive contact can include: personal interviews, a telephone interview, a mail survey, events, or focus groups. For example, Green Bay, Wisconsin, used focus-group sessions with executives to explore their primary business clusters. Northbrook, Illinois, used a telephone survey to reach 83 percent of the targeted companies within three weeks. The Galesburg Regional Economic Development Council in Illinois used a mail survey in combination with personal visits to extend their reach to protect volunteer time for large employers. These firms received a mail survey. If answers trip a warning signal, the company may receive a call or a personal visit.

Each of the four forms of contact has advantages and disadvantages. The outcome of an event or focus group is dependent on who shows up, how talkative they are, and the skills of the facilitator. Also, a focus session involves only a small percentage of the full body they represent. Findings can, therefore, be misleading. A mail survey can reach a large number quickly but is impersonal. Response rates tend to be low, but respondents tend to be less critical. Answers to open-ended questions are often sketchy. A telephone survey is quick and efficient but lacks the personal contact of a visit. Open-ended questions can be explored with follow-up questions as needed. A personal visit is difficult to coordinate and time consuming, but provides an opportunity to begin a personal relationship. Open-ended questions can be explored as needed.

Partnering

An executive contact program can be undertaken in partnership with other groups. For example, the North Dakota Department of Development & Finance, Small Business Development Council, and the Manufacturing Extension Program all collaborate on existing business calls. Each contributes manpower to make the calls. Each of the partners gains information important to their individual programs.

> ### CONTACT OPTIONS
>
> - Events/ focus groups
> - Mail
> - Phone interview
> - Personal visit

> ### POTENTIAL EXECUTIVE CONTACT PARTNERS
>
> - Chambers of commerce
> - Economic development organization
> - Local, county, and state government
> - Manufacturing extension program
> - Municipal, cooperative, and public utilities
> - Small business development council

Another advantage of working with partners is that business executives will have fewer interruptions from well-meaning organizations trying to offer assistance. Too many different groups reaching out to help a limited number of businesses reduces everyone's opportunity. In one situation in Florida, an organization had difficulty securing appointments because of meeting fatigue. This is a growing issue. Consequently, identifying and collaborating with other organizations that are doing or considering executive interviews is an important step in the planning process.

The Strategic Information Tool
(Survey or Interview Forms)

An essential step in building an executive contact program is to decide what will be discussed with area executives during the interview. Most economic development organizations prepare questions to help organize the interview and explore important issues. The challenge here is not what question to ask, but rather, how to limit the appetite to ask the next question. There are always more interesting questions to ask than there is time available.

The challenge is deciding *why* to include a question. Research shows that 53 percent of interviews are devoted to confirming easily obtained information, such as parent company and facility size. This means for an average 30-question survey, 16 questions pertained to gathering data of absolutely no strategic value. Just asking these questions demonstrates to a company executive that no one in the organization did their homework. This is not the image any organization wants to project.

Approximately 25 percent of the interview was spent identifying and/or documenting problems limiting business growth or thwarting the attraction of new companies. Many questions were intended to document a known problem. For example, in Illinois the cost of workers compensation and unemployment insurance has been a perennial problem. Numerous economic development organizations ask about these problems on their survey. Unfortunately, this question invites the standard "knee-jerk" reaction from executives but generates no new information or insight.

ANALYSIS OF SURVEY QUESTIONS		Figure 3
Type of Questions	**Percent**	**Questions**
• Confirmation question	53.2	16.0
• Assistance questions	10.6	3.5
• Problem identification question	25.3	8.0
• Predictive questions	4.3	1.0
• Industry intelligence questions	0.6	0.0
• Company intelligence questions	5.2	1.5
• Buyer/supplier linkage questions	1.1	0.0
Source: Blane, Canada Ltd.		

For this reason, when documenting a known problem, focus on the problem's consequences. For example, in California energy costs, availability, and reliability are issues for every company because of the 2001 energy crisis. Therefore, an appropriate line of questioning could be: How has the energy crisis specifically impacted the company? How has the company adjusted its business practices to minimize the negative consequences of the energy crisis? What are the long-term implications of these changes? These questions explore the nature and consequence of the problem instead of just confirming that the problem exists.

Knowing community-related problems is important. Creating goodwill is valuable. Offering assistance is useful. But, in an environment of global competition, these issues do not drive corporate-location decision making.

A New Conceptual Framework

A new framework for increasing the strategic value of information gathered through the business retention process *must*:

- Acquire information relevant to the decision-making process of companies
- Build company-specific knowledge
- Create a process to transform unconnected pieces of information into relevant, accurate and useable strategic knowledge
- Focus information resources on helping identify marketing opportunities and predicting companies at risk

The executive contact program should be viewed as a five-step process:

Step 1: Compile employer information.
Step 2: Conduct CEO interviews.
Step 3: Compile and analyze the data.
Step 4: Blend findings into the marketing plan.
Step 5: Evaluate, evaluate, evaluate.

Step 1:
COMPILE EMPLOYER INFORMATION

Company background information should be collected through research or by phone from company contacts prior to conducting the CEO interview. Then, the interview can focus on questions that provide valuable information, the interviewer is better prepared to relate to the company, and the CEO sees that the organization has done its homework.

Step 2:
CONDUCT CEO INTERVIEWS

The redesigned survey should be used to conduct a competitive analysis and capture strategic information: customer satisfaction, predictive information, and marketing research. The essence of the information gathered should help leadership understand the factors that will drive the community's economy in the future. A focus on the future requires the collection of strategic information that will allow the user to evaluate every company on such critical factors as:

- Value to the community
- Growth potential
- Technological adaptation and leadership
- Risk of downsizing and/or leaving
- Satisfaction with the community

Gathering *predictive* information is critical. It helps the development executive anticipate changes impacting a community's economic base. Market intelligence documents or quantifies competitive advantages and weaknesses affecting retention and/or attraction.

Predictive information and market research data cannot be easily captured in a mailed survey. These questions do not lend themselves to multiple choice or short answers. A telephone interview or personal visit is the best way to uncover this type of information. Each interviewer should probe for clarification by following answers with a second or third question, such as asking for examples of specific examples.

The proposed competitive intelligence approach is supported by proven market research and techniques used regularly in other industries. More than 140 economic development organizations are using these principles as the foundation of their existing business program.

Preparing Questions

Assessing the community's portfolio begins with asking the right questions. The following sample questions cover three areas of interest: customer satisfaction, predictive information and market research. These questions are just a few examples of the approach developers could use to predict behavior, evaluate satisfaction, and improve economic development marketing. This list is not exhaustive, nor are these questions designed to be blended into an existing survey instrument. Each community must determine what specific questions will produce information of the greatest strategic value to leadership.

Customer Satisfaction

Important indicators of customer satisfaction are attitudes and how they have changed. Uncovering negative attitudes helps identify problems, whereas positive trends could indicate progress.

Sample Questions

1. Has your attitude toward doing business in this community changed during the last two years? *Yes No*
2. If yes, has it improved or deteriorated?
3. Why?
4. Rate the following public services on a scale of 1 – 6 (high).

Predictive Information

To predict company behavior, learn about factors that drive expansion and relocation. For example, if the company has another facility with the same production capabilities already in place, production can be shifted quickly in response to changes in business conditions. The possibility of a quick shift increases the risk level for communities with a similar facility.

INTERVIEWER'S QUICK TIPS

Executive interviews are a critical component of most existing business programs. The following tips will help the Interviewer create a positive experience for both the interviewee and the interviewer while maximizing the quality of the information gathered.

The interviewer plays a critical role. This person is the eyes, ears, and mouthpiece for economic development in the community.

Poor quality, incomplete, or unreadable information will reduce the value of the information to leadership.

Background Information

Compiling background information on the company is a prerequisite of an executive interview. Compiling background information demonstrates professionalism and provides a level of credibility to the interviewer and the program. Furthermore, executives expect and appreciate preparation. To do less is a signal that we really don't care enough to do our homework.

Appointment Call

During the appointment call, it is essential to *sell* the visit. It is important for the economic development group to establish a personal contact with area executives.

3 Rules of Interviewing

1. What you hear in the room *stays* in the room. Do not share information collected with others outside the program.

2. It is customary for an executive to offer a beverage. ***Do not, under any circumstances, accept beverages during an interview.*** A beverage can:

   - Become major distraction (where to put it)
   - Limit your ability to take notes
   - Cause a significant interruption (if spilled)

3. Be cautious when asking about family pictures. Photos can be old and family circumstances could have changed, creating a potentially awkward situation.

Before the Interview

Both the interviewer and the recorder, if different people, should practice the questionnaire at least two times, out loud prior to the first interview. Note any questions that are confusing, and ask the program administrator for clarification.

Opening the Interview

During the opening, small talk off the subject of the business should be limited to two or three minutes to avoid wasting the executive's time.

During the Interview

Watch the clock. Stay focused. Try to maintain a conversational tone to put the interviewee at ease. Move through the questions at pace, but don't rush, especially when the executive is responding to an open-ended question. Listen. If there are follow-up questions that will help you understand the response, ask them. Do not ask "Why" questions. "Why" questions turn a conversation into an interrogation.

Encourage the executives to share their stories about the company and issues. ***Don't overreact to something said when you know or believe the facts to be different.***

Listen, listen, listen carefully.

Make notes, lots of notes. Memory is not nearly as accurate as a note. Even an incomplete note is valuable if reviewed and elaborated after the interview.

Assistance

Economic development organizations are limited in the types of assistance they can provide; therefore,

> *Don't try to solve a problem on the spot.*
> *Don't make any promises.*

Confidentiality

Confidentiality is critical to the success of the executive contact program; therefore,

- Discussion and notes from the interview are confidential.
- Don't discuss what you learn with anyone outside the program.
- Reports provide only aggregated information, not company-specific information.

After the Interview

After the interview, once off the company's premises:

- Add clarifying detail to interview notes.
- Make adjustments as needed.
- Describe any follow-up required.
- Return the survey forms to the designated contact for data entry.

Returning Completed Forms

If you are responsible for sending the completed survey instrument and notes to someone else for data entry, *always* make a photocopy before mailing or handing it off for delivery. Destroy your copy once you have confirmed receipt by the person responsible for data entry.

Interview Supplies

Always bring along a good writing surface so notes can comfortably be taken when balanced on one leg. Carry extra pens and paper.

Carry extra business cards in case other company executives are invited to join the interview.

Carry extra copies of the survey form in case the executive asks to see it.

If forms will be faxed to the recorder, remember pencil notes *do not fax clearly.* Always use a pen.

SOURCE: *Synchronist Business Information System™ Interviewer's Guide,* Eric P. Canada, 630-462-9222, *ecanada@blanecanada.com*

Sample Questions

1. Does your company have a sister facility producing the same or similar products? (List city and state or country.)
2. Are the plant and equipment at the sister facility older or newer?

For many companies, the driving force in plant location is proximity to market. When growth is in a different geographic region than production, pressure increases to move or expand production in the growing market. Being unaware or complacent of a company's growth patterns could cost expansion opportunities. Valuable insight is gained through understanding a company's market area and direction of their growth.

Sample Questions

1. Where are the company's top three markets served from this facility?
2. Where is your company's market growing fastest?
3. What is the company's top international market?

Market Research

Understanding advantages and disadvantages of doing business in a community from the executive's point of view can provide valuable marketing insights on how the product can be improved. Community problems can be addressed and opportunities can be leveraged. The answers also help leadership understand community satisfaction.

Sample Questions

1. What are the advantages of doing business in this community?
2. What are the disadvantages of doing business in this community?
3. Where are your primary competitors located? Why?

Marketing Support Information

Executive interviews are an opportunity to cultivate valuable information for business attraction marketing. For example, workforce is always an issue. Every community says it has a productive workforce, yet few have evidence to back up the statement. Hence, at minimum, the organization should define a few questions on key business issues. These questions should be designed to create specific, measurable information on issues such as:

- ✓ Workforce availability
- ✓ Workforce quality
- ✓ Workforce reliability
- ✓ Workforce productivity
- ✓ Workforce skill gaps
- ✓ Supplier gaps
- ✓ Expansion plans
- ✓ Growth drivers
- ✓ Business activity indicators
- ✓ Growth barriers

Sample Questions

1. On a scale of 1 to 6 (high), how would you rate the reliability of the workforce in the community?
2. Is the company experiencing recruitment problems with any employee positions or skills? *Yes No* If Yes, what problems, positions, skills, etc.?
3. Would you give an example of how this is impacting the company?
4. What are the barriers to increasing the company's investment in the community?

One question should address whether the CEO has suppliers that he or she wishes were located closer to the facility. This question can be used to identify companies or industries that can be contacted for investment in the community. If a number of area companies identify a specific product needed, such as boxboard fabrication, this provides a stronger hook for pursuing companies in that business if a known demand for the product can be demonstrated.

Local Issues

The focus of the strategic information tool is on the company, its industry, and its relationship to the community. Beyond strengths and weaknesses, it does not focus on community issues. To investigate these issues and maintaining continuity in the interview, conduct a mail or telephone survey on special issues as they arise or segment the survey into two parts. The first part consists of the core questions that do not change. A second part would be devoted to special issues and would change as new issues arise. Local-issue questions would change as issues changed.

Survey Length and Design

It is always important to respect the time of executives willing to meet. Forty-five minutes to an hour is considered reasonable. To keep the interview to less than an hour, each question should do double or triple duty. For example, the question "Are there any barriers to the company's expansion in the community?" reveals three things:

First, a yes indicates a company at risk of leaving or taking growth elsewhere.

Second, problems of doing business are specified.

Third, problems are prioritized by their impact on risk.

A casual interview style with a 30-question survey will require about 45 minutes for an on-site interview or 35 minutes for a telephone interview. The interviewer's skill and the interviewee's desire to elaborate affect the length of time required. The form of the question also affects the interview length. There are four basic question formats:

- **Simple** (yes/no)
- **Compound** (multiple choice)
- **Complex** (multiple parts, e.g., arrange in order of importance)
- **Open-ended** (solicits a comment)

Complex and open-ended questions take longer to ask and answer. A survey with only complex and open-ended questions must include fewer questions to fit within the available time. Open-ended questions, when combined with a simple or compound question, enrich the findings by providing a context to aid understanding. Also, a survey of all yes/no and multiple-choice questions will sound like an interrogation.

Complex and open-ended questions are more difficult to tabulate and analyze than simple or multiple-choice questions. Moderation is key. Focusing on important questions and blending simple, compound, complex, and open-ended questions will produce the most interesting interview and most valuable information.

To reduce the number of questions, use this "acid test":

- Will the answer help determine the company's status in the community's portfolio (value, growth, risk, or satisfaction)?
- Does the question provide insight into more than one of the four critical factors?
- Will the interview last too long?

The Assistance Trap

The last dominant theme of the executive interview form is the "assistance" question. More than 10 percent of the questions included in typical surveys were directed at identifying forms of assistance that could be provided.

Most economic development organizations wish to assist companies but are limited in what they can provide. In most cases, economic developers provide time, contacts, and persistence. Economic development organizations do not set law, do not regulate, do not have an endless supply of money to distribute. Therefore, development organizations must rely on a partner, such as government or utility representatives, to address the concerns of businesses executives.

Any offer of assistance will create an expectation on the part of the executive. Meeting this expectation will prove difficult for the economic developer who must rely on a third party. Failing to meet an executive's expectations could damage the developer's credibility and harm future economic development efforts.

Also, a large number of executive meetings could yield an overwhelming volume of requests if assistance is offered. When this happens, priorities must be set. Consequently, some responses will be delayed, perhaps for a long time.

Therefore, the best practice for offering assistance is, don't make any promises that can't be kept. Train volunteers not to make any commitments. Use the interview to gain an understanding of the company and to identify problems. If a direct request is made, take down the details and offer to get back to the executive later. After the meeting, consider the company's requests and check to see if others can help before returning with an offer to help the company. This is an enlightened approach to dealing with the assistance trap.

Step 3:
COMPILE AND ANALYZE THE DATA

There are two levels of analyzing information collected in an interview or survey: company-specific comments and comments from all companies interviewed related to a specific question or group of questions.

Company Level Analysis

First, use the survey results to answer the following questions:

1. Is this company is at risk for downsizing, closure, or relocation?
2. What assistance can/should be provided to this company?
3. Is there evidence the company is considering expansion locally or elsewhere?
4. Is this a high-value company or a growth company?
5. Is the company committed to the community?
6. Regarding these findings, what steps, if any, should be taken by the organization?
7. Is there a marketing opportunity to be pursued?

This company screening should be completed immediately following the personal or telephone interview, and any necessary follow-up action should be scheduled as soon as possible. If the company's information that needs to be acted upon is confidential, ask permission to discuss details with prospective assistance providers.

Typically 60 to 80 percent of the company executives interviewed will ask for something to be supplied after the interview. These information requests range from supplying the name of a contact, providing information on a training program, to helping with an expansion. The majority of information requests will be similar and are easily filled.

Complicated follow-up requests will require a tracking procedure. At a minimum, the tracking procedure should identify the company, the contact, the issue, the assistance needed, the date assigned, who has responsibility for follow-up, and a target date for completion. This will help the program administrator track each follow-up task to completion. Many organizations use contact management software like Act! or Goldmine for this purpose. A spreadsheet or database program can also be used.

Each company should receive a post-visit letter prepared by the program administrator. The letter should express thanks for the executive's time, reinforce the meeting's importance and explain how the findings will be used. This letter can be used to supply requested information using prewritten "plug-in" paragraphs or enclosing brochures. Even if no information was requested, a post-visit letter should always be sent.

After the company risk analysis and follow-up response, each survey should be scored to determine the company's value, growth potential and satisfaction. These might be categorized high, medium, or low based on how an executive responded to questions for each factor.

Group Analysis

The goal of analyzing numerous survey results is to find recurring comments that identify opportunities or suggest potential problems. The condition of the community's product, community services, and attitudes toward the community, are of particular concern during group analysis. Compare different answers to a question to spot community-wide trends. Problems can be spotted by comparing answers to a question. One community's interview results showed that a number of companies that were getting pressure from their clients to obtain International Organization for Standardization (ISO) quality certification.

The comments and insights identified during this analysis can help identify the community's real strengths and weaknesses. A meaningful competitive advantage useful in business attraction may emerge from this group analysis. The competitive advantage can then be used in business attraction marketing.

LEADING EDGE OF EXECUTIVE CONTACT

Technology presents some dramatic changes in the way existing business programs are viewed and supported. For years, economic development professionals have been deploying contact management and relationship database software to increase the productivity of the executive contact program. These tools have allowed better reporting, follow-up, and tracking of programs. However, as in the past, each organization developed its own system and tools. Consequently, funding limitations have hampered the deployment of technology.

The leading edge in executive contact programs is the use of standardization combined with customer managed databases to enhance productivity. Two systems have emerged over the past four years for use by economic development professionals. These systems provide two different views of how to apply standardization, database technology, and the Internet to increase efficiency, improve customer services, and increase the quality of information for decision-making.

Team Pennsylvania Business Calling Program

An Internet-accessed database provides the core of the existing business program for Team Pennsylvania. Built on database technologies used in corporate applications to improve access to information for their broadly distributed partners. Pennsylvania is entering the third year of use resulting is a substantial, comparable business information base covering economic development topics.

Strengths: Regional partnering encouraged. Standard information set (database) across a broad region. Client information page for service tracking. Ubiquitous access to company information for any partner with an Internet browser and password. User-executed broadcast e-mail. Key word search capabilities. Urban, regional and state application. Tech support.

Weaknesses: Independent database, no contact management interface. No automated reporting or analytical capabilities. Costly software customization, programming, and hardware leasing. Volunteer involvement discouraged.

Current Uses: State of Pennsylvania; Erie, PA; Buffalo, NY

Provider: Business Retention Technology (BRT), Erie, PA, 814-456-6162, *www.brt-inc.org, lwardi@team.org*

Synchronist Business Information System®

The first "standardized" existing business software product for economic development organizations. The Synchronist System uses portfolio management concepts to determine a company's value, growth potential, risk, and satisfaction providing the first ever company-to-company comparative information. Desktop version has been in use since 1998. Internet version became available in 2001.

Strengths: Regional partnering encouraged. Standard information set across a broad region. Export data to contact management program. Tech support, training, and training tools. Point-and-click automated analysis and reporting. More than 40 preformatted reports. Local, regional, or state application. Desktop or Internet versions.

Weaknesses: Independent data set. Limited linkage to contact management software. Set questions required for analysis function.

Representative Users: Dubuque, IA; Raleigh, NC; Louisville, KY; Putnam County, FL; States of Iowa, Ohio, North Dakota, and Washington; northeastern IL and metro Chicago, IL; plus over 100 communities.

Provider: Blane, Canada Ltd., Wheaton, IL, 630-462-9222, *www.blanecanada.com, info@blanecanada.com*

The most frequently used methods to evaluate findings during a group analysis include:

Frequency	Totals, percents, and distributions displayed in tables, pie charts, and graphs
Key word frequency	Number of times a select word is used
Trends/problems	Recurring themes from the responses of different companies
Quotable quotes	Individual comments that summarize the feelings of a broader group
One-ups	Powerful, insightful comments that suggest an emerging issue/problem

Responses should also be grouped by company size, industry, location, market, or other shared characteristics to be studied. It will be possible to identify trends limited to a specific geographic area or a group of companies. In one situation, five responses from an older business park showed the narrow roadway was causing delivery truck problems.

An analysis of groups of responses should be conducted regularly as new surveys are added to the information base. Economic development organizations have identified and addressed many significant issues in this manner.

Analysis Support Tools

Group analysis can be performed manually or electronically. The choice will depend on the number of surveys involved and the time, skills and funds available. The other consideration for data management is how the information will be used for future reference or research. Specifically, as the value of the information increases, by focusing on strategic information the number of ways the findings can be used increases if it is easily accessible. The classic file cabinet/box approach is not always conducive to repeated use. Therefore, use an electronic storage system with spreadsheet or database software. While contact management software is fine for company background information, it has limited capacity for recording responses to questions. Reporting can also be more cumbersome with contact management software.

The trend today is toward more staff-driven programs with fewer volunteers conducting interviews. Program design is also moving away from periodic or blitz campaigns to ongoing programs in which interviews are conducted weekly or monthly. Both trends support investing in some software to aid analysis and provide access to the data.

Avoid overbuilding the form or database. If the tool is too complicated, the next person may not be able to understand it. Also, don't use an intern to construct a database program who will not be available later to service the program.

The greatest value of an electronic reporting/tracking tool is accessibility. At a minimum, the company background information will be available to update for the next round of visits.

Accessibility to interview answers could be important for three reasons. First, when a company calls to ask for incentive assistance in the future, it would be useful to look at: the company's individual question responses; their value, risk, and growth potential; and other similar companies in the community prior to making the decision. Second, the findings can be queried for specific research after the fact. For example, the mayor may ask how many people complained about building permits or zoning. Third, data accessibility is especially valuable when staff changes occur because the prior work is always available for quick reference.

An electronic reporting/tracking tool also provides the ability to research the evolution of issues from year to year. While it is easy to compare a summary or report to see some year-to-year trends, improvement, or deterioration over time may not be visible without analyzing the individual answers to relevant questions.

The Statistically Valid Option

Statistical analysis is concerned with the probability the information collected represents the universe as a whole. To create a statistically valid survey, a rigorous methodology is used to avoid skewing findings by question structure, sample selection, or interview technique. As a result, statistical validity reduces the burden to defend the findings.

Unfortunately, statistical analysis dramatically increases the cost to conduct an interview or survey. Also, the highly structured methodology limits what questions can be asked. Finally, professional interviewers must conduct the survey to ensure the validity of the interviews or survey, so there is no room for volunteer or staff involvement.

Few economic development organizations use statistically valid surveys because the survey's purpose is to uncover problems and trends, the exception rather than the norm. The economic developer is interested in knowing if the exception represents a potential trend for the organization or the community. For example, if two companies need room to grow and there is no industrial property available, these two companies have a problem. At the same time, the other 98 companies interviewed may be content with their current space. The two companies with a space problem are clearly not representative. Still, the lack of industrial space is a problem for the companies and a potential problem for the community.

Step 4:
BLEND FINDINGS INTO THE MARKETING PLAN

The Report

Reports, like the existing business programs, are highly personalized to the community, organization, and program leader.

An official report is unnecessary for an executive contact program where follow-up interactions are specific to each company. A simple activity report is adequate.

If the organization's goal is to affect changes—within the organization or community—then a report is critical. The report records and organizes the findings, conclusions, and recommendations so they can be shared with leadership and influencers. The report builds the case for action by providing evidence to document why action is necessary.

SAMPLE REPORT OUTLINE

1 Acknowledgments
2 Title page, Table of Contents, date, sponsor
3 Summary of the report
4 Introduction
   • Purpose of the interview
   • Relevance to the community
5 Summary of findings
6 Recommendations to local organizations
7 Plans for implementation
8 Responsibility for Implementation
9 Appendix
   • Tabulation of results
   • Methodology
      – Members of the committee
      – Procedure for selecting and interviewing businesses
   • Data tabulation and analysis procedures
   • Survey instrument

There are at least five levels of reporting:

- ► Company-specific meeting notes, no compiled report, activity report.
- ► Basic information, simple tabulation, totals, percents, and distributions, informal reporting.
- ► Moderate information, trend and key word analysis, summary reporting, and conclusions.
- ► Strategic information, year-to-year continuity, quotes, special insight into an emerging issue, extensive reporting, recommendations, accessible database for follow-up research.
- ► Highly sophisticated, statistical analysis, extensive reporting, recommendations.

As a final note on the report, the quality and detail of the report matters little. What really matters is what leadership is willing to act on. In short, slick, colorful, and expensive reports won't change the outcome if there isn't substance in the information, a clear need for action, or a willingness by leadership to act.

Sharing the Findings

One component of reporting easily overlooked is the need to report back and keep stakeholders informed. Feedback is important to connect the results with the starting point, the executive contact program. Sharing the findings is also critical for building support for action on any recommendations. Frequently, economic development professionals get so involved in the process, they forget to take credit for accomplishments. The most common practice is to use a newsletter to provide feedback to participants and share findings with leadership. A printed report distributed at meetings is another common practice. Unfortunately, both assume participants/leadership read newsletters and attend meetings. Publishing a downloadable report on the organization's website is becoming increasingly popular. These channels are limited. To expand awareness, it is important to engage the community's print and electronic media. Community and business leaders are far more likely to read the newspaper than an organization's newsletter. Releasing the report with a press release will generally get an article in the paper. Most often the coverage will focus on the most controversial element of the report. Therefore, work with the editor or business writer to create articles on different aspects of the report and their implications for the community. A modest investment of time here can produce significant dividends.

Connecting with Marketing

The next step in the executive contact program is to decide how the new information affects business attraction marketing. Questions were included in the survey to support marketing efforts. Other questions, however, provide insight into the condition of the product from the user's perspective. Consider the following questions. Then, share your thoughts supported with evidence from interviews with the individual(s) responsible for business attraction marketing and the individual(s) responsible for improving the community as a product for economic investment.

- *What are the implications for future marketing activities?*
- *Do local plant managers need community information packaged specifically for off-site decision-makers?*
- *Is more internal marketing needed with local executives?*
- *How should the organization respond to changing attitudes about doing business in the community?*
- *Are there supplier opportunities for business attraction to be pursued?*
- *Can executives open doors through their affiliations to help with business attraction?*
- *Are there product problems (available land, zoning, permitting, workforce) that need to be addressed?*

Step 5:
EVALUATE, EVALUATE, EVALUATE

Every phase of the executive contact process and results should be evaluated. Feedback, follow-up, and tracking are extremely important. Initially, all results are short-term. The short-term evaluation focuses on the process and company-specific actions taken.

- *Were all contacts made?*
- *Were company information needs followed up and completed?*
- *Were any significant issues identified?*
- *Were volunteers adequately trained?*
- *What can be done to improve the process?*
- *What worked, and what didn't work?*
- *What should be done differently next time?*
- *How does leadership feel about the results, and why?*

One short-term change that should be avoided is changing the interview questions too dramatically or frequently. Not every trend is evident in one round of interviews. The best executive contact programs have some unchanging questions. Local issues, as discussed before, supplement the base questions.

Long-term evaluation focuses on the big-picture items that impact groups of companies and improve the community or the community's business climate. Such changes will take longer to accomplish. Consequently, long-term evaluation requires tracking actions over time to evaluate results. In one case it became clear that companies needed room to grow. The lack of industrial land forced the development organization to build two new business parks, one in the community and another in the county. Securing organizational and political support, raising millions of dollars, dealing with reluctant land owners, and overcoming topographical challenges took nearly four years. The result was delivered after four years of work—600 acres of prime industrial and business park space for growing area companies as well as new companies.

BUSINESS DEVELOPMENT:
A Serious Alternative
to Business Attraction

How can an economic development organization adopt a growth-oriented strategy without total reliance on business attraction? The best approach to economic development for many communities can be characterized as business development. Under this proven economic development strategy, the economic development organization becomes a hub connecting companies and business support programs to stimulate and/or accelerate the growth of companies in the community.

Business development is:

- Proactive management of the local economy
- A proven economic development strategy
- Focused on existing employers to help them grow sales outside the community.

Government procurement programs and international export development programs were early economic development services targeted at business development. Each of these programs was aimed squarely at growing existing companies. Contemporary examples could include actions like those following. While some of these examples are from areas that do not have an active focus on business development, the projects described are perfect examples of the type of activities undertaken by those with business development programs.

As shown in the examples on the following page, services may simply constitute referrals to an existing public and/or private service provider elsewhere in the community or region. In other cases where no service is available, an existing organization may help the company find a private consultant. For example, business owners nearing retirement frequently face the prospect of closing their business for lack of a successor. If this is a significant issue, the business development program may form a business brokerage network to help business owners sell, avoiding abandonment of the business. The bottom line in business development is finding ways to help existing companies survive and thrive.

SUCCESSFUL BUSINESS ATTRACTION

Some years ago, **Advance Green Bay Area Development** (Wisconsin) found that small manufacturers were having difficulty achieving ISO-9000 certification. Since ISO certification was becoming a supplier requirement, these small companies were at risk of losing current business and being frozen out of future opportunities. These small companies could not afford the cost of an expensive consultant to help achieve ISO certification. In response, Advance formed an ad hoc group of eight firms. Each participant put up a portion of the funding to cover a consultant's fee. Each participant shared in the services provided. Ultimately, each company achieved ISO certification. This action by Advance Green Bay preserved jobs and created an opportunity for eight area companies to grow their businesses.

In **Kentucky**, two small furniture manufacturers jointly bid on a contract that was too large and complex for either company to win alone. Together, they were able to craft a winning bid bringing new work to the community.

Greater Louisville Inc. (Kentucky) has created a "client services center." Staff members make calls on existing companies and are charged in part with trying to develop networking opportunities to connect (buyer-supplier, collaborative partnerships) companies from their three-county service area.

In **North Dakota**, the Manufacturing Extension Partnership program provides services to improve manufacturing operations in the state. The first step in the development of the program was to assess the capabilities and growth potential of existing companies, identify services needed to improve manufacturing processes, and direct client companies to public and private sector services for assistance. Individualized services are provided to qualifying candidates. Independent providers offer many services using a combination of state and federal funds to reduce the company's direct cost.

Weak interaction between business executives slowed growth in the emerging technology-business cluster in eastern Idaho. In response, **Eastern Idaho Economic Development Council** formed the Forum for Information Technology. By bringing together employees from several firms the group arranged custom training courses through the community college using state funding. Using group clout, they are working on a regional network connection point for high-speed broadband, Internet access for a group of users.

A thin workforce and revolving door human resources policies led **Fond du Lac County Economic Development Corporation** (Wisconsin) to create an employee retention service to help companies put systems in place to retain employees. The fee-based service is available to any employer.

In 1997, **Development Thunder Bay** (Ontario) helped create Forestry Thunder Bay, a public-private partnership. The partnership has since created an e-business buyer/supplier tool *http://www.northernsupplier.com/*. Today, more than 300 of the largest regional suppliers are now registered and more than $1 million in business has been tendered. The site guarantees a buyer supplying basic information at least three quotes from regional suppliers within 48 hours.

CREATING A BUSINESS DEVELOPMENT PROGRAM

The fatal characteristic of government procurement and export development programs was that they were programs with a one-size-fits-all approach. The assumption was that any company could sell to the government or overseas. Unfortunately, if a company did not have a suitable product, the program was of no use. Consequently, these programs were inappropriate for most communities. Where the business base was large enough, they still struggled to justify their existence, then quietly disappeared.

The better model for a business development program is the Manufacturing Extension Program (MEP) of the U.S. Department of Commerce's National Institute of Standards and Technology. The MEP makes it possible for even the smallest firms to tap into the expertise of knowledgeable manufacturing and business specialists. MEP centers have the ability to assess a company's capabilities and to direct technical and business solutions in a wide range of areas to help build the companies capabilities.

The beauty of the MEP is that it is market driven. The services offered are dependent on the situation and needs of the individual company. While their focus is manufacturing, it is not a specific type of manufacturing. This gives the MEP center latitude to focus on producing results.

In most communities, business owners and managers are not well connected. They do not have many meaningful networking opportunities. The "networking" events hosted by chambers and civic organizations are heavily attended by vendors with something to sell. Under a business development model, like the MEP, the economic development organization serves as the network hub by conducting assessments, exploring needs, and directing public and private services to area companies to them grow their business.

Maintaining an open structure without a specific industry allows the most benefit. Creating cross-industry links and coalitions allows development organization to play a valuable role. Furthermore, understanding the needs of growth companies helps a community prepare for the future instead of building for the past.

Business development is not entrepreneurship. Entrepreneurship programs focus on helping an individual start a business. In a business development program, the primary focus is working with companies that already have proven business models. Target companies have employees, a client base outside the area, and sales. Most importantly, they have the potential for more sales. Business development is about identifying the economic potential of existing companies, and helping these companies reach that economic potential. Growing revenue streams create opportunities for expansion and new employment. In addition to the economic and employment value, a community is building future business and civic leaders by helping local companies grow.

Business development can use a variety of staff skills, particularly analytical and problem-solving skills. Since the process is relationship-based, rather than transaction-driven as with

business recruitment, it requires the ability to cultivate successful, ongoing relationships. A grasp of the entrepreneurial personality and business is also helpful. When resources allow, staff with business and management experience can fill gaps and provide services that are otherwise not available. Where skills are not available on staff, retired executives can be recruited for assistance.

SERVICE CATEGORIES	SERVICE DELIVERY PARTNERS
Process improvement	
Business management	Community colleges
	University professors
Financing	MEP
Human resources	Other businesses
Marketing	Private consultants
Research	
Product development	

This business development plan will work for both large and small communities. Randolph County, Illinois, with a population of 35,000, is an example. The county's economic developer, Ed Crow, clips articles from newspapers and business periodicals with information or leads useful to area business executives. Those leads might include school plans to purchase 25 computers or a telephone system bid notice. Articles are collected in envelopes labeled with the business names. If time sensitive, the article will be dropped off or faxed to the business executive. Dozens of businesses have bid on sales they would never have known about. One implement dealer sold a tractor 50 miles away. The goodwill has been bountiful and the cost has been negligible. Crow's efforts deliver more than 70 business development leads to business leaders each month.

As an example of a low-cost program, the Greater Moncton Economic Commission, NB, Canada has sometimes joined one of their corporate citizens at the table to sell to prospective clients. According to the commission, "As partners, we are selling the company, the community, and the workforce." The commission has supported OAO Technology Solutions (a large systems-information technology company providing application development and maintenance), as one example, in their quest for new business. This approach has successfully helped secure new business for their Moncton operation and OAO Technology Solutions continues to grow.

ECONOMIC GARDENING

Economic gardening—a new movement in the United States and a form of business development—can serve as another model for creating a business development program. The premier economic gardening program is Littleton, Colorado's New Economy Program. Widely modeled, Littleton's economic gardening program is sponsored by the city. It consists of a very sophisticated business resource center and a skilled staff with research, business, and management backgrounds. Area companies are invited to events to learn about the research and assistance that can be provided. Staff can conduct market feasibility studies to help companies identify and/or prove potential new markets for their products. Once a prospective market is identified, resource center staff will also help develop a custom mailing list for a promotional campaign. Additionally, executives can come to the resource center to use research resources. Littleton provides services and support to any company or entrepreneur on request.

GROWING MOVEMENT

Economic gardening is a growing movement, especially in areas where business attraction has been more challenging or growth issues have emerged. These programs form a body of work for reference and inspiration. A few of the U.S. communities engaged in economic gardening are Santa Fe, New Mexico, and San Bernardino and Chino, California.

Two Approaches

The approach recommended for business development begins with a strategic assessment and understanding of area companies.

This market research can be conducted concurrently with the executive contact program using the strategic information approach described. Understanding the needs of growth companies provides insight into how existing service providers or available government programs can be the most valuable. A revitalized business retention and expansion program can form the cornerstone of the assessment process by focusing on identifying growth companies.

Business development services may be directed toward companies fitting established criteria, to push services to the companies most capable of generating new jobs in the community. The criteria for a business development program could include:

- Profitable business with 25 to 75 employees (lower in rural areas)
- Solid growth potential
- Growth-oriented management
- Majority of product/services sold outside the region

The alternative approach is to take all applicants on a first-come, first-served basis. This may be necessary for programs sponsored by a unit of government as in Littleton, Colorado. In their case, service delivery is reportedly somewhat self adjusting. More sophisticated companies with stronger managers tend to ask more sophisticated questions and receive more service as a result.

BENEFITS OF BUSINESS DEVELOPMENT

The benefits of economic gardening and manufacturing extension, which mirror those of the business development program model, include:

- Reduce leaks by substituting local products or services for products or services currently purchased outside the community
- Help existing companies draw new sales dollars from outside the area
- Create more potential to pay above-average wages
- Build the economic base, adding new jobs and cash flow to support other business and government

- Increase the use of existing public and private programs for existing businesses
- Support the resource needs of existing businesses, rather than competing with their needs as business attraction can
- Highlight strong business role models
- Create a positive self-sufficient attitude within the community or region
- Spawn success stories boosting community confidence
- Draw attention from others outside the region creating attraction opportunities

BUSINESS DEVELOPMENT AND ECONOMIC DEVELOPMENT STRATEGY

The ultimate model for economic development was once considered to be a blend of business retention/expansion, business attraction and a third element, perhaps tourism or entrepreneurship. Today, the model has been strengthened by upgrading business retention and expansion as part of business development.

If the goal is good-quality jobs, increased wages, and new corporate investment, the most powerful economic development strategy is business development.

Business development is an alternative to traditional attraction strategies for communities where a business attraction strategy is undesirable or inappropriate. In other communities, a business development program can be implemented in parallel with a business attraction strategy.

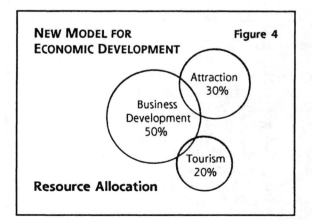

NEW MODEL FOR ECONOMIC DEVELOPMENT   Figure 4

Attraction 30%

Business Development 50%

Tourism 20%

Resource Allocation

The complete economic development strategy should be a combination of elements led by business development. In Figure 4, resource allocation of 50–30–20 has been assigned by leadership. This economic development strategy:

- Focuses resources on the best opportunity
- Makes business retention/expansion become an integral part of a more comprehensive approach to existing business
- Leverages the executive contact/assessment phase to collect information beneficial to business development, business retention, as well as business attraction programs
- Improves community infrastructure, making it more attractive to prospective investors
- Generates positive growth success stories documenting the good business climate for regional and/or national media
- Works to diversify the economy

Focusing on portfolio management and upgrading retention and expansion into a business development program provides all the benefits of a classic relocation and expansion program. Companies with problems and/or expansions are identified while community problems are isolated.

There are no firmly established rules for what constitutes a business development strategy. The final design for a community could be a blend of all of the elements described. A business development strategy is an opportunity for innovation and creativity. But, beyond this, portfolio management creates an integrated, proactive economic development strategy capable of generating the thrill of successful business attraction, and much more.

FINAL THOUGHTS

Economic development organizations have done a good job of generating results, short-term and long-term, from existing business programs. Professionals have a lot to show for their work with business retention and expansion. However, reframing retention and expansion is a huge opportunity for economic development organizations to build more value for the community and the organization. Viewing the existing business base as the community's economic portfolio clarifies the community's dependence on maximizing the portfolio's value. This defines a clear role for the economic development organization. Furthermore, maximizing portfolio value requires strategic information, a hands-on management approach, and selectively directing resources to growth companies to help them achieve their potential. This is clearly a proactive strategy, presenting a compelling argument for additional resources. Starving existing business programs to devote 80 percent of the available resources to attraction is a flawed strategy. Investing resources to build the economy from the inside out is equally important because, as we all know, without a strong existing business program, the attraction advocates among us would have less to sell.

SOURCES

Books and Manuals

Andreasen, Alan R. *Cheap But Good Marketing Research*, Dow Jones-Irwin, Homewood, IL, 1988.

Canada, Eric P. *Economic Development: Marketing for Results!* Chicago Spectrum Press, Evanston, IL, 1995.

Combs, Richard E. and John D. Moorhead, *The Competitive Intelligence Handbook*, The Scarecrow Press, Inc., 1992.

Gerber, Michael E. *E-Myth Revisited: Why Most Small Businesses Don't Work and What to Do About It*, Harper Collins, New York, 1995.

Mathey, Charles J. *Competitive Analysis*, American Management Association, New York, NY, 1991.

Morse George, and Scott Loveridge. *Business Retention and Expansion Visitation Program: Initial Manual for Starting New BR&E Visitation Programs*. Manual, CD-Rom, and video. BREI, c/o Northeast Center for Rural Development, 814-863-4656.

Rich, Ginger, editor. *Keeping Business Healthy, Happy and Local: Business Retention and Expansion Primer*, Second Edition. Washington State Department of Community, Trade and Economic Development, 2002.

Networks and Contacts

Business Retention Expansion International (BREI), an association for the advancement of retention and expansion efforts of existing businesses. *http://www.brei.org*.

ED Marketing Letter, a monthly e-mail newsletter, various issues. Blane, Canada Ltd., ISSN 1527-5175 *http://www.blanecanada.com*.

Department of Commerce's National Institute of Standards and Technology, Manufacturing Extension Program, *http://www.mep.nist.gov/*.

About the Author . . .

Eric P. Canada is a psychologist by training, an entrepreneur at heart, and a developer by choice. He is a nationally recognized authority on existing business programs and business retention. He is author of the award-winning article, "Locked in the Twilight Zone: Business Retention Fails the Strategic Value Test!" His business retention software, Synchronist Business Information System™, is in use in more than 150 statewide, regional, and community economic development organizations. Mr. Canada is recognized for his signature innovations in business retention including portfolio management, predictive surveys analysis, and company assessment ranking covering value, growth potential, risk, satisfaction. Mr. Canada, a Partner with Blane, Canada Ltd., can be reached at 630-462-9222 or *ecanada@blanecanada.com*, *http://www.blanecanada.com*.

EXECUTIVE CONTACT PLANNING CHECKLIST

✔

PROJECT TITLE _____ PROJECT NUMBER _____

This checklist highlights many of the important issues to be addressed when setting up an executive contact program. The checklist moves through each major stage of the planning process. The individual issues are in a general order; however, there are very important questions in each section that will impact resource requirements and early choices. Therefore, it is best to review all of the questions before beginning to make choices. As you read through the questions, circle those that will be affected by known resource constraints. Ultimately, these issues will determine the nature of your executive contact program and should be addressed first. Once these resource related decisions have been made, other issues can be addressed.

General Issues

Who will organize, manage, and assume responsibility for the completion of the executive contact program?

_____

What area will be covered?   ☐ Community ☐ County   ☐ Multi-county
                             ☐ Regional   ☐ Other: _____

The program format be:

☐ a Blitz (Limited duration, e.g. 2 days, one month)
☐ Ongoing (certain number of contacts each week/month)

If blitz, will it be repeated?
☐ No planned recontact   ☐ Every year   ☐ Every 2 years

If ongoing, how many contacts will be made monthly? _____

Will the contacts be made by: ☐ Visit   ☐ Mail   ☐ Phone   ☐ e-mail

If personal visits, how many firms will be targeted for contact? _____

What criteria will be used to select firms for contact?

☐ Largest employers   ☐ Representative sample
☐ Industry group   ☐ Geographic area (industrial park, etc.)

What type of firms will be targeted for contact?

☐ Industrial   ☐ Agri-industry   ☐ Service
☐ Retail   ☐ Technology   ☐ Other: _____

Who will compile the list of existing companies to be contacted? _____

PROJECT TITLE _____ PROJECT NUMBER _____

Who will write and produce advance appointment letters to targeted executives?
_____

If personal visits, the interviews will be conducted by:

☐ Individual interviewer   ☐ Teams of interviewers

If visits, who will make the contacts?

☐ Staff   ☐ Volunteers   ☐ Consultant(s)
☐ Strategic partner(s) (utility, government agencies, educational institutions, etc.)

If volunteers will be conducting interviews, who will train the volunteers?

☐ Staff   ☐ University   ☐ Utility   ☐ Consultant   ☐ Other: _____

How will the program be funded?

☐ Budget ☐ Grants   ☐ Special assessment   ☐ Other: _____

What resources will be needed?   *Estimated amount or value*

☐ staff time required   _____
☐ volunteer time required   _____
☐ cash expenditures anticipated   _____
☐ value of in-kind support   _____
☐ staff or volunteer time to manage short-term follow-up _____
☐ staff or volunteer time to manage long-term follow-up   _____
☐ staff or volunteer time for ongoing management   _____

Is training required in preparation for the planning/design of the executive contact program?

☐ Yes   ☐ No

Promotion

How will members and/or the public be made aware of —

The program? _____

Sponsoring organizations? _____

Findings? _____

Will the program be promoted before it is implemented to alert business executives in the community?   ☐ Yes   ☐ No

PROJECT TITLE _____ PROJECT NUMBER _____

Will an internal report be prepared?　　☐ Yes　　☐ No

What type of report will be prepared for public distribution?　　☐ Complete　　☐ Summary

Who will receive the report? *(check all that apply)*

☐ Media
☐ Member/investors
☐ Elected leaders (local, state)
☐ Issue related audiences
☐ School districts
☐ Other: _____

☐ Board members
☐ Survey respondents
☐ Training institutions
☐ Colleges/universities
☐ Economic development organizations

Approximately how many copies will be needed for distribution? _____

How will the report be distributed? *(check all that apply)*

☐ Personal delivery
☐ E-mail
☐ Other: _____

☐ By request
☐ Website (downloadable)

☐ Direct mail
☐ Public meeting

When will media coverage be encouraged?

☐ At the beginning of the program
☐ When contacts are being made
☐ Once the findings are prepared

If this is an ongoing contact program, how will media interest be encouraged periodically throughout the year? _____

Survey Instrument

Who will development/provide the survey instrument?

☐ Staff
☐ Partner
☐ Consultant
☐ Committee

Will different types of survey instruments be required for different types of companies?

☐ Yes　　☐ No

EXECUTIVE CONTACT PLANNING CHECKLIST

✓

PROJECT TITLE _____ PROJECT NUMBER _____

Information Management

How will individual responses be handled? _____

How will confidentiality of company-specific information be maintained?
_____

How will responses from executives be stored?

  ☐ Paper filing system ☐ Entered into a spreadsheet
  ☐ Entered into an electronic database

If an electronic database will be used to aggregate information, who will create it?

  ☐ Staff   ☐ Outside service provider (university, partner, etc.)
  ☐ Consultant ☐ Other: _____

If data entry is required, who will do it?

  ☐ Staff   ☐ Outside service provider
  ☐ Consultant ☐ Other: _____

How, if at all, will the information gathered from these executive interviews be used in the next round of contacts?
_____

Analysis

Will there be a formal evaluation of the results? ☐ Yes ☐ No

Who will perform the analysis?

  ☐ Executive ☐ Staff ☐ Committee ☐ Consultant ☐ Other: _____

How will responses from executives be analyzed?

  ☐ Individually reviewed for actions
  ☐ Entered into a spreadsheet
  ☐ Entered into an electronic database
  ☐ Analyzed as groups (industry, geographic, size, etc.)

PROJECT TITLE _____ **PROJECT NUMBER** _____

Beyond tallying for totals, calculating percents, and distribution of responses, what additional analysis will be performed?

_____

_____

_____

Will the committee or staff meet after the findings are tabulated to draw conclusions and identify actions to address the findings?　☐ Yes　　☐ No

Follow Up

Who will track company-specific actions for completion? _____

Who will track actions taken for completion? _____

Who will manage company-specific follow-up actions? _____

Who will be responsible for follow up actions with the individual companies?

_____

Who will be responsible for initiating actions to help groups of companies or improve the community's business climate?

_____

Who will be responsible for managing actions to —

    Change programs? _____

    Change local government business policy? _____

    Change resource allocation? _____

Who will help work on the actions to stimulate —

    Changes in programs? _____

    Changes in local government business policy? _____

    Changes in resource allocation? _____

PROJECT TITLE _____ PROJECT NUMBER _____

Evaluation

What are the three or four most important things we want to learn as a result of the executive contact program?

1. _____
2. _____
3. _____
4. _____

What results will be satisfactory —

Short-term? _____

Long-term? _____

[To the person responsible for planning:]
What are your personal expectations for the executive contact program?

_____
_____

What are board members' expectations for the executive contact program?

_____
_____

How important is the executive contact program to the organization's mission?

_____
_____

What problems are likely to occur during implementation?

_____
_____

How can these problems be avoided?

_____
_____

CHAPTER 6

MARKETING TECHNIQUES
Attracting Companies to Your Community

Lindy Hoppough
Director of Editorial Services, Chabin Concepts

Roger Brooks
Principal, Destination Development

———— ◆ ————

Marketing in economic development is the process of educating, encouraging, reminding, and influencing targeted industries on the positive aspects of expanding or locating a business in the community. The goal of marketing is to generate inquiries and leads.

Methods used to market a community include direct mail, trade shows, personal visits, advertising, public relations, and special events. The community may decide on a mix of these methods. Each has its pros and cons. The key to any effective marketing program is to employ the most effective method for the company being targeted.

IS THE COMMUNITY READY TO BE MARKETED?

In the computer industry, it's called "vaporware"—the promise of a product that doesn't yet exist. Likewise, in economic development, the community shouldn't invest money in marketing unless it has something to sell.

In the narrowest sense, the community's product is available real estate that meets a company's needs. Before beginning a marketing program, ask:

- Is the infrastructure (transportation, access, utilities, proper permitting, etc.) in place?
- Is there adequate sewer and water capacity?
- Is the pricing on land, commercial leases, construction, etc., competitive?

Sites and buildings don't exist in a vacuum. The practitioner also is selling the community. Evaluate the community's marketability based on these criteria:

- Does the community have a competitive fee structure (e.g., permitting and impact fees, business licenses, etc.)?
- Is permitting handled in a timely manner?
- Is there adequate labor for the industries being targeted?
- Do transportation issues need to be resolved?
- What incentives and financing options—from both public and private sources—can the community offer?
- Are the operating costs of companies in the community competitive with what similar companies spend to operate in other communities?

Addressing the issues mentioned in these questions will make the community more marketable.

But when it comes to "closing the sale," you'll need to be able to answer perhaps the toughest questions: "Why would a company pick this community over the dozens of others that want them there?" "What is it that makes our community more competitive?" "How can that business make more money in our community than in Somewhereville?" The wrong answer, by the way, would be "our quality of life is better."

THE MARKETING PLAN

All practitioners have been guilty of "patchwork" marketing—an ad here, a brochure there, a website developed two years ago and then forgotten. This method requires little effort but yields disappointing results.

Research and planning are critical to an effective marketing plan. Research may show that a community's slogan, "A Bit of Italy in Northern Minnesota," doesn't resonate with the targeted audience. A community may market itself in one publication for years and then learn, through research, that its target market reads another publication. A full-page ad in *Fortune* magazine might create a big splash, but an ad in one of the site location periodicals may yield more qualified leads and be less costly. And what about follow-up? An ad or brochure will do little to sell a community unless there's someone to facilitate the contact.

The community's marketing plan may not be organized exactly like the outline shown in the table on page 97, but it should address all of the issues shown.

GOALS AND OBJECTIVES

Goals and objectives keep a marketing program on track and provide a yardstick for measuring results. A *goal* expresses a general desired outcome of the marketing program:

- ► "Achieve greater recognition among corporate site selectors."
- ► "Supplement the existing agriculture-based economy with an expanded presence in biotechnology."
- ► "Improve awareness of loan programs among existing businesses."

An *objective* describes how success will be defined. Objectives should be measurable. They should not describe what the practitioner will *do* (e.g., "send out 2,000 brochures") but, rather, what he or she hopes to *accomplish*:

- ► "Generate 100 leads within the next year."
- ► "Locate two new companies in the next year, representing a combined increase of 40 employees."

- ► "Package enough loans to generate the creation of 100 jobs over a two-year period."

From the objectives, you can build the *action plan*—the "to-do list"—that describes the specific methods, materials, and personnel required to achieve the goals. The action plan forms the rest of the marketing plan.

AUDIENCE(S)

The marketing plan should include the target industries' SIC or NAICS codes, the desired size range (usually defined by the number of employees), and the geographic areas in which these industries are concentrated. This information can be used for ordering mailing lists or targeting media in a particular locale.

Going beyond the basics with a detailed industry profile will help pinpoint the unique needs of a particular industry. Some industries place the highest priority on available labor that fits their occupational profile, while the critical factor for others may be operating costs or quality of life. Use this information to gear the marketing message to their needs.

The audience for the marketing campaign is not limited to the target industries. Larger corporations often use site location consultants. This is a different breed than the owner/operator. Corporate site selectors tend to be more savvy regarding demographic data, costs, and incentives. They are motivated to look for the best deal and less moved by qualitative issues that could be important to an owner or manager who is relocating with the company.

Developers are an often overlooked audience. They may be the first to know who's looking in the area. They may be looking themselves. Make them partners by providing regular updates on projects and available resources.

Retention should be part of the community's program, so local businesses are another target. Know who they are and which ones are growing, shrinking, or fleeing.

The local, regional, and national news media are another audience for the community's marketing efforts. While press releases and

CONTENTS OF A MARKETING PLAN

1. Goals and Objectives	What are we trying to accomplish? • Achievable • Measurable
2. The Audience	Who are we targeting? • Industry types • Geographic distribution • Size of company
3. The Product	What are we marketing? • Real estate • Labor • Operating costs • Incentives • Streamlined location/permitting process • Market access • Existing business community
4. The Message	Why would a company come to this community? • Benefits • Positioning • Key message points
5. Methods and Materials	What activities will reach our targets and contribute to accomplishment of our goals? • Advertising (print, electronic, audio) • Telemarketing • Direct mail • Website • Relationship with influencers and associations What collateral materials are necessary to support those activities?
6. Timeline	A schedule of all activities: • Advertising • Trade shows • Visitations • Direct mail • Follow-up contact
7. Sales Plan	The "other half" of marketing • Screen leads • Sales call schedule • Face-to-face meetings • Qualify leads, send proposals
8. Budget	Line-item budget
9. Monitoring and Evaluation	Monitor scheduled activities and results on a monthly basis

editorial meetings allow less control over the message and placement, a positive article will be much more credible than a paid ad. Obtain the editorial calendars of economic development periodicals and trade publications for target industries and look for opportunities.

Finally, investors in the community are another audience of its marketing efforts. Keep them informed and offer them opportunities for input to maintain their commitment.

In summary, the community's target audiences for marketing may include any or all of

the following:
- Target industries (owner/operators and managers)
- Corporate site selectors
- Developers
- Existing local businesses
- News media
- Investors

PRODUCT

A successful practitioner knows his or her community well before marketing it. Before developing the message, compile as much information about the community as possible. First, consider the community's attributes from the perspective of someone operating a business.

- *What are the community's strengths?*
- *What are its weaknesses?*
- *How does it compare with competing communities?*
- *What opportunities does the community offer businesses?*
- *What specific services and programs does it offer?*
- *What specific details can be included about the community's ratings, rankings, resources, labor, operating costs, etc.?*

These specifics will help transform the message from a ho-hum notice such as "We have labor" to a more engaging sound bite like, "The best brains in the business."

In addition, consider the extraneous image factors that may work into the message. If the community is located on the East Coast, it might be autumn leaves or the colonial spirit. In the Southwest, the community's marketing message might emphasize desert or Native American themes. Ask these questions to discern the community's image:

- *For what is the community best known?*
- *For what does the community want to be known?*
- *Are there any recognizable landmarks or famous people in the community?*
- *What sensory factors, such as tastes, scents, and colors, are associated with the area?*
- *Are there local products or companies that could potentially fit into a campaign?*

When community leaders in one agricultural community were surveyed, they identified two prominent scents in the area: orange blossoms and manure. Manure? Skipping past the obvious digs at marketing, what can we do with *manure*? Probably nothing. Then again, consider the fertilizer ad that portrayed a skier poised to take off down a dark and fertile slope: "Bandini Mountain: Man dares to go where only cows have gone before." Humor, used effectively, will stand out against most economic development campaigns in circulation today. Don't reject any ideas in this information-gathering phase of the marketing plan.

MESSAGE

Let's face it, there are only so many factors a company will consider: labor force, market access, incentives, etc. Thousands of cities, counties, states, and countries are all selling some variation of these factors. In fact, a cursory review of advertising used in the mid to late nineties found five using the same slogan: "Open for Business." The goal is to find a unique angle on a common theme, often called the positioning statement.

A positioning statement works behind the scenes to guide the marketing message. An effective slogan expresses the community's position in a memorable way. Here are two examples, one from economic development and one from consumer product marketing:

Positioning statement: "A high-absorbency paper towel that cleans up messes faster than other brands."
Slogan: "The quicker picker-upper."

Positioning statement: "One-of-a-kind research and development facilities where the best minds collaborate to invent the technologies of tomorrow."
Slogan: "Bridging the Americas for International Trade"

MESSAGE CONTENT

All the information a community presents to a prospect, or fails to present, sends a message. The community's message is communicated through its logo, slogan, general appearance, tone of communication, as well as the text of the marketing materials.

While each marketing tool has its own message requirements (these are described more fully in the section on marketing methods), marketing communication in economic development should include these principles:

- *Consistency*—Remember the goals and positioning statement at all times. Use one logo and use it the same way on all pieces. Are all elements compatible, or does the design say "sleek" while the copy says "geek"?

- *Benefit-Oriented*—Always approach marketing from the company's perspective. For example, if a prospect visits the community's website, would they relate better to a link for "business development" or "location opportunities"?

- *Call to Action*—With each step, the prospect should become more committed. If they put down the brochure, they might not pick it up again. Give them a reason to click, a reason to call, a reason to fill in the blanks and drop it in the mail.

MARKETING TOOLS

Direct mail is the most common means of getting a community's marketing message to companies. The key to a successful direct marketing program is developing a message and a delivery mechanism that will capture a prospect's attention and elicit a response. Follow-up is essential.

Trade shows offer a face-to-face encounter and leave prospects with the knowledge that there is an individual who can be of assistance when a site-selection process is underway.

Sales calls, sometimes referred to as trade missions, are targeted visits to a particular area where multiple prospects are located.

Advertising, especially in trade and development magazines, is one method that can be effective if a commitment is made over a sustained period of time. The basic principle behind advertising is to consistently position the community's identity and image with the target market.

Public relations articles and stories that portray a community in a positive light are also an effective communications tool. A community needs to develop good relationships with local, regional, and national media.

Special events can give a community the chance to showcase itself. This event must be well coordinated and give guests the chance to meet with local business leaders, view key sites and offer recreation opportunities.

Online marketing through various channels is changing the face of marketing. One benefit of this type of marketing is that it indicates that the community is technologically adept. All indications are that it will be a growing force in the field of marketing.

Using these tools, and applying them consistently, creates the appropriate mix of marketing to appeal to the type of company the community would like to attract.

MARKETING METHODS WITH USAGE AND RATINGS					
METHOD	PROS	CONS	TARGETS	USAGE %	RATED HIGH %
Direct Mail	Simple. Effective.	Need to carefully target recipients; requires follow-up to be successful.	Smaller companies; big ones get too much.	19%	4%
Trade Shows	Meet prospective leads face-to-face, out of the office.	Expensive, requires planning, requires follow-up.	Larger firms and firms with distributed sales forces.	19%	9%
Personal Sales Calls	Meet prospective leads face-to-face.	Time-consuming to coordinate; requires follow-up, expensive.	Any level. People still buy from people.	18%	24%
Public Relations	Provides third-party credibility.	Difficult to place stories, takes time to develop.	Any level. Don't be shy—send a copy.	5%	5%
Special Events	Lots of face-to-face time. Happy memories.	Takes lots of planning and extensive use of volunteers.	Invite companies that would fit your area.	12%	24%
Internet Presence	Nearly a requirement today, much like an 800 number.	Results mixed on the actual effectiveness of online promotion.	Will be used at all levels of company.	59%	15%
Advertising	Ability to cover a large audience.	Message may be lost to a large audience; can be costly.	Helpful in larger companies where staff specialize in their field, e.g., real estate.	9%	1%

Note: Numbers can be misleading. Growth Strategies Organization (GSO), a respected observer of economic development marketing trends, published these numbers. However, the simple numbers do not tell the full story. GSO found that the more money an organization spent on a method, the more often it ranked that method highly effective. These numbers also do not account for organizations that started a method, then gave up or stopped funding the program before results were achieved. In a similar study done by Development Counselors, International, face-to-face methods also achieved the highest ratings for effectiveness. In some cases, face-to-face meetings may have been the result of advertising or public relations.

Tool No. 1:
DIRECT-MAIL CAMPAIGNS

One of the most popular marketing techniques is direct mail—the process of sending prospects literature or promotional material about the area. Direct mail is most effective when it is sent directly to a person who can make or influence a location decision. This requires a high-quality direct-mail list.

List brokers, magazines, trade publications, credit report companies, and organizations such as Dun & Bradstreet are good sources for direct-mail lists. Generally, there is a minimum rental for a one-time use of 5,000 names at rates of $50 and up for 1,000 names. Good sources of names will include:

- Lists of industry trade association members
- Rosters of trade show attendees
- Trade magazines that list the industry leaders who wrote articles for the publication
- Industry directories
- Lists of exhibitors at trade shows or industry conferences

Whether the names come from a list broker or one of the sources listed above, ask the following questions:

1. *How often are the lists updated?*
2. *How are nonqualified persons weeded out of the list?*
3. *Are there telephone numbers available for follow-up purposes?*
4. *Are extended fields, like revenues, locations, and employment, available?*

WHAT THE DIRECT MAIL MESSAGE SHOULD INCLUDE

Communities sometimes spend tens of thousands of dollars creating beautiful direct-mail pieces. These are helpful for the prospect to understand the community, but not absolutely necessary. At a minimum, include the following information:

- A contact person for the prospect to respond to via phone, e-mail, or regular mail
- A few key facts about the community and what it has to offer *this particular business*
- Testimonial(s) from the community's business leaders
- An invitation to visit the community, or an offer to call on the company
- A call to action that provides the prospect with an easy next step, such as calling for a free CD or industry profile

Another effective strategy is to send a letter written on the letterhead of a company currently located in the community whose CEO is willing to talk about the community's assets and benefits.

> **TIP:** Brevity is key here. In exchange for brevity, studies show the prospect will accept multiple communications without complaint. Postcards make excellent vehicles for cost-effective direct-mail marketing, with the added benefit that they are almost always read, even if the recipient discards them.

WHO SHOULD RECEIVE THE DIRECT MAIL

Title of Person	Input on location decisions
Chairman	Will make or approve final decision
President	Will make or approve final decision
Vice President, Sales	Will influence decision at high level
Vice President, Manufacturing, Marketing, or Customer Service	Will influence decision, depending on type of company
Vice President, Human Resources	Will have near veto power re: labor
Chief Technology Officer	Will have near veto power re: telecommunications
Vice President, Real Estate	Will have influence in early stages

Tool No. 2:
TRADE SHOWS

Trade shows are an excellent opportunity to meet many prospects at one event. Additionally, trade shows provide a unique platform to showcase the community to a cross-section of an industry in the space of a few days. This total immersion into a group of industry leaders provides instant feedback and information critical to making the community and its offer more appealing.

The main drawback of trade shows is the high cost. Trade shows are not cheap, nor are they for the fainthearted, as it takes a brave suspension of reality to pay a union electrician $300 to plug in the booth to the AC outlet. Large companies at big trade shows like COMDEX regularly spend $150,000 to $300,000 just for their trade show booth and furniture.

The savvy community, however, can attend and work a major trade show at a fraction of these costs, if the community plans well. Additionally, the cost of the trade show is offset by some of the benefits that cannot be achieved in any other setting.

TRADE SHOW BENEFITS:

Face to face—Communication with CEOs and other decision makers on neutral ground.

One on one—Opportunities for brief encounters or extended conversations with decision makers without staff, gatekeepers, and other potential critics.

Hook and go—The ability to start a conversation at one venue, such as the trade show floor, and continue it in depth at a hospitality suite.

Critical mass—The chance to compare the reactions of many leaders within the same industry.

The compression of time—Reaching 100 or more industry leaders in a single day rather than taking months using other methods.

The compression of geography—Avoiding the need to travel to 100 different businesses, which is time-consuming and expensive.

A natural environment for networking—The opportunity to share a marketing letter with the local utility, the state, and other political entities—a common and accepted practice at trade shows but not elsewhere.

TIPS FOR THE TRADE SHOW

Since trade shows are of great value, the wise community will choose to use this method, but will do so at the lowest possible cost. Here are some tips to lower the cost of trade show participation, while increasing the effectiveness of economic development efforts:

- **Tag along.** Find out which trade shows the state department of economic development plans to attend. Ask if the community can participate.

- **Tag along some more.** Ask the local utilities, the local telecommunications company, and any large local businesses if they attend trade shows. Ask if the community can participate.

- **Buddy up.** Partner with surrounding communities. Workers for almost any new project will come from a 20-mile radius of the new site, so it only makes sense to include other nearby communities. This will reduce cost and provide additional staffing for the booth.

- **Walk before running.** Attend a trade show as a participant or guest before exhibiting at one. At the trade show, determine if walking the floor gives just as much access to industry leaders as having a booth.

- **Get a jump.** Get the list of attendees ahead of time. Pick favorites and write letters inviting them to stop by and visit the booth or hotel suite or meet for coffee. Try to set up appointments prior to your arrival. This will maximize your chance of success by providing you time to know the prospect.

- **Borrow a booth.** Ask if the local school district, bank, or utility has a traveling trade show display. Many times, these portable displays are brand-neutral, so the graphics can be changed to make it look like a dedicated and expensive booth for the community.

- **Plan ahead.** Mail the community's brochures, fact sheets and, other information to the hotel or a nearby office ahead of time to avoid last minute, heavy overnight mail. Keep the original boxes, make some return address labels ahead of time and send the surplus back to the office in the same method. ▶

TOOL NO. 3:
PERSONAL VISITS TO THE PROSPECT

Studies by multiple organizations over the last 15 years have identified the personal sales call as the most effective way to create interest in the community. When economic development is viewed as a sales process—even though it is a complex sale—success rates nearly always increase. Most people buy things from people, not from brochures, letters, or videos.

Getting an appointment is usually accomplished over the telephone, sometimes in the dreaded cold-call method. Do not be surprised if it takes 30 to 40 telephone calls to get one contact. In larger companies, it might take 50 to 70 cold calls.

If there is a good salesperson in the community—perhaps a young retiree who has sold goods and services professionally—that person can usually improve those numbers by a factor of 10. It would be worth hiring a person with extensive and proven sales skills to make these appointments.

Companies that make appointments for economic developers sometimes charge $200 to $300 per appointment scheduled. Keep in mind that power buys from power, and the best way to meet with a CEO is to put a leader on the phone to ask for the appointment.

Once the appointment is made, the fun begins. An entire book could be written about the right way and the wrong way to make a personal call on a high-ranking industry leader to get that person interested in the community. Here are a few tips when calling on industry leaders in person:

Make a friend—Cordiality rules, even today. Establish rapport. Look around for hints, such as pictures of children, spouses, dogs, sailboats, diplomas, etc. on the wall or desk. Ask appropriate questions about their children, interests, and hobbies.

Find the need—Pretend the meeting is about the company, not the community. You may have to travel 500 miles to meet with the company's representative, but this meeting is critical to determining the company's needs and how the community can provide the solution.

- **Gather intelligence.** While attending a trade show, observe what kind of booths draw a crowd. The expensive booth space and high-dollar graphics don't always attract a high volume of visitors. Sometimes it's the small, inexpensive booth with ice cream cones that draws the crowd.

- **Get the good stuff.** Obtain as much information as possible about the people who visit your booth. Modern trade show managers usually offer a name-badge-scanning device for a small fee. Use this service! The prospect must have the badge to get in, and an unobtrusive hand-held scanner can capture a name, title, and address in the blink of an eye, even if the prospect is only there for the ice cream. If this scanning service is not offered, offer a drawing for an expensive golf club or shopping spree and collect business cards in a big fish bowl. It's been done, but it works. *(Hint: Desirable items that cost $400 to $500 are fine. No need to give away a $4,000 vacation in Fiji. Make sure the giveaway item can be gender-neutral.)*

- **Go early and stay late.** CEOs attend the first day of a conference or trade show more often than any other day. CEOs of smaller companies will be there in person during set-up time. Keep a few rolls of expensive gaffer tape (not duct tape!) available just to help out other booth workers. This informal time is a great way to make a person-to-person connection. The same trick applies during take-down time.

- **Get around town.** Other prospects who are located in the trade show's city will not attend because they are in a different industry. Offer to meet these prospects the day before or the day after the show. Conversations during the trade show will bring you up to speed on the area and on local business leaders.

- **Follow up.** Gather business cards at the trade show, and be sure to call the people you've met when you get back home. Otherwise those cards won't have any value.

Be Like Baba—Be like Barbara Walters on an interview. Ask questions that need a bit of emotion to be answered. Ask questions that seem innocuous, but get right to the point.

Listen for the pain—If the prospect is allowed to talk, eventually he or she will mention that there is one or more pain point in the company. This pain point is the key to the economic development professional's success.

Say the magic words—Noted management guru Tom Peters, when asked how to size up a company quickly, said ask two questions to discern a company's likelihood of success:

1. What's the company's business?
2. How's business?

Asking those two questions in various forms throughout the interview will produce a flow of vital information.

MARKETING— WHAT <u>NOT</u> TO DO

In 1999, Development Counselors International partnered with the International Development Research Council to perform a survey of perceptions of U.S. corporate leaders of companies with revenues of $100 million and at least 250 employees. The survey identified some of the *least* helpful things that communities do in the name of marketing. Here are a few:

- *Too much quality-of-life information*
- *Bulky, generic information that does not address specific needs*
- *Unusable or inflexible incentives*
- *Site information that does not meet the company's criteria*
- *Political meetings and greetings from functionaries who don't provide any value in the process*
- *Not respecting confidentiality of a prospect's interest*
- *Contacting CEOs and presidents directly without having any reason to do so*
- *Arranging time-consuming meetings with few results.*

Be patient—Don't present the community's benefits until the time is right. Many communities start spouting about labor, taxes, quality of life, incentives and which country club the CEO would prefer before they know the slightest thing about the company's needs or desires.

Walk the walk—Ask for a quick tour, if possible. Like the "How's business?" question, a tour requires the tour guide to tell about the company and to point out where things are being changed, improved, or phased out.

Talk the chalk—Instead of a canned Power-Point presentation, it's usually more effective to be in a position to walk to a blank white board and make a "chalk talk." Just holding the dry erase markers will evoke feelings of confidence. Additionally, the prospect will think that the person holding the marker has knowledge to impart.

Don't go too high too fast—Calling high in the organization is generally good, but calling too high too fast could put the economic development professional face to face with a decision-maker before he or she knows the true business needs. It will be a VSM (Very Short Meeting). Once this meeting has been blown, there's nowhere to go but out the door!

TOOL NO. 4: ADVERTISING

Advertising is a broad term, and there are hundreds of ways to approach this marketing method. There is one critical key, however, that most economic developers miss:

> *The key to advertising is to find the vehicle —a magazine, a radio show, a blimp, or whatever—that is already successfully reaching the desired audience.*

If the above test is not met, don't buy any advertising in that medium! Do not rely on promises that this or that method can be tailored to suit needs if it has never done so before.

Advertising is a science. General Motors hires Tiger Woods to talk about Buick automobiles on televised gold matches because that method *sells Buicks*. If it didn't sell Buicks, they wouldn't do it. The savvy advertising buyer asks for the names and phone numbers of others who have successfully used this medium to generate leads.

Some communities place advertising in trade magazines, such as *Plastics Today*; some in general magazines like *Forbes*, and some in economic development topical magazines like *Expansion Management* or *Plants, Sites and Parks*. Some run ads in newspapers. The important aspect of these periodicals is their circulation.

All publications worth considering subscribe to some kind of independent audit service to assure advertisers that the magazine is actually being sent to the promised number and mix of people. The Audit Bureau of Circulations is one such service. Any top-quality magazine or newspaper should be able to provide a potential buyer with an audit statement that details who actually received the magazine in the past year or so. Magazine recipients are listed by zipcode, state, industry, and title, and by how recently have they renewed their subscription.

There are two types of print advertisements: general or image ads, and response ads. The former is designed to get the reader to think nice thoughts about the community. The latter is designed to get the reader to inquire about the message or offer.

Experience shows that economic development advertisements generate virtually no leads on their own, *unless* an irresistible offer is made, such as "call for a chance to win free land," or the magazine offers a response mechanism to go with their display ad. This response mechanism is referred to as a bingo card. To obtain more information about an advertiser, the reader can circle a predetermined number on a postcard in the back of the magazine. The cards are mailed back to the magazine, which then passes on the lead to the advertiser. Ask how the magazine qualifies these leads, because there is no standardized method for how this gets done, or for whom.

The budget for ad size and creativity will have a lot to do with response, but probably the most important factor with display advertising is repetition or frequency. Don't start this type of campaign without plans for frequency.

Follow up is everything. Failing to get back to someone who responds to the message is worse than never having placed the ad in the first place.

Tool No. 5:
PUBLIC RELATIONS

Public or media relations involves using publicity through radio, television, newspapers, magazines, and motion pictures to tell the community's story. Local politicians can say their community is a well-kept secret about to burst with opportunity for those who act quickly, but it's not nearly as effective as if *The Wall Street Journal* would say that on its front page.

The best part of the public relations campaign is that the cost is very minimal.

First, develop a message and then deliver it. Press releases are one way to communicate the message with media outlets. They should be clear, well written, and delivered by hand, fax, or e-mail to convey their timeliness. Media people are extremely competitive, and a press release mailed four days ago won't be considered new and fresh. Note that despite people's perceptions, the local newspaper staff thinks their publication is timely.

It's key to maintain a list of local editors, reporters, and photographers and update it monthly. Calling to check spellings, street addresses, phone numbers, and e-mail addresses provides a great opportunity to chat with the editor or reporter about the community's message, and to find out what they are thinking about the community.

Also, maintain a list of editors and reporters for national media outlets, such as *The Wall Street Journal, USA Today,* the major television networks, and CNN. The community may not hold much interest for CNN or *Fortune* magazine today, but if something important happens, the economic development professional must be comfortable dealing with the media.

Some media relations people work to get mentions in national news or motion pictures by virtue of their location. International Falls, Minnesota, is often the coldest place in the lower 48 states and its public relations people don't let the national media forget that fact. *Sleepless in Seattle* could have just as easily been *Sleepless in Sacramento,* and the public relations people in Seattle are gratified that it wasn't.

Other ways to achieve the benefits of free publicity are to write articles for a publication or a column for a newspaper or magazine. Hiring a professional writer (and photographer) for these free-lance jobs is a good idea.

10 STEPS TO GETTING YOUR STORY OUT
1. Develop a nose for news
2. Build your media data base
3. Target the media
4. Build media relationships
5. Develop the pitch
6. Write effective news releases/ pitches
7. Get the news out
8. Follow up and follow through
9. Establish your agency as a source
10. Be proactive, not reactive

Developed by Jennifer West, APR
Rockey West Public Relations, a division of Hill and Knowlton, <www.rockeycompany.com>.

Why do public relations campaigns work?

- Articles are written by third parties. A third party has more credibility.
- Articles are read three times more often than advertisements.
- Placed articles offer a greater return on investment than advertising space, according to public relations firms. These firms often claim that $3 of publicity is attained from every $1 spent on a public relations campaign.

TOOL NO. 6:
SPECIAL EVENTS

Since the ultimate goal of most marketing campaigns is to get the prospect to visit the community, often the direct approach is best. Special events are the way that some cities bypass the hype and get the prospect's feet on the ground in the community. Typical events are sports games, recreational opportunities, and business familiarization tours. Examples:

TIP: Maintain a library of professional photographs, including the community's downtown, special events, historical sites, housing, neighborhoods, retail areas, schools, lakes, people at work, etc. Be sure to obtain a photo release (written permission) from any people in the picture. Do this in advance so there will be no delay in providing a photo to the media.

SOME DOS AND DON'TS FOR SPECIAL EVENTS	
• Do invite interesting people. If one interesting CEO agrees to come, others will, too. • Do allow time for the participants to get to know one another. Positive memories will be of great value to the visitor and will serve the community well. • Do house the participants at the nicest lodging available. • Do provide all meals for participants.	• Don't cram participants into crowded vehicles. If the van holds 15 passengers, take 9 or 10 in two vans. Use plenty of comfortable vehicles to do the job well. • Don't make the special event all work. About one-third of the time should be spent on business, one-third on play, and one-third on free time. • Don't be overbearing by trying to close the deal. Spend time listening to the prospects' problems.

▶ The State of North Carolina hosted more than 50 CEOs and site-selection consultants to Pinehurst when the US Open golf tournament was held there.

▶ Williamson County, Tennessee, invites prospects to a two-day showcase where business leaders and executives host the prospect for tours of schools, business parks, and attractions.

▶ Oklahoma City, Oklahoma, invites site-selection consultants to the city for the Senior PGA Tour events when held there.

▶ Lander, Wyoming, hosts celebrities and business executives at the annual Single Shot Antelope Hunt. Each participant, armed with one bullet blessed by a Native American medicine man, is guided by an expert and a few local business leaders.

▶ The Kansas City Area Development Council invites prospects to spend time there during the NASCAR races held northwest of the city.

The key is to invite business leaders up to four months in advance before, so that their calendars will not be full and they will be more likely to attend. Most communities pay all expenses to these events. Some pay all except the airfare. Spouses and significant others are often encouraged to attend, but their expenses are usually not covered.

The event doesn't need to be a football game, a quail hunt, the Olympics or a movie premier. Some communities invite prospects to visit and discuss business.

TOOL NO. 7: ONLINE PROMOTION

The last marketing tool, online promotion via the website, is probably the most important link a community will have with site selectors and those companies that want to relocate. It is often the first introduction they have with your community and oftentimes will determine if there are any other meetings. The website is your most important **communication** tool with your customers or prospects.

At the end of this chapter are checklists for website design and data, items to consider to make online searching of your website as user-friendly and informative as possible. Remember the "three-click syndrome": if they can't get where they want to be in three clicks, they probably will be off your website and on to your competitor's. On a website, the saying "more is less" is very true.

SALES PLAN

Marketing opens the door and invites prospects in; sales convinces them to stay. As shown in the comparison of marketing tools, personal contact is rated as the most effective method. Have a sales team in place, prepare a call schedule, and track prospects. Be ready to answer the prospect's questions quickly, accurately, and professionally. The chapter, "Closing the Deal," offers more suggestions; see pages 161–172.

BUDGET

The budget should be at the forefront during the planning process. National economic development organizations estimate the minimum annual marketing budget needed for results is $25,000. A rule of thumb for estimating total expenditures is $1 per person minimum in communities of 25,000 to 100,000 and $1.50 per person in cities with 100,000 or more people.

COMMUNITY SIZE	MINIMUM MARKETING BUDGET
0 to 25,000	$25,000
25,000 to $100,000	$1 per person population
100,000 and up	$1.50 per person population

Consider advertising, where repetition is the rule. If the community plans to advertise in a magazine, plan on running the ad a minimum of three times to build recognition. In 2002, the cost of a half-page, two-color ad in one of the site selection magazines was approximately $4,000 per issue. Running the ad three times would have cost $12,000, not including design costs.

If your community's economic development budget can't justify that kind of expense, add a fund-raising component to the marketing plan, or consider alternative approaches for shoestring budgets to get the best results:

- Read *Guerilla Marketing* for great ideas on low-cost marketing techniques.
- Look for cooperative promotional opportunities with neighboring communities, regional economic development organizations, or the state. Collaboration gives the community more "bang for the buck" on big-ticket items such as advertising.

- Local businesses can be another source of cooperative marketing. Ask them if the community can tag along on their next trade show exhibit. Existing businesses are some of the best promoters of the community. Find business leaders who can contact prospects or visit them. Sharing an advertisement in an appropriate trade magazine could provide good exposure for both the community and a local business in that industry.
- *For items that would exceed the budget, prepare a wish list of unscheduled opportunities. Donors may be interested in funding a specific activity.*

MONITORING AND EVALUATION

Creating measurable objectives at the beginning of the marketing plan simplifies monitoring and evaluation. A simple summary table (see example below) will show whether the marketing plan achieved its objectives. Remember that not all marketing activities are tied directly to lead generation; some create awareness or lay the groundwork for a follow-up call. Document the usefulness of such activities to reassure investors and board members of their worth.

Project management software, such as ACT!, is highly recommended for tracking leads and contacts. Use it to schedule follow-ups, note individual needs, track which marketing pieces have been sent to which companies, and create summary reports showing how many leads and prospects have been generated.

Example: SUMMARY OF MARKETING ACTIVITIES

ITEM	DATE	QUANTITY DISTRIBUTED	COMMENTS
Postcard Mailing #1	Oct. 1	500 mailed	1 call
Brochure Mailing #1	Nov. 1	500 mailed	1 call, 10 reply cards received
"labor" ad, PSP, 1/4-page 4-color	Nov.		5 leads
Press release on new Loan Fund	Nov. 12		Times ran story in business section; received 2 calls as a result
Website	FY 2003-04		1,000 hits, 100 requests for information, 5 leads

FINAL THOUGHTS

For the scientifically minded, marketing will cause nothing but indigestion. There is no magic formula for success, no rulebook to fall back on. At best, there are guiding principals, and sometimes even the "experts" can't agree on them. Some advertising professionals will cringe at the thought of Mr. Whipple begging, "Please don't squeeze the Charmin," while others will point out that Mr. Whipple sold a *lot* of toilet paper. If everyone used the Mr. Whipple approach, it would soon lose its effectiveness.

In economic development, the communities receiving the most attention are usually those that "broke the rules" in some way:

- Amarillo Economic Development Corporation offered an $8 million check to companies locating in Amarillo and received free exposure in the *Wall Street Journal* for doing so.
- Tacoma, Washington, ran a black and white "film noir"–style cartoon campaign that was unusual enough to be picked up by the *New York Times*.
- Fairfax County Economic Development Authority sponsored news programming on National Public Radio and received national exposure with each underwriting announcement.

In each case, the approach was effective because it hadn't been tried before. Be bold, be different, but never be so clever that you lose sight of your message or your audience.

SOURCES

Articles

"Colour Blindness: Colour Blind Design Hints and Tips," *www.delamare.unr/edu/cb/design/html.*

McEnroe, Kate. "The Best State Sites for Site Seekers," *Site Selection*, Jan. 2001, p. 38.

Nielsen, Jakob. "Eyetracking Study of Web Readers," *www.useitcom/alertbox/200000514.html.*

———. "How Users Read on the Web," *www.useitcom/alertbox/9701a.html.*

———. "Web Research: Believe the Data," *www.useitcom/alertbox/990711.html.*

Books

Bangs, David H. *The Market Planning Guide: Creating a Plan to Successfully Market Your Business, Products, or Service,* Upstart Publishing Company, Inc., 1998.

Beckwith, Harry. *Selling the Invisible: A Field Guide to Modern Marketing,* Warner Books, 1997.

Bly, Robert W. *Business to Business Direct Marketing: Proven Direct Response Methods to Generate More Leads and Sales,* McGraw-Hill, 1998.

Bly, Robert W. *The Copywriter's Handbook: A Step-by-Step Guide to Writing Copy That Sells,* Henry Holt, 1990.

Caples, John and Fred. E. Hahn. *Tested Advertising Methods,* Prentice Hall Trade, 1998.

Castro, Elizabeth. *HTML for the World Wide Web.* Berkeley, CA: Peachpit Press, 1998.

Levinson, Jay Conrad. *Guerrilla Marketing,* Houghton Mifflin Company, 1993.

McEnroe, Kate. *The Economic Development Series: Web Sites.* Dubuque, Iowa: Kendall/Hunt Publishing Company, 1999.

Sullivan, Luke. *Hey Whipple, Squeeze This: a Guide to Creating Great Ads.,* John Wiley & Sons, Inc. 1998.

Trout, Jack, with Steve Rivkin. *The New Positioning,* McGraw-Hill, 1996.

About the Authors . . .

Lindy Hoppough is Director of Editorial Services at Chabin Concepts, a private economic development consulting firm that has assisted more than 100 communities with business development strategies. With Audrey Taylor, President of Chabin Concepts, she co-authored *So You Want to Make a Company's Short List, Huh?*, a guide to data collection for economic development. Ms. Hoppough can be reached at *lindy@chabinconcepts.com.*

Roger Brooks, founder of the team Destination Development in Olympia, Washington, has worked in the tourism development and marketing industry for more than 20 years. He has assisted communities and resorts throughout North America by recruiting more than $3 billion in private investment, developing architectural and event themes, and developing successful award-winning marketing programs. His love is working with rural communities, shaping diamonds-in-the-rough into true gems. Mr. Brooks can be reached at *rbrooks@chandler-brooks.com.*

MARKETING CHECKLIST ✓

PROJECT TITLE _____ PROJECT NUMBER _____

Marketing Goals

Are our goals measurable?   ☐ Yes ☐ No
Are our goals achievable?   ☐ Yes ☐ No

Audience

What industry types are we targeting?   _____
What size companies are we targeting?   _____
Where are our targets located?   _____

Product

What are our strengths and weaknesses?   _____
What are our competitors' strengths and weaknesses? _____
What are our benefits?   _____
What is our positioning statement?   _____

Message

Is the appearance and message consistent in all pieces?   ☐ Yes ☐ No
Is the message benefit oriented?   ☐ Yes ☐ No
Is there a call to action?   ☐ Yes ☐ No

Methods, Materials, and Costs

Activity	Related Materials	Personnel	Est. Hrs.	Cost
_____	_____	_____	_____	____
_____	_____	_____	_____	____
_____	_____	_____	_____	____

Are all of our goals and objectives addressed with the above activities?   ☐ Yes ☐ No
Is there adequate follow-up for lead generation activities?   ☐ Yes ☐ No
Is there adequate personnel to accomplish the activities?   ☐ Yes ☐ No

Sales Plan

Do we have software or another system in place to track leads and schedule follow-up calls?
         ☐ Yes ☐ No
How will we qualify leads? _____
Can we provide a proposal within 48 hours?   ☐ Yes ☐ No

PROJECT TITLE _____ PROJECT NUMBER _____

1. <u>Getting Found</u>   YES   NO

Can the site be found relatively easily through a search engine?   ___   ___

*(Use **www.google.com**; suggested key words:*
   "[Name of Location]"
   "[Name of Location]" and "Economic Development"
   "[Name of Location]" and "Industrial"
Other key words: state, MSA name, site selection, location selection, facilities location,
relocation, real estate.)

Are appropriate keywords in meta tags, including typical misspellings?   ___   ___

(Also include both county and city names, as some users will know one but not the other.
If your economic development corporation has a name that doesn't identify the area
(e.g., "The Business Center"), it is particularly important to include the location names.)

Has an appropriate descriptive sentence been added to the meta tags?   ___   ___

(Many search engines will display this information, rather than the first few words
on your website. This gives you more control over what the potential visitor will see
in the search engine.)

**Does the text in the home page include typical keywords that would be entered
in the search engine?**   ___   ___

(See suggested words above.)

**Does the home page title contain appropriate language that would be found by
search engines?**   ___   ___

*(By **title**, we are referring to the title that appears at the top of the window; the page title*
is entered in the meta tag for the page.)

Other factors that can't be checked at the site, but do figure in:

Has the site's URL been registered with all major search engine services?   ___   ___

(Software is available to do this automatically.)

**Have related sites been contacted to arrange links to your site, e.g.,
communities, related agencies, state, associations?**   ___   ___

**If Flash graphics are used in the home page, is an alternate page or
crawler-friendly page also used?**   ___   ___

(ALT tags can't be used with Flash graphics, so search engines will ignore them;
additionally, some people search web with graphics turned off. Text-to-speech
converters need ALT tags to "read" screen for sight-impaired computer users—
ADA makes universal access a must, particularly for publicly funded sites.)

WEBSITE DESIGN CHECKLIST

PROJECT TITLE _____ PROJECT NUMBER _____

2. Technical Matters

	YES	NO
Is the total home page size 40k or less, to allow for rapid downloading?	___	___
Are tables split for faster loading (i.e., first table loads so the user has something to look at while the second table is loading)?	___	___
Does the page work on different browsers (Explorer, Netscape, AOL)?	___	___
Are ALT tags used on all graphics [text label that appears as placeholder for graphic while user is waiting for graphic to download] so user doesn't have to wait for graphics to move on?	___	___
Is the image height and width included in the code for every image to reduce download time?	___	___
Are graphics preloaded* for the next level down?	___	___

*(*Load the graphics at the bottom of the home page, but set them at 1 x 1 pixel—it makes the next page come up instantly. However, don't get carried away with too many preloaded graphics.)*

3. Navigation

	YES	NO
Does your site have the customer in mind?	___	___
Who is/are the target audience(s) and how will they find the info they need?	___	___
Are there pull-downs that can lead the customer to the right area for information?	___	___
Is there always an identifying label to tell the user where he or she is in the site?	___	___
Can the user get to the home page from any other page?	___	___
Can the user get where they need to go in three clicks or less?	___	___
Are all pages laid out consistently (e.g., links appear in the same spot on every page)?	___	___
Are text links used appropriately?	___	___

(Hyperlinked words are unambiguous; "click here" wording is avoided.)

	YES	NO
Can pages be accessed via more than one route to accommodate different user needs?	___	___

(e.g., population data can be reached from both the labor and community overview sections)

WEBSITE DESIGN CHECKLIST

PROJECT TITLE _____ PROJECT NUMBER _____

	YES	NO

If the site is large (20 pages or more), is there a site map to help the user locate information? ____ ____

Have hyperlinks been added to narrative text wherever possible? ____ ____

(A major advantage of web text is that words and phrases can be linked to related information, yet interactivity is rarely used to its full potential.)

Have you appropriate links to other resources? ____ ____

Have you limited visitor registration components to the "request more information" stage? ____ ____

4. Appearance

What is the general impression one gets from looking at the site?

☐ Professional	or	☐ Amateurish
☐ Corporate	or	☐ Mom and Pop
☐ Flashy	or	☐ Mellow
☐ Bureaucratic	or	☐ Businesslike
☐ Customer-oriented	or	☐ Self-promoting

Do animated gifs enhance or distract from the message? ____ ____

(9 times out of 10 they distract)

Do colors and/or background patterns enhance or interfere with readability?

If the site will be viewed by a large number of males, are all important elements distinguishable to someone who is color blind? ____ ____

(Red/green/brown/gray/purple may not be distinguishable from each other; use strong light/dark contrast.)

Will a visitor be enticed to look beyond the home page? ____ ____

Are fonts large enough to read? ____ ____

Are a limited number of fonts used? ____ ____

Is contrast used in font sizes to enhance readability? ____ ____

Are related items grouped together to establish logical relationships (proximity)? ____ ____

WEBSITE DESIGN CHECKLIST

PROJECT TITLE _____ PROJECT NUMBER _____

5. Content   YES   NO

General Content:

Are exit links used appropriately?   ___   ___

*(Good: links provided to peripherally related sources of information.
Bad: links to other sites used for primary information, unless the link goes to
the precise information; don't make the user leave your site to go on a scavenger hunt.
For example, provide your visitor with a summary table of all taxes; provide a link to all
taxing bodies to obtain additional information and forms.)*

Is objective information presented, rather than marketing hype?

Is scannable text* used where possible?   ___   ___

*(*e.g., use of bullets and subheads, highlighted keywords, one idea per paragraph,
that allow reader to quickly grasp the content of the page)*

Is text as concise as possible?

**Does the home page contain a succinct, one- or two-sentence summary of
the company's position and purpose, phrased in terms of user benefits?** ___   ___

*(Mission statements do not belong in home pages. In some cases, a photo or
illustration may say it all, but some search engines look at the words used in
the home page, so this is an argument for including some minimal text.)*

Is there an appropriate balance of text and graphics?   ___   ___

*(At least one eyetracking study of news-related sites found that of users' first
three eye fixations, 78% were on text, and only 22% were on graphics. Some users
didn't even look at graphics until their second or third visit to a page.)*

Economic Development:

**Is your data up to date, particularly employer list and size, new
announcements about companies or actions taken that will assist companies,
availability of properties, announcements about availability of a particular
skill base due to a company's downsizing?**   ___   ___

*(Removal of outdated information, e.g., locations that are no longer available,
is just as important as adding new data.)*

Is there an adequate depth of information to make it useful to site selectors? ___   ___

(Users go to websites to get more information, not to download a brochure.)

PROJECT TITLE _____ PROJECT NUMBER _____

	YES	NO

Does your site contain data that site selectors can't obtain elsewhere? ____ ____

(e.g., available sites and buildings, local employers, size and union affiliation; prevailing wages for primary manufacturing and office occupations, full information on taxes, including telecommunications and utility taxes)

Are you alienating users by requiring them to fill in a form, or otherwise identify themselves, in order to obtain information? ____ ____

(Instead, make an offer to provide them something additional that they can't get online— a brochure, a free gift, a customized proposal.)

Are user-oriented words used? ____ ____

(Examples: say "locating your business" instead of "business development," "business recruitment" or "expansion opportunities" rather than "retention," or "how to report a pothole" instead of "Public Works Dept." For specific departments, you might want to have links from both, to accommodate different user needs.)

Is the information understandable for someone unfamiliar with the area? ____ ____

(Will they know what county to click for information if presented with a map of the state?)

Is it easy to find contact information from every page?

Can the information be downloaded quickly?

Can a user pick and choose the information they want to download?

What format is the download? ____ ____

(Site selectors prefer Excel spreadsheets. If the user cannot download Excel worksheets, find a method to provide that information within 4 hours.)

6. Response System

Is there an email contact on each page? ____ ____

Can a customer request additional information from the site directly to a person? ____ ____

Can the customer submit information and request a Proposal for Siting? ____ ____

Can the customer order information via the website? ____ ____

Is the response time to questions less than 4 hours? ____ ____

PROJECT TITLE _____ PROJECT NUMBER _____

Demographics

- ☐ Population
- ☐ Population growth estimates
- ☐ Median age
- ☐ Population by age
- ☐ Median household income

- ☐ Labor force size
  (If possible, define by time rather than geography, i.e., 30-minute commute.)
- ☐ Labor force participation rate
- ☐ Unemployment rate history

Education

- ☐ Percent of adults graduated from highschool
- ☐ Percent of adults with some college
- ☐ Percent of adults graduated from college
- ☐ Median years of education

- ☐ Identity of community colleges, colleges, and universities
- ☐ Name, size of student body, major programs
- ☐ Special training programs, with contact names
- ☐ Discussion of any special school to work initiatives

Employer Profiles

- ☐ Industry breakdown
- ☐ Occupation breakdown
- ☐ Identity of major manufacturing and service employers
- ☐ Who they are
  - ☐ Major functions and occupation groups
  - ☐ Number of employees
  - ☐ Significant developments—hiring programs or downsizing
  - ☐ Full time/part time mix
  - ☐ Union affiliation
  - ☐ Case histories

Labor Costs

- ☐ Starting and median wages for major manufacturing and office occupations
- ☐ Unemployment insurance rate for new companies (i.e., x% for the first $X of payroll)
- ☐ Contact name and number for worker compensation quotes

Sites and Buildings

- ☐ Pictures are not critical, but asking price is important
- ☐ Remember to include office buildings and retail or other spaces that may be appropriate for adaptive reuse.

PROJECT TITLE _____ **PROJECT NUMBER** _____

Sites and Buildings (continued)

☐ For sites:
   ☐ Map of location, maybe topo
   ☐ Size
   ☐ Neighboring uses
   ☐ Zoning
   ☐ Access to site
   ☐ Utility service
   ☐ Asking price
   ☐ Ownership

☐ For buildings:
   ☐ Map of location
   ☐ Schematic of layout
   ☐ Size
   ☐ Ceiling height
   ☐ Bay size
   ☐ Construction material
   ☐ Previous use
   ☐ Neighboring uses
   ☐ Access to building
   ☐ Utility service, including telecommunications
   ☐ Parking availability
   ☐ Zoning
   ☐ Asking price
   ☐ Ownership

Transportation

☐ Major highways
☐ Passenger rail, if any
☐ Freight rail service
☐ Port service
☐ Passenger air service
   ☐ Airlines
   ☐ Major markets served
   ☐ Type of service: jet or commuter

☐ Private passenger air service
☐ Freight air service
☐ Overnight package delivery
☐ Truck terminals
☐ Community bus or train service

Business Amenities

☐ Local banking services
☐ Nearest bulk mail facility

Taxes

☐ State level personal and corporate income tax rates
☐ City income tax if any
☐ Sales and use tax: state rate and local option rates
☐ Property tax rates, assessment ratios for major jurisdictions
☐ State telecommunications tax

Regulatory Environment

☐ Typical permitting time for different types of businesses

☐ Nonattainment status
☐ Monitoring restrictions for telephone use

WEB DATA CHECKLIST

PROJECT TITLE _____ PROJECT NUMBER _____

Utilities

☐ Names and contact numbers for electric power, gas, water, sewer, local and long distance telecommunications providers (contact names should be people who can discuss rates and availability of service)

☐ Electric power: Provider(s), status of deregulation, typical rates

☐ Gas service: Provider(s), status of deregulation

☐ Water and sewer: Provider(s), capacity, excess capacity, expansion plan

☐ Telecommunications: Local and long distance providers, cellular providers, long distance points of presence, fiber availability, central office switch locations, digital switching

Quality of Life

☐ Education—public and private K-12 schools, test scores, teacher/student ratios, etc.

☐ Climate—typical temperatures, rainfall, snowfall, days of airport, and school closure due to weather

☐ Crime—FBI statistics, if available

☐ Culture and recreation—golf courses, theaters, museums, etc.

☐ Cost of living—housing cost, including apartment rental, preferably from a third-party source
　　☐ Description of typical homes, neighborhoods, prices
　　☐ Comparative cost of living statistics from third-party source, if available

Incentives

☐ State programs
　　☐ Training
　　☐ Tax credits
　　☐ Loans and grants

☐ Local programs
　　☐ Abatements, tax increment financing
　　☐ Discretionary funds

☐ Private programs

☐ Case studies

This checklist is adapted from Kate McEnroe's *The Economic Development Series: Web Sites* (Dubuque, Iowa: Kendall/Hunt Publishing Company, 1999.) Reprinted with permission.

CHAPTER 7

DUE DILIGENCE
A Commonsense Approach

David Wingate, CEcD
Finance Specialist,
Washington State Office of Trade and Economic Development

———— ◆ ————

When investment and job-creation opportunities present themselves to many economic developers, the first tendency is to embrace the project with open arms. But an astute economic developer will first ask whether he or she can justify taking such an opportunity into the public arena. This chapter will help the economic developer conduct a successful due diligence effort.

Due diligence is the industry term for doing one's homework. It means finding out as much information as possible to ensure that, as a dealmaker, the economic developer's time is spent doing business with a company that has the essential integrity and financial capability necessary to close a deal. Due diligence means investing enough time at the beginning of negotiations with a prospect to ensure that the resources of time and capital are directed efficiently in the future.

WHY DUE DILIGENCE IS IMPORTANT

There are various reasons for conducting due diligence at the beginning of a relationship with a prospect, but none are as critical as preserving the economic developer's integrity. Every deal places the economic developer's reputation on the line. Each time that risk is taken, the potential for un-employment is presented in very real terms. The deals that are presented into the public arena should only reach that stage after being researched thoroughly.

It is also important for economic developers to know that some businesses perceive the profession as a means to cheap financing or free money. These unscrupulous companies will seek communities that display a certain level of desperation. Occasionally, they will set up investment or expansion scenarios that may potentially dupe the community out of its valuable resources. A greater understanding of the company's background at the forefront of negotiations can prevent the economic developer, and the community he or she represents, from becoming the victim of a scam.

Community assets are another reason for conducting a due diligence effort. The profession has yet to experience an economic development program that has unlimited assets to throw at deals. When an economic developer enters into negotiations with a prospect, he or she is making good faith commitments on community assets that may be pledged toward successful deal closure. As this occurs, these assets are no longer available for other opportunities that may present themselves. While most deals are considered in a linear fashion, there are times when multiple deals must be addressed simultaneously. When this occurs, the community may be forced to choose between deals or to apply limited amounts of incentives to multiple deals. Imagine how embarrassing it would be to have Deal A be lost to another community with a stronger incentive package and then have Deal B implode due to improper due diligence at the front end of negotiations.

And speaking of eleventh-hour embarrassments, how long does an economic developer expect to be employed when deals blow up late in the negotiation process? One of the first responsibilities of an economic development professional is to cull the deals from the dogs as soon as possible. Then, only credible deals are moved into the public arena, the reputation of the professional is protected, and the closure rate of the community is held at its maximum possible level.

STEPS IN THE DUE DILIGENCE PROCESS

No due diligence process is executed the same way for every project. In economic development, every deal is different. Therefore, the practitioner must be flexible and able to work in an unstructured environment. Having said that, the basic steps for conducting a successful review of a prospect are as follows:

1. Meet with the prospect
2. Define the project
3. Research the company
4. Research the industry
5. Visit corporate headquarters and/or a plant of comparable size
6. Summarize the findings
7. Get a second opinion

Step 1:
MEET WITH THE PROSPECT

An economic developer worth his or her salt will develop an ability to assess the character of an individual sitting across the table from them. Therefore, a luncheon or afternoon with a prospect is an essential first step in the due diligence process. Evaluate the prospect by considering the following:

- *How do they dress?*
- *How do they conduct themselves?*
- *Do they look you in the eyes when they talk?*
- *Are they sincere and focused about their plans?*
- *Do they leave you with a good feeling about their ability to conclude this deal?*

These basic characteristics tell the economic developer about the character of the prospect. Before dessert is served, the first test will be either passed or failed.

Step 2:
DEFINE THE PROJECT

Get the project defined on paper. The process of reducing it to writing allows for a couple of advantages:

- It confirms the statements made by the prospect.
- It provides a vehicle for accurately conveying the project to the appropriate parties necessary for gathering consensus on the deal.

The Washington Office of Trade and Economic Development has a standard Business Investment Data Form which can be used as is or customized for your personal use. Regardless of how it is designed, it is important to use one to define the project. The form should be quite detailed.

In most instances, filling out this form in person with the prospect on the first meeting is an inappropriate use of both the economic developer's and the prospect's time. What is appropriate, however, is to state in this first meeting something to the effect of: *"We have some basic forms that we use to define the projects we address. They are detailed and will require a little time to complete. I'd like to send one along as a follow-up to our meeting. Can you or someone on your staff complete it and get it back to me when possible?"* The answer will most always be "Yes."

Step 3:
RESEARCH THE COMPANY

Once a company provides the basic information in the questionnaire, the economic developer is then presented with an opportunity to begin the real research necessary to make a quality decision regarding pursuing the deal. Information can be obtained both formally and informally. To conduct formal research, use library reference books and online research databases such as DIALOG, Lexis/Nexis, Westlaw, Ward's Business Directory of the United States, Dun & Bradstreet, Standard & Poor's, Moody's, etc. Trade credit reports will verify if the company pays its bills. A Uniform Commercial Code (UCC) search in the state where the business has its headquarters will reveal liens filed against the company's assets.

One of the most commonly referenced credit reports is the Dun & Bradstreet Report. This report—an industry standard—can usually be obtained for free from one of the following:

- Local banker
- Commercial insurance agent
- State Department of Commerce
- Utility Economic Development Office

A Dun & Bradstreet Report will provide an overview of the company, including credit rating, history, management, owners, operations, locations, financial, trade credit, and UCC filings.

Working one's network is another valuable method of revealing information. The community's economic development team can gather data through phone calls. The following ideas may yield results:

▶ A local banker on the team can contact a correspondent banker in the business's community.

▶ A local utility person can contact someone at the utility serving the business's community.

▶ Contact some of the business's suppliers.

▶ Someone on the team may know someone in the business's community and be willing to contact them.

Finally, the Internet provides a wealth of information on a company. For publicly traded companies, an hour of research will provide more information than most economic developers will have time to read. However, for larger privately held companies, there is often a large volume of information available as well.

To get started, log on to CEO Express, *www.ceoexpress.com*. This website links all of the world's information sources into a single space and provides the economic developer with a single source for tracking information on a company. In the search box at the top of the page, type in the name of the company and hit return. Usually, this will yield large amounts of information that will create a background of knowledge about the company.

Another great resource is Smart Money, *www.smartmoney.com*. Log onto this page and enter either the company name or stock sym-

bol in the search engine. The following sites also offer useful information about businesses:

The Street, *www.thestreet.com*
Bloomberg, *www.bloomberg.com*
Moody's, *www.moodys.com*
Standard & Poor's, *www.standardpoor.com*
Factiva, *www.factiva.com*

THE ULTIMATE COMPANY REVIEW

Economic developers should feel comfortable requesting three years of audited financial statements from the company. With these in hand, the economic developer possesses the ultimate business analysis tool. Learn how to analyze financial statements via the highly acclaimed courses provided by the National Development Council, *www.ndc-online.org/*.

If the risk is high, obtain a litigation search on the business and personal credit reports on the principals. An attorney or services such as Lexis/Nexis can conduct a litigation search. This will show if the company is involved in any lawsuits (product liability, class-action, pollution violations, fraud, etc.) or has ever filed for bankruptcy. Personal credit reports can be obtained with the help of a local banker or revolving loan fund. Personal credit reports will show liens, judgments, collections, bankruptcies, and repossessions. Written permission of the individual is required to order a personal credit report.

If incentives and public financing are not issues for the business, obtaining financial statements or their business plan or completing a due diligence checklist may not be necessary.

Step 4:
RESEARCH THE INDUSTRY

Researching an industry is somewhat similar to researching a company. In most cases, a company will be experiencing similar trends to its industry, so if the industry is in an expansion mode, a well-run company has a good probability of experiencing the same.

*If the company shows glowing financials but the industry does not,
a red flag should be raised by the economic developer
signaling the need for closer scrutiny than usual.*

Conversely, if an industry is contracting or receding, most businesses in that industry will be experiencing similar economic pressures. The two are interconnected.

This is important, because some companies see economic development incentives as a saving grace for getting out of financial trouble. A prudent economic developer who has done his or her homework well will know what's happening with the company *and* the industry they represent. If the company shows glowing financials but the industry does not, a red flag should be raised for the economic developer signaling the need for closer scrutiny than usual.

Resources for Industry Trends

- Local Banker
- Department of Commerce
- Local Universities
- Your Stock Broker
- Internet
- Growth Strategies
- Harris
- Manufacturer's Directory

So how does the economic developer review the industry? It's pretty much the same process as that of reviewing the financials for the company. In this instance, however, the local banking community is an even more valuable asset. Most bankers regularly receive reports on industry trends and updates. These bulletins provide a good overview of what's happening in that sector, thereby affording them the same briefing knowledge that is being sought by the economic developer. In many instances, these documents can be obtained by calling a banker who may also be a board member.

Another reliable source of information is the state Department of Commerce. As with bankers, the agency often compiles its own industry briefings and trends analysis.

A third resource could be an economist at a local university. Many economics department heads are keynote speakers for business luncheons and can provide economic insight and commentary. In order to prepare for these presentations, the professors do a great deal of research regarding various sectors. In many cases their data is current and can be quickly given or e-mailed to the practitioner.

A stock broker is another source of industry knowledge. If there is an investment advisor in the community, he or she will have a wealth (no pun intended) of information at their disposal about various business and industry sectors. A close relationship with some of these individuals provides the economic developer access to a valuable information source. Also, while many people are moving away from full-service brokers, there are still a good number who use partial service, such as Schwab or Fidelity—trading services that have excellent online company- and sector-analysis services for their customers. Additionally, the economic developer's own 401k programs may provide investment advice that can be accessed to review various sector trends and analyses.

Lastly, there is the Internet. Many of the resources listed in the previous section also have sector-analysis services. In many cases, these can be accessed for free by investing an afternoon doing the research. Usually, these are high-level reviews that provide a good overview.

SOURCES AND DIRECTORIES FOR DUE DILIGENCE

Most public and university libraries have the resources required to investigate a North American company and many international companies. The library's reference desk can provide help.

Online Databases

ABI/Inform is a database of business articles that can be used for current and historical information dating to 1971. This replaces the old Business Periodicals Index.

Company Intelligence (Co-Intell) includes the date of financial data, which reveals how current the numeric information is.

DIALOG is a conglomeration of about 3,000 databases. Associations provide trade, industry, and company data. *http://www.dialog.com*, 800-334-2564.

Disclosure presents three to five years of financial information for companies. Call 1-800-638-8241 to request annual reports and other SEC filings for $35 plus shipping.

Dun & Bradstreet Online Information Services, *http://www.dnb.com*, 800-234-3867.

Lexis/Nexis has approximately 5,000 databases. *http://www.lexisnexis.com/documentsolutions/default.htm*, 800-634-9738.

Westlaw has approximately 7,000 law databases. *http://www.westlaw.com*, 800-344-5008.

Online Reference Books

Credit Reference Directory of U.S. Businesses from American Business Information, Inc. provides general company information and payment history. Online equivalent: TRW/Credit, DIALOG, and Information America.

Directory of Corporate Affiliations lists corporate affiliations of U.S. public and private companies, regional offices, divisions.

Dun & Bradstreet Million-Dollar Directory of America's Leading Public and Private Companies, arranged by Standard Industrial Classification (SIC) industry and geography.

Moody's provides financial analysis of companies listed on the New York and American Stock Exchanges.

The Reference Book of Manufacturers is a guide to information on more than 400,000 U.S. manufacturers.

Standard & Poor's provides financial analysis for more than 55,000 publicly traded companies but not about private companies. It also has a news file that tracks the Dow Jones wire service for the latest earnings, sales, and stock quotes.

Ward's Business Directory of U.S. Private and Public Companies from Gale Research is a directory of more than 142,000 companies arranged alphabetically, geographically, and by industry. It lists financial information, executive structure, products, and services offered.

References to Research Small Companies

Directory of American Firms Operating in Foreign Countries. Volume 1 alphabetically lists American firms with operations abroad; Volumes 2 and 3 list American firms' foreign operations, by country.

International Directory of Company Histories provides the historical development of 1,250 of the world's largest and most influential companies. Companies chosen have achieved US$2 billion in annual sales or are a leading influence in a particular industry.

Principal International Businesses: The World Marketing Directory, Dun & Bradstreet. Categorized by SIC codes.

World Business Directory, Gale Research, Inc. Analysis of 100,000 businesses involved in international trade.

World Trade Resources Guide provides contacts for organizations, agencies, banks and other financial institutions, chambers of commerce, government agencies, research centers and services, trade associations, business libraries, computerized databases, and consultants.

Worldwide Branch Locations of Multinational Companies, Gale Research, Inc.

Information on Private Companies

Owners and Officers of Private Companies is a directory of private U.S. businesses providing hard-to-find data on personnel and companies—105,000 private company executives from 43,000 top private firms. Search by company name index, personal name index, SIC code, or geography. Lists address, telephone, sales, employee number, SIC, type of business.

Other Information Sources

Burwell's Directory of Fee-Based Information Services lists commercial research firms and brokers by country, state, company, subject, and service.

Croner's A-Z of Business Information Sources has an international scope and is a directory for company product, market, and consumer information.

Who Knows What lists organizations that provide business information.

The Worldwide Government Directory provides information on 175 governments and 100 international government agencies worldwide.

Step 5:
VISIT CORPORATE HEADQUARTERS AND/OR A PLANT OF COMPARABLE SIZE

A site visit to the corporate headquarters or another plant the company operates that is similar in size to the one they are considering may be the single most important step in the due diligence process. The economic development team would benefit greatly by seeing the business in operation to verify the truth of the business's statements. Pictures taken to document the trip can be used to brief community leaders who are not able to participate in the site visit while also substantiating the viability of the prospect company.

Multiple visits may be warranted to view the plant on different days and times. While in town, walk around their community. Visit other local businesses and ask questions. If the company has shift labor, a stop at the local watering hole may provide a climate within which the economic developer can ask more direct questions to those employees who work now for the company.

A red flag at this point is if the prospect company tries to restrict visits to the corporate offices. In some cases this is legitimate due to the proprietary nature of the production process. In others, this is an attempt by the company to hide old and dilapidated equipment or a poor work environment. The economic developer must judge why certain facts and facilities are shared or withheld during the due diligence process.

THINGS TO LOOK FOR WHILE ON SITE

— *Is the operation orderly, clean, and professional?*

— *Do employees and management know what they are doing?*

— *Do the production line and operations seem to run smoothly?*

— *How are visitors and the firm's customers treated?*

— *Does management seem to have information readily available?*

— *Ask employees how they feel about the company.*

Step 6:
SUMMARIZE THE FINDINGS

At this point, a great deal of information will have been gleaned about the company, its expansion plans, and the relative fit within the community. The result of this work will be a pile of fragmented information, photos, financial statements, and miscellaneous documents sitting in a file (or pile) in the economic developer's office.

Now comes the task of compiling and summarizing the data. The purpose of this exercise is twofold:

- The economic developer will want to consolidate all information into a review of the prospect company.
- The information can then be shared with other community leaders as needed to influence the decision-making process.

Each project will generate different amounts of information. If the economic developers produce due diligence reports in a consistent format, however, they will be able to retrieve them quickly while also enhancing their integrity with the board and community.

Review the due diligence checklist at the end of this chapter and apply those sections that are relevant to the risk or investment the business is requesting from the community. The higher the risk/investment, the more detailed and complete the due diligence checklist should be.

Step 7:
GET A SECOND OPINION

The need for this last step increases substantially as the size of the deal increases. In the practice of economic development, a project team should be formed around each project. The size of the team is proportional to the size of the deal. Small projects may only involve the economic developer, while large projects may involve a team consisting of a board member, local banker, Department of Commerce representative, a utility member, a realtor or real estate developer, etc.

DUE DILIGENCE REPORT — Suggested Format

1. **Executive Summary**
   Summarize the project, the company and the incentive/financial package.
2. **Strengths and Weaknesses**
   Be honest. There is no perfect company just as there is no perfect community. On a single sheet of paper in the due diligence report, list the strengths (pros) the company presents for locating in the community on the left column and the weaknesses (cons) on the right column.
3. **Company Financial Statements**
   The three-year, audited financial statements come next in the report. If the economic developer took the NDC finance course listed earlier, the "Quality Indicator Checklist" should precede the financial statements.
4. **Industry Review and Analysis**
   A summary of the industry (or sector) trends is helpful.
5. **Site Plans**
   Information about the proposed site development should come next. A site plan (or building footprint), investment plans, environmental impacts, transportation access, etc. are all valuable items to address at this point.
6. **Corporate Site Visit Report**
   A review of the findings of the corporate site visit should come last.
7. **Miscellaneous**
   Any other valuable information gleaned about the company or project should conclude the report.

On large deals, one or more members of the project team should be involved in the due diligence process. The final corporate and project review discussed in Step 6 should receive a second look by a team member before being presented to the organization's board. This allows the economic developer to have their findings reviewed and critiqued privately before submitting them to the board of directors.

Due to the complex nature of the information gleaned during the due diligence process, the second opinion may actually be a number of partial second opinions. A banker may review the financial statements, while a stock broker may review the industry trends. A board member who accompanied the economic developer on the trip should review the findings of the site tour.

A second opinion will confirm the findings achieved during the review process as well as spot grammatical and editorial corrections. As individual sections receive sign-off, they can be compiled into the final report that is shared with select decision-makers in the community.

KEY ATTRIBUTES* . . . OF A GOOD DEAL

1. **The deal is made possible because a business organization adheres to the profit-making motive** and has specific corporate objectives, requiring the deployment of business resources.

2. **The business and the local practitioner have done their due diligence** and have concluded that the possibility exists for a good fit between company and community.

3. **The business provides the practitioner with a completed questionnaire** covering the essentials of the project and continuing well beyond, searching for subtle aspects about the community. The implication is that the more exhaustive the transacting parties are in doing their homework, the better the chances for a good deal.

4. **The business provides timely and qualitative responses** to the local practitioner's questions and needs for information.

5. **The business understands its market** and has increased sales during the last three years.

6. **Incentives should not be necessary for the transaction to ensue,** even though the business may demand them. Incentives must be incidental to the project; they can never be the main reason for the transaction to take place. If the practitioner is aware of a nearby competitor with more or less the same deal, incentives can act as a tie-breaker.

7. **Information about the business is readily available** through Dun & Bradstreet. (This means the business is not a start-up and has had inquiries through D & B before.) Some of the smaller businesses targeted by small rural communities—under $1,000,000 in sales and fewer than 25 employees—may not have had an inquiry before. Search all sources; ask for a credit check by a third party.

8. **The business is interested in meeting key community leaders** and in how things happen in the community. This reveals that the business is concerned about how it will be perceived in the community and that the company intends to be around for a long time.

9. **The business settles in the community without a disproportionate impact on the infrastructure of the host community.** If the business is a bean processor and the community's sewage treatment system is barely capable of handling the discharge, future development opportunities may be compromised. A good transaction contains an appropriate fit between the company's use of the infrastructure and the community's ability to provide an infrastructure.

INVOLVING OTHERS IN THE PROCESS

The development team should include a banker, a commercial real estate developer, an attorney, and a representative from a Small Business Development Center. Representatives from the local community college and a local revolving fund can help with due diligence and research.

DUE DILIGENCE COSTS

Most of costs relate to research. The D&B report costs between $60 and $100 for a member. A local banker or large city economic development council or state partners could split this cost or donate it to the organization.

An attorney will generally charge between $150 and $250 to do a litigation search. Lexis/Nexis (800-634-9738) charges the following rates, which vary from state to state and with

KEY ATTRIBUTES* . . . of A BAD DEAL

1. **The business would be the only employer of its type in the community.** This doesn't mean the deal is bad, but the economic development team would have difficulty effectively screening this business.

2. **The business needs financing or incentives** in order for the project to take place. Studies show that companies choosing location based upon a financing need are likely to be marginal companies from the beginning.

3. **The business owner/manager does not appear to know his or her business** and the circumstances in which it will grow.

4. **The business does not know its market** and/or has a declining sales trend.

5. **The business is a start-up.** This is not a deal killer if there is plenty of equity, good management, and a strong market. It is, however, a red flag. It means a higher risk of failure. Studies show that more than 70 percent of new businesses fail in the first three years of operation.

6. **The business does not respond in a timely manner** with adequate information.

7. **The business is inconsistent.** Local practitioners should closely observe business management styles and, if possible, try to learn something from the venture about employee relations. Compare what is observed with what the prevailing practices are within the community. An inconsistent management style or one that disrupts labor peace in the community is definitely undesirable. At times of low unemployment rates in many parts of the United States, labor pool considerations become much more important.

8. **The business has a disproportionate impact on community infrastructure.** Certain food processors, for example, may require extensive use of water or sewage treatment. Capacity of the community system to meet current and future needs will impact not only the business's ability to grow and expand, but also the community's ability to accommodate the business's future growth.

9. **The business is reluctant to have the local practitioner and community leaders visit its current site of operations.**

*Key Attributes was developed by James Hettinger, President, Battle Creek Unlimited, with assistance by Janette A. Burland. This information first appeared in **Race To Recruit: Strategies for Successful Business Attraction**, edited by Maury Forman and James Mooney. Reprinted with permission from the editors.

PRINCIPLES FOR SUCCESSFUL DUE DILIGENCE	
Use information from reliable sources. Rumors should be considered but should be verified with reliable sources.	**All information obtained during due diligence should be held in strict confidence.** Always ask the business for permission to share information before it is released.
Information must be timely.	**Present information in a clear and concise format** so lay people can understand it.
Information must be thorough.	**Learn from mistakes.**
Information must fit the purpose and be applicable to the situation or need.	**Trust intuition and gut feelings.** Intuition often comes from experience.
Dare to be Diligent! People lose their jobs because it is *easier not to be diligent.*	

the number of jurisdictions (or court districts) that need to be searched:

Legal or litigation search	*$50-$70 plus $1.50 per page for attachments*
UCC search	*$40-$60 plus $1.50 per page for attachments*
Federal, state and local tax lien search	*$30-$40 plus $1.50 per page for attachments*

Search companies in every state capital that provide similar services. Before approving a litigation and lien search, be sure the risk the community is being asked to take is large enough to justify the cost.

Personal credit reports generally cost about $20 for members. Membership costs can be shared with a local banker or revolving fund.

Businesses can get their own D&B by calling 800-234-3867. Individuals can get their personal credit reports by calling Equifax at 800-685-1111.

The primary cost of due diligence is time spent by local staff and the development team. The due diligence process continues as long as the business is operating in the community.

WAS IT WORTH IT?

In reading this chapter an economic developer might think, "Hey, due diligence is a lot of work!" Yes, it takes effort to qualify a pros-

pect, quantify the project, and determine the fit with the community, but that is why the economic developer was hired.

Due diligence is one of those areas where the economic developer can provide true value-added service to the community(ies) he or she serves. Many of the services and specialties of the economic developer can be provided by others in the community. The economic developer who provides needed services will be the greatest success.

Due diligence weeds out the bad deals at the front end of the negotiation process. It ensures that the community's assets and the economic developer's time are directed toward projects that will become winners, not losers.

As projects close in the community, the economy is enhanced, and the community is able to close additional deals while providing essential public services. Few economic developers would argue against these measures of success.

Looked at differently, the economic development professionals will invest their time in basically one or two activities: finding ways to close deals and bring projects to fruition, or finding new work after they lose their jobs. A successful due diligence program facilitates the accomplishment of the first objective and avoids the second. Most practitioners would argue that the due diligence process was worth the effort.

FINAL THOUGHTS:
THE ENRON IMPACT

As this book was going to press, the Enron implosion was unfolding daily in the media. Enron was at one time perceived to be the seventh largest company in America. Its demise was predicated by corporate and personal greed. Enron personifies the need for good due diligence.

The saga is elevated to a higher catastrophic level by the fact that Enron's accounting firm, Arthur Andersen LLP, released audited financial statements each year that made the company appear to be highly profitable. Prior to the Enron collapse, Arthur Andersen was considered to be one of the most credible accounting firms around the globe. As Enron purchased and built additional assets throughout the world, its credit-worthiness was reviewed and approved repeatedly due to the

THINGS TO WATCH FOR	
The company refuses to provide information or the owners are unwilling to provide personal information and/or will not guaranty.	The business is slow or late in delivering requested information, especially historical financial information.
The company should see the economic development professional as an ally or advocate and be willing to share information on the project and their company's performance. If the business is not asking for a local investment of any kind, there may not be justification for requiring financial information. However, if the business does want local investment and risk taking, refusal to provide financial information is a deal killer.	The company does not want the economic development team to visit its current location. Perhaps they have something to hide or have not been honest.
	The business does not know its market and/or has a declining sales trend.
The company lies or misleads the economic development team on one matter.	The business has a bad reputation in its community or industry.
Liens, judgments, or lawsuits show on the business or the owners' credit reports.	The business appears to be of poor quality during a site visit.
Poor credit history of the business or owners.	The business has problems with neighbors, the city, or the county where it is located.

Indicators that the business has poor motives for wanting to relocate:

- **The business places importance on the availability of incentives at the expense of other, more fundamental business location factors.**

- **The proposed project financing is given priority at the expense of other, more fundamental business location factors.**

- **The business insists that the project is being done only to provide jobs for the community.** Any company that claims it can create jobs without being concerned about the bottom line will not be in business long and the jobs it creates will be temporary.

false claims made in its financial statements provided by Arthur Andersen.

Economic developers impacted by Enron's fraud, after having conducted even the most extensive review of the company, would most certainly have felt a sense of frustration as the company collapsed. While their frustration was ultimately relieved by the exposure of Enron's unscrupulous business practices, they can feel comfort in knowing that even the best financial minds were fooled. Enron taught the economic development community some very valuable lessons:

► When presented with what appears to be the most credible audited financial statements, the economic development practitioner must consider that they may be looking at nothing more than a numerical fairy tale.

► The numbers alone do not tell the story of the company. Although somewhat hidden from the popular press, the energy industry knew at a minimum that things were not well in the Enron camp. Economic developers who were working their network could have flushed out anecdotal information if they were reviewing Enron deals in the fall of 2001.

► Even the best get duped once in a while. The government, the investors, and the employees of the company all fell for Enron's story. Once the final chapter is written, we may find that Enron's fairy tale was scripted by a handful of people with very senior positions in the corporate ladder. As these individuals withheld vital information from the public, the world was led to believe that company was a viable and growing entity.

A due diligence exercise that turns up falsified information is still better than no due diligence at all. When the unfortunate occurs and the deal collapses at the eleventh hour, as it did for some communities in the case of Enron, the economic developer who can produce a project file (or report) documenting the fact that they did their homework will survive the experience. They'll be better off for having done their homework and will feel secure in the knowledge that their credibility in the community is both protected and enhanced as a result of having done so.

SOURCES

Alexandra Reed-Lajoux, Charles, *Art of M&A Due Diligence*. McGraw Hill, 2000.

Bing, Gordon, *Due Dilligence, Techniques and Analysis: Critical Questions for Business Decisions*. Greenwood Publishing Group, 1996.

Crilly, William, *Due Diligence Handbook*. AMACOM, 1997.

Kahn, Michael, *Due Diligence*. Dutton/Plume, 1995.

Rankine, D., *Commercial Due Diligence*. Prentice Hall, 1999.

About the Author . . .

David Wingate, CEcD, works as a Finance Specialist for the Washington State Office of Trade and Economic Development and covers seven counties in Northeastern Washington. He helps small businesses access capital where jobs are created or retained. He works primarily in timber-dependent, high-unemployment communities and prioritizes businesses owned by women and minorities. He has more than 30 years experience in banking, commercial finance, and rural economic development in both the private and public sectors, including Seattle First National Bank, SAFECO Commercial Credit Co., Inc., the National Consumer Cooperative Bank, and United Security Bank. Mr. Wingate can be reached at *dwingate@plix.com*.

PROJECT TITLE _____   PROJECT NUMBER _____

The following outline is a guide to business analysis. It is intended for professionals who review loan applications, recruit businesses, or have other direct contact with private companies. Sections I through IV constitute a minimum level of knowledge about a business. Not all of the topics will be relevant for a particular project analysis.

		TO	
	DONE	DO	N/A

I. REFERENCE CHECK

A. Call personal references, as well as industry contacts who may know the principals.

B. Call suppliers and customers, as well as former co-workers. ___ ___ ___

C. Call educational institutions to verify degree claims. ___ ___ ___

D. Investigate past relationships with banks and creditors. ___ ___ ___

II. LITIGATION REVIEW

A. Assess the status and outcome of any legal action taken by, or against, the company or its principals. Specifically:
  1. Litigation which may adversely affect the business. ___ ___ ___
  2. Any criminal records. ___ ___ ___
  3. Any "gray areas" such as divorce suits or personal liability actions which may affect the conduct of business. ___ ___ ___

B. Request information on any bankruptcy proceedings, past or present, which affect the principals or the company. ___ ___ ___

III. BUSINESS OVERVIEW

It is important to know the background of the company. If you are working with a business plan or an annual report, you will find the information there. At a minimum, the following items are ones which should be clearly stated and easily explainable.

A. **General Description**
  1. Brief history of company, including sales and profits. ___ ___ ___
  2. Business objectives (e.g., expansion, capital improvement, new product line). ___ ___ ___
  3. Products or Service:
     a. Product description. ___ ___ ___
     b. Competitive advantage (e.g., weight, size, cost), including technology review. ___ ___ ___
     c. Proprietary status (e.g., who holds patent rights). ___ ___ ___
  4. Current and projected market share. ___ ___ ___
  5. List of board members. ___ ___ ___

B. **Industry Overview**
  1. Current market trends ___ ___ ___
  2. Status of competition ___ ___ ___
  3. Pricing ___ ___ ___

C. **Other Issues.** *These are potential red flags which should be carefully screened.*
  1. Has the business changed names or location? ☐ YES ☐ NO
     If so, why? _____
  2. Has there been recent turnover of principals? ☐ YES ☐ NO

TO
DONE DO N/A

   3. Were there recent product changes? ☐ YES ☐ NO
   4. What is the status of suppliers? _____
   5. What is the competition's view of this company and its products?

   _____

  D. **Financial Background**
   1. Balance sheet   __ __ __
   2. Income statement   __ __ __
   3. Cash flow   __ __ __
   4. Has the business prepared a source/use statement? ☐ YES ☐ NO

IV. **PROJECT INFORMATION**

  A. What is the basis of the contact? Is the company's objective to, e.g., seek
    funding, relocate, restructure, or expand? _____

    _____

  B. If the company is seeking financing, what are the financial requirements of
    each of the following items (whether or not the company is seeking funds
    for them)?
    1. Research   __ __ __
    2. Product development   __ __ __
    3. Working capital   __ __ __
    4. Machinery and equipment   __ __ __
    5. Real estate or leasehold improvements   __ __ __
    6. Marketing   __ __ __
    7. Other (specify: _____) __ __ __
  C. What funding sources are involved in the project (whether or not the agency
    is being asked to participate)?
    1. Equity—evidence of which should be documented.   __ __ __
    2. Private Lenders.   __ __ __
       If from an institution, are there letters of commitment? ☐ YES ☐ NO
       What are the rates and terms? _____
       Are there special terms? _____
    3. Public Agencies. Who is participating—federal, state, or local government?
       Ports or nonprofit agency? _____
       What are the terms and conditions? _____
       Has a separate review been completed? ☐ YES ☐ NO
    4. What past investments have been made in the company, and by whom?

    _____

    _____

  D. What are the requirements for second round financing?
    1. Bank interest: _____
    2. Venture funding: _____
    3. Stock offering: _____

V. OPERATING PLAN

This component of the review is the one through which the public sector can usually interact best with the business. After the initial review, this is a logical place to begin the more thorough analysis.

A. **Geographic Location.** *It is important that the following issues be understood by the economic development professional as well as by the business.*

	DONE	TO DO	N/A
1. Labor rate.	—	—	—
2. Labor availability.	—	—	—
3. Level of labor force training (and how additional needs can be met).	—	—	—
4. Proximity to distributors and customers.	—	—	—
5. Proximity to suppliers.	—	—	—
6. Tax structure (from all sources).	—	—	—
7. Utility rates and requirements.	—	—	—
8. Zoning and applicable local laws.	—	—	—
9. Local source of components (ease of supply).	—	—	—

B. **Facilities and Improvements**

1. Current development plans.	—	—	—
2. Expansion needs.	—	—	—
3. Office and manufacturing floor space requirements.	—	—	—
4. Machinery and other capital requirements.	—	—	—
5. Lease vs. purchase requirements—should reveal costs; planning should be consistent with three- to five-year period.	—	—	—
6. Review appraisals or rehab cost estimates where appropriate.	—	—	—

C. **Manufacturing Plan**

1. Describe manufacturing process (include major subcontract decisions).	—	—	—
2. Discuss "make or buy" decisions.	—	—	—
3. Show details of expected overhead expenses.	—	—	—
4. Discuss inventory required for various sales levels.	—	—	—
5. Describe inventory control systems, as well as quality and production controls.	—	—	—
6. Discuss flow of material and purchasing structure.	—	—	—
7. Determine how quality can be ensured.	—	—	—

D. **Employment**

1. Discuss the immediate job requirements and pay structure.	—	—	—
2. Project mid-term and long-term job requirements.	—	—	—

E. **Product.** *Frequently the first question asked of a business is, "What's the product?" As such, it is usually overemphasized. Understanding the product does not mean understanding the company.*

1. Describe current status of the technology and design. Indicate existence of engineering prototypes, field test items or pre-production units (as appropriate).	—	—	—
2. Discuss program for completing the development work, including major tasks, significant milestones, and overall "time to market."	—	—	—
3. Identify key technical people who will participate in the development process.	—	—	—

	DONE	TO DO	N/A

4. Identify and discuss anticipated development problems and approaches to their solutions. Include discussion on the timing of product introduction and its effect on costs. ___ ___ ___

5. Show details of product costs, including design, development, field testing, tooling and consulting. ___ ___ ___

6. Discuss patent status and other technology protection. ___ ___ ___

VII. FINANCIAL REVIEW

Not all of the information listed below will be needed. Failure to provide requested material, however, should be regarded as a red flag. Items such as tax returns should be requested (and treated) with sensitivity.

A. For existing companies: financial statements and tax returns for the last three years, including profit and loss (P&L) statement and balance sheet. ___ ___ ___

B. Interim financial statements (less than 60 days old). ___ ___ ___

C. Projections, including:
   1. Pro forma balance sheet showing effect of financing. ___ ___ ___
   2. Two-year project P&L. ___ ___ ___
   3. If start-up (or below break-even), cash flow statement for 12 months, or three months beyond break-even point. ___ ___ ___
   4. Break-even analysis (itemization of fixed and variable costs), including cost-volume projections. ___ ___ ___

D. Discussion of assumptions. *(Accountants' notes should accompany all statements and projections. This is a particularly important point, often overlooked. The notes frequently contain clues to the answers sought unsuccessfully in the pro formas.)* ___ ___ ___

E. Current financial statement of affiliate or subsidiary company. ___ ___ ___

F. Current financial statement from each principal with 10 percent or greater share of business. ___ ___ ___

G. Consider requesting personal tax returns. *This is an optional step but is useful when where a greater level of certainty is sought. This is routinely required by banks making larger loans.* ___ ___ ___

H. **Ratio Analysis.** *With existing companies, spreadsheets should be prepared to determine viability of the business—with and without a new debt structure. Although ratios can be misleading, the following provide important baseline data:*
   1. **Debt to Equity**—*compares company financing through lender-investors against that provided by owner-investors.* ___ ___ ___
   2. **Quick Ratio**—*compares current assets (those which can be immediately converted to cash) with current liabilities.* ___ ___ ___
   3. **Percent of Sales Growth**—*change in sales over the last four quarters, as well as over the previous three years.* ___ ___ ___

VIII. MARKET ANALYSIS.

There is frequent confusion between the market analysis and the marketing plan. The analysis is concerned primarily with assessment of the prevailing market conditions. It considers the environment in which new products must compete. The marketing plan (Section IX) deals primarily with how the new product will be marketed.

	DONE	TO DO	N/A

A. **Market Potential**. Define markets and discuss history and future trends. ___ ___ ___

B. **Customers**
   1. Who are major purchasers? What are their characteristics?
   _____
   2. Significance of prices, quality, service, and environmental pressures. ___ ___ ___
   3. Buying and ordering patterns. ___ ___ ___
   4. Actual contacts—and results. ___ ___ ___

C. **Market Size and Trends**
   1. Quantification of total market of interest. ___ ___ ___
   2. Past growth rates and reasons for growth. ___ ___ ___
   3. Forecast of future trends (3 to 5 years). ___ ___ ___
   4. References and sources of data and estimates. ___ ___ ___

D. **Description of Market Niche**. Also determine that the target market will provide for a reasonable return on investment. ___ ___ ___

E. **Competition**
   1. Assess direct competition, including comparative matrix of products, showing price and performance. ___ ___ ___
   2. Assess competitor's capabilities. ___ ___ ___
   3. Describe successful competitors—consider how market share will be gained at their expense. ___ ___ ___
   4. Generic competition—describe other means of providing the same or similar customer benefits; discuss potential competition and customer alternatives. ___ ___ ___
   5. Describe how the competition can be expected to react to the introduction of your product, and how to counter that reaction. ___ ___ ___

F. **Market Share and Sales**
   1. Discuss the basis for sales projections; include customer commitment, reaction of competing and extraneous factors (such as social changes). ___ ___ ___
   2. Describe, in table form, estimate of total market (dollar volume), projected sales, and estimated market share that these sales represent. *Estimates should include both total number of units and total income by quarter for the first two years, and annually thereafter.* ___ ___ ___

IX. MARKETING PLAN

A. **Product Plan.** Describe approach to product family, including market targets, features and timetable for introduction—support the need for multiple products. ___ ___ ___

	DONE	TO DO	N/A

   B. **Sales and Distribution Plan.** Describe sale and distribution of products. ___ ___ ___
      1. Discuss basis for choosing distribution channels (or direct sales), effectiveness of that channel, and ability to command attention. ___ ___ ___
      2. Address sales commissions and margins for retailers and wholesalers. ___ ___ ___
   C. **Pricing.** Describe basis for current and future pricing—is it based on current competition? Discuss penetration strategy and value as perceived by the customer. ___ ___ ___
   D. **Promotion.** Describe advertising plan and sales promotion—how do these support sales estimates? Are public relations a problem? Can they be used to the company's advantage? ___ ___ ___
   E. **Service and Warranty.** Is this being used as a marketing tool? Describe approach and implementation plan—discuss effect on pricing and profits. ___ ___ ___
   F. **Marketing Strategy.** Are the elements listed above combined into a single coherent market strategy? Is it understood by the whole team? To what extent is the company truly "market driven"? ___ ___ ___

X. **MANAGEMENT TEAM**

   A. **Organization**
      1. Describe the roles of key managers, their primary duties and the proposed organizational structure. Determine whether managers have worked together previously. ___ ___ ___
      2. Indicate where key functions are not being met. ___ ___ ___
         a. Discuss proposed solutions. ___ ___ ___
         b. Determine whether contractual help is required (e.g., design, marketing, accounting). ___ ___ ___
   B. **Management Personnel.** Include detailed resumes for each key member. Stress past accomplishments in similar roles (include specific successes such as sales, productivity improvement or technical breakthroughs). ___ ___ ___
   C. **Management Compensation and Ownership**
      1. State salary to be paid to each key person. ___ ___ ___
      2. Describe stock ownership plan. ___ ___ ___
      3. Discuss equity positions and performance—dependent stock options or bonus plans? ___ ___ ___
   D. **Board of Directors.** Identify board members and include a background statement, as well as a summary of benefits each will bring to the company; include investments made into the company. ___ ___ ___
   E. **Management Assistance and Training Needs.** Describe candidly the strengths and weaknesses of the management team and board of directors. Discuss the kind, extent, and timing of support needed to overcome any weakness. ___ ___ ___
   F. **Supporting Professional Services.** Discuss professional services retained by the firm. Address plans to acquire future services. Review costs. ___ ___ ___

XI. **OVERALL SCHEDULE.**
This review ties together all major tasks and events on a common timeline. It shows the interrelationships of product development, production, marketing and sales. The schedule should recognize those activities which could cause slippage in the timeline. It should also identify milestones critical to the venture. __ __ __

XII. **CRITICAL RISKS AND PROBLEMS**
   A. Identify and discuss the major problems and risks likely to be encountered in the venture. Indicate which business plan assumption or potential problems are most critical to the venture. Describe plans for minimizing the effect of unfavorable developments in each risk area. __ __ __
   B. Prepare sensitivity analysis and include affects of sales reduction, increases in fixed cost, and monthly burn rate. __ __ __
   C. Prepare report on site visits and meeting with principals. __ __ __
   D. **Capitalization**
      1. Show the names of current stockholders (over 10 percent) and number of shares held. __ __ __
      2. Indicate how many shares of common stock are reserved for future key personnel. __ __ __

XIII. **APPENDICES**
Carefully review any exhibits that may be attached to the business plan. Examples include credit reports, product brochures, news articles, market research data, description of technology, and supporting exhibits to the financial statements. __ __ __

NOTES or COMMENTS:

_____

*This information first appeared in **Race To Recruit: Strategies for Successful Business Attraction**, Chapter 11, "Is It a Deal or a Dog?" by James Hettinger, with assistance by Janette A. Burland. Reprinted with permission from the editors, Maury Forman and James Mooney.*

DEAL OR DOG CHECKLIST ✓

PROJECT TITLE _____ PROJECT NUMBER _____

	YES	NO
Is the educational attainment and skill level of the local workforce a good match with labor needs of the suspect and its product?	—	—
Are local training programs in place which can overcome discrepancies in workforce skill levels and readily adapt to incorporating new manufacturing or management technologies, as required by the suspect?	—	—
Is local representation in organized labor within the range of acceptability for the suspect?	—	—
Are local natural resources (water, land, or air quality attainment) in adequate supply for the production process of the suspect?	—	—
Has the suspect historically remained amenable to complying with local environmental regulations?	—	—
Has the suspect the capital and resources for this relocation or expansion?	—	—
Will incentives not make or break the deal?	—	—
Has the suspect provided careful details regarding infrastructure, housing, educational, and workforce skill level, utility and natural resource needs, or other specific aspects which indicate a good match between the suspect and the community?	—	—
Has the suspect responded to your questions in a timely and thorough manner?	—	—
Have you been able to compile research, articles, and other data about the suspect?	—	—
Is the suspect enthusiastic about meeting key community leaders?	—	—
Is the suspect well-acquainted with such aspects of the business as competition and research and development status?	—	—
Does the suspect recognize the circumstances under which the business will thrive and grow?	—	—
Does the suspect have a business plan?	—	—
Will the suspect bring a presently imported good or service to the local business and industry mix?	—	—

EVALUATION: *If you checked more than 10 of the 14 boxes in the "yes" column, you may begin to consider your suspect a prospect. On the other hand, more than four check marks in the "no" column indicate the suspect is suspicious, indeed. When suspects are dogs, cull them out and spend your time more productively with truly good deals.*

---

*This information first appeared in **Race To Recruit: Strategies for Successful Business Attraction,** Chapter 11, "Is It a Deal or a Dog?" by James Hettinger, with assistance by Janette A. Burland. Reprinted with permission from the editors, Maury Forman and James Mooney.*

CHAPTER 8

ECONOMIC IMPACT ANALYSIS
An Analytical Approach to Economic Development

Jim Mooney, CED
President, Development Services (DeSCo)

——— ◆ ———

Economic impact analysis is one of the unique services that economic developers can point to as something they, and only they, are providing to the community. It is one of the most important skills an economic developer can have.

An economic impact analysis (EIA) is a projection of the direct, current public costs and revenues associated with growth in a local jurisdiction. The most important components of this analysis are:

Direct Impacts—Those generated by the project itself and impacting the unit of government under study are of greatest importance to an EIA. Direct impacts are the most accurate, reproducible, and defensible results from an investment into a local economy.

Costs and Revenues—Both should be addressed when conducting an EIA. Economic developers love to talk about the benefits that will be produced by the projects brought to the community. They rarely discuss the costs of development. However, when costs are included in the impact discussion, the practitioner's credibility in the community is strengthened, as is the accuracy of the reporting.

Local Jurisdiction—For any business prospect, a number of taxing jurisdictions would impose costs and fees on them as the business locates or expands in the community. An EIA, however, should only include those taxes and fees levied by the unit of government for whom they are calculating the impact analysis.

Current—This term typically means any revenues or expenses incurred in the current fiscal year. A skilled practitioner knows, however, that he or she must take a long-term view, because a project may have a positive impact initially but could have negative consequences in later years. If the economic-impact time is too short, the practitioner could easily end up with an incorrect assessment of the project's impact on the community.

What time span should the impact analysis cover? Here are some recommended guidelines:

- If debt occurs, the EIA should be the same length as the bond.
- If no debt occurs and the project breaks even on day one (more on this later), the analysis should be based on the impact over five to ten years, depending upon the character of the community.
- If the project is expected to break even in future years, the analysis should be based on twice the length of the break-even period.

An EIA is a communication tool that bridges the technical and social sides of economic development. The practitioner's job is to develop the report, deliver it in a clear and concise manner, then use the information to influence the decision-makers in the community.

THE IMPORTANCE OF AN EIA

An EIA develops parameters that guide decisions for encouraging and closing projects.

When used in partnership with decision guidelines developed in advance of the meeting with the prospect, an analysis manages community expectations during the negotiation process.

Conducting an EIA consists of eight primary steps:

1. Decide which method to use.
2. Determine project revenue.
3. Calculate project costs.
4. Calculate first-year cash flow.
5. Consider the incentive package.
6. Calculate net first-year cash flow.
7. Calculate secondary benefits.
8. Make key-decision parameters.

Step 1:
DECIDE WHICH METHOD TO USE

There are three common methods of calculating an EIA:

- Average costing
- Marginal costing
- Comparative costing

Average costing lists the costs of running the community on a per-capita basis. This method is quick, the data is easy to assemble, and the process is easily understood.

Marginal costing assumes that each sector of the community (police, fire, parks, streets, etc.) has certain carrying capacities. If growth occurs within the carrying capacity of the sector, there is no impact on the community. When the growth exceeds the carrying capacity, additional staffing and equipment are needed to accommodate the growth. Marginal costing is more accurate during the short term but is more difficult to explain in the public arena.

Comparative costing makes a comparative analysis of the community with communities of comparable size that are experiencing similar growth and investment opportunities. While it is the most accurate method of calculating impact, it is also the most complex and time-consuming.

This author prefers average costing because it is quick, accurate, and easy to explain to the public.

Step 2:
DETERMINE PROJECT REVENUE

Three things are required to determine project revenue:

- The state's and community's assessing practices
- The tax rates levied in the community under study
- The prospect's investment, broken down into land, real, and personal property

Assessing property. In any community, property will have two values: the market value and the assessed value. Market value is the price paid for the property at the time of sale. Assessed value is the value that is reported on the books for taxing purposes.

The economic developer's responsibility is to understand how market value is converted to assessed value. Assessed value is defined as some percentage of market value. Typical ratios are 100 percent, 66 percent, 50 percent, or 33 percent of market value. In a few states, the assessing level is graduated. For example, the first $100,000 of value is assessed at one rate while the next $100,000 of value is assessed at another (typically lesser) rate. On the west coast of the United States and in the western provinces of Canada, the most common assessing percentage is 100 percent of market value.

Property is assessed at the county level by the county assessor. In theory, this practice is standardized through assessing manuals and training provided by the state or provincial governments. In practice, however, property assessment varies at the local level.

For example, one assessor might look at a piece of equipment and value it one way while another, using the same techniques and practices, could assign a value slightly less or greater than the first. Therefore, the economic development professional must know and understand the assessing perspective of the local assessor. Often, as a result of this individual's perspective, the actual results of the assessed value may be anywhere from 95 percent to 105 percent of market value, even though the formal practice may call for 100 percent of market value.

Tax rates. The taxes levied by the municipality, county, school districts, state, and other jurisdictions should be printed on the community profile data sheets. The economic developer should understand these taxing practices and how they are applied to property in their service territory.

Investment by category. This is simply how much the prospect intends to spend on land, buildings, and personal property. The land investment includes acquisition and improvement costs. Building costs include the cost to build or acquire and renovate buildings. All other costs are considered personal property—the machinery, equipment, and furnishings a company puts into its facility. ▶

The revenue to be produced from the project can be calculated using these three expenses. To illustrate, assume a company spends:

- $700,000 for land
- $2,400,000 for the building
- $4,750,000 for machinery and equipment

In our sample community, property is assessed at 100 percent of market value and the property tax rate is $22/1,000 of assessed value. Also assume that the local government taxes all property. In this situation, the revenue projection would become:

Table 1

CALCULATION OF PROJECT REVENUE (000's)

	LAND	REAL	MACHINERY AND EQUIPMENT
Value	700	2,400	4,750
Assessed Value (100%)	700	2,400	4,750
Taxes 22 ÷ 1,000	(700 x 22) ÷ 1,000 = 15.4	(2,400 x 22) ÷ 1,000 = 52.8	(4,750 x 22) ÷ 1,000 = 79.2
		Total:	15.4 + 52.8 + 104.5 = 172.7

Step 3:
CALCULATE PROJECT COSTS

In order to calculate the project costs, three items are needed:

1. The most recent, non-grant, non-user fee budget for the unit of government under study.
2. Population figures from the same year as the budget year.
3. The details of the incentive package.

General fund budget. The budget should be the general fund budget for the unit of government for which the economic impact is being calculated. Grants and user fees should be excluded from these calculations, as they are one-time revenues generated for the municipality. The amount of the general fund budget that is tax base–generated is the number used in this calculation.

Population figures. These should correspond with the year of the budget, because the community's budget is influenced by the population, among other things. A common mistake is to use the population figures from the latest decennial census while using the most recent budget figures.

Once these items are assembled, the costs for the unit of government can be calculated. Let's make the following assumptions:

- The community has 12,225 residents
- The general fund budget is $5,500,000

Under this scenario, the costs to run the community are:

Table 2   CALCULATION OF PER CAPITA OPERATING COSTS

Municipal Population	12,225
Municipal Budget	$5,500,000
Per-capita Costs	$5,500,000 ÷ 12,225 = $450/resident

Now, let's make some more assumptions. The project being negotiated has the following characteristics:

- 200 employees
- 32.3 percent of whom will become residents (see Table 8)

▶

- Population density is 2.86 people per household (pph)

Then, the additional costs to be incurred by the project could be calculated as:

Table 3   CALCULATION OF ADDITIONAL ANNUAL COSTS CREATED BY PROJECT

Employees	200
Percent to be new residents	32.3%
Cost per resident (table 2)	450
Population density	2.86 pph
Additional Costs	200 x 32.3% x 450 x 2.86 = $83,140

Step 4:
CALCULATE FIRST-YEAR CASH FLOW

Most of the work of the first-year cash flow has already been completed. By taking information generated previously, the first-year cash flow can be determined:

Table 4   CALCULATION OF FIRST YEAR CASH FLOW (000's)

Additional Revenue (Table 1)	173.2
Additional Costs (Table 2)	83
Net Cash Flow	173 – 83 = 90

Table 4 shows that there will be an additional $90,000 of revenue for the community in the first year of the project. Many practitioners of economic development would stop here and and claim the project to be a successful venture. To do so would leave the community with an incomplete analysis of the project's impact. Other factors must be considered in the analysis process.

Step 5:
CONSIDER THE INCENTIVE PACKAGE

The impact of the incentive package(s) negotiated on behalf of the prospect must also be considered. For this sample project, assume the following (generous) incentive package:

Table 5

INCENTIVE PACKAGE

Road Improvements	$ 145,000
Sewer Plant	800,000
Workforce Training	22,000
Tax Abatement	133,000
Total Incentive Package	$1,100,000

Step 6:
CALCULATE NET FIRST-YEAR CASH FLOW

The previous five steps have determined the preliminary data for this analysis. At this point the net first-year cash flow can be calculated as follows:

Table 6

NET FIRST-YEAR CASH FLOW

Gross Revenue (Table 1)	173
− New Costs (Table 2)	83
= Net Cash Flow (Table 4)	90
− Incentives (Table 5)	1,100
= Bottom Line	<1,010>

By including the incentives in the equation, the economics change dramatically. Projects that may have generated a great deal of revenue and pride for the community actually become much less attractive when incentives are included.

Step 7:
CALCULATE SECONDARY BENEFITS

The secondary benefits from a project in a community come from two sources: The amount of money that the company and the employees spend in the local economy.

Company Spending. Companies support the local economy when they buy local goods and services to support their primary business activity. To calculate the multiplier effect of corporate spending, two figures are needed from the company:

- The amount of spending on cost-of-goods-sold (COGS)
- The percent of COGS expended in the local economy

COGS can be obtained directly from the corporate operating statement. Most corporate operating statements will look something like this:

> Sales
> − Adjustment to Sales
> = Net Sales
>
> Net Sales
> − Cost of Goods Sold (COGS)
> = Operating Profit

COGS represents what the company spends to provide its product or service.

The second number to be determined is the amount of COGS to be spent in the local economy. This number can be obtained by either asking the prospect what portion of COGS they anticipate will be spent in the local economy or by negotiating this value, such as 15 percent of all supplies must be purchased in the county.

For example, assume that the company spends $5,000,000 on COGS and that 10 percent will be spent in the local community. The local expenditure would be $500,000. This figure can then be multiplied by the industry- or location-specific multiplier to obtain the indirect impact of the corporate spending in the local economy. For this example, assume the multiplier is 1.45[1].

---

[1] For a complimentary copy of the latest BEA multipliers, contact the author at *mooney.devserv@verizon.net*.

THE MULTIPLIER EFFECT

Practitioners love to talk about the multiplier effect of a project but might not understand the term. The Bureau of Economic Analysis (BEA) provides a great example of how the multiplier effect occurs:

> The input-output tables can show how an increase in consumer demand for motor vehicles will affect the rest of the economy. It will likely cause an increase in the production of motor vehicles, which could result in increased steel production and which, in turn, could require increases in the production of chemicals, iron ore, limestone, and coal. It could also require an increase in the production of upholstery fabrics, which could require more natural fibers, more synthetic fibers, and more plastics and which, in turn, could require increases in the production of electric utility services and plastics materials and resins.

Here are some important points to keep in mind:

► Multipliers differ by industry and by location. A plastics plant that moves to a town of 50,000 people will have a different impact (multiplier effect) than a distribution center in that same community. The same plastics plant placed into a community of 10,000 people would have a different impact (multiplier effect) than when placed in a community of 50,000 individuals. Moving that project from the West Coast to the East Coast would have an entirely different impact again!

► The calculation of multipliers used to determine secondary benefits is a highly location- and industry-specific practice. Organizations such as Regional Economic Multiplier, Inc. (REMI) specialize in the calculation of multipliers for location-specific determinations. REMI are considered by many to be the best at what they do but charge large sums of money to perform this service.

Two agencies in the U.S. Department of Commerce also calculate these numbers on an industry-wide basis: the Economics and Statistics Administration, and the Bureau of Economic Analysis. More information is available at:
http://www.bea.doc.gov/bea/dn2/i-o.htm.

Table 7 — CALCULATION OF CORPORATE SECONDARY BENEFITS

COGS	PERCENT LOCAL	MULTIPLIER	TOTAL
5,000,000	10%	1.45	$725,000
$5,000,000 x 0.10 x 1.45 = $725,000			

Employee Spending. When calculating the impact of employee expenditures, several key constants must be kept in mind. These constants have been derived from studies performed on development projects on a national basis.

Table 8 — KEY CONSTANTS TO REMEMBER

Percentage of new employees who will build homes	20.0%
Value of homes as a percentage of income	230.0%
Percentage of new employees who will become residents	32.3%
Propensity for localresident consumption	85.0%
Propensity for non-resident consumption	10.0%
After tax income available for nonessential spending	33.0%

Remember that these percentages are merely averages. For example, when a company moves to a large urban community with expensive housing costs, the actual percentage of new employees who will build homes may fall. The same project in a rural community with less expensive homes may see a much higher percentage of homes built by the employees.

A practitioner must determine early in ▶

the project cycle how to adjust percentages in Table 8 to reflect his or her community. Then, the constant should be used consistently.

Secondary impacts should be determined next for a project. The secondary impacts on employees will be different for those who reside in the community and those who reside elsewhere. Therefore, employee expenditures can usually be calculated as follows:

Table 9a   CALCULATION OF EMPLOYEE EXPENDITURES

	DISTRIBUTION OF NEW JOBS	AVERAGE EXPENDABLE INCOME	PROPENSITY TO CONSUME LOCALLY	ECONOMIC BENEFIT
Residents				
Non-Residents				

Total Employee Expenditures $_____

Here's how to calculate each cell of the table:

Distribution of New Jobs—The number of new jobs for new employees who will become residents is simply the number of jobs created by the project (200 in the example) multiplied by the constant for the number of new employees who will become residents (32.3% from Table 8). The number of non-residents is the number of new jobs minus the answer to the above equation. The math looks like this:

    Number of Resident Workers
    200 x 32.3% = 65

    Number of Non-Resident Workers
    200 – 65 = 135

Average Expendable Income—Again, from Table 8 we see that roughly 33 percent of a person's salary is allocated for ▶

discretionary spending. If the workers in the sample project are paid $35,000 annually, then the expendable income becomes:

    $35,000 x 33% = $11,550/year

Expendable income is the same regardless of where the worker resides.

Propensity to Consume Locally—Table 8 shows that people who work and live in the community (resident employees) will spend, on average, 85 percent of their disposable income in that community. Those who reside outside the community will spend 10 percent in that community.

Multiplier—For the sake of example, assume that the multiplier is 1.45.

With these numbers derived, Table 9 can now be completed as follows:

Table 9b   CALCULATION OF EMPLOYEE EXPENDITURES

	DISTRIBUTION OF NEW JOBS	AVERAGE EXPENDABLE INCOME	PROPENSITY TO CONSUME LOCALLY	ECONOMIC BENEFIT
Residents	65	11,550	85%	638,138
Non-Residents	135	11,550	10%	155,925

Total Employee Expenditures   **$794,063**

To determine the total secondary impacts of the project, add the results of Table 7 and Table 9:

Table 10

CALCULATION OF SECONDARY PROJECT IMPACTS

Corporate Spending	$ 725,000
Employee Spending	794,063
Total Secondary Impact	$1,519,063

Step 8:
MAKE KEY-DECISION PARAMETERS

The data obtained above can be used to determine the key-decision parameters. These are ratios and guidelines used to help focus the decision making that results from the EIA. Here are five key-decision parameters to help guide the impact of a project:

- Cost/benefit analysis
- Incentives/job ratio
- Return on investment
- Incentives/wage ratio
- Break-even analysis ▸

Cost/benefit analysis. The cost/benefit analysis compares the direct revenues to the direct costs of the project to determine the ratio between the two. The goal is to obtain a ratio greater than one. The degree to which this ratio exceeds the value of one is proportional to its strength in impacting the local economy. For the sample project, the cost/benefit analysis becomes:

Table 11   COST/BENEFIT ANALYSIS

	FORMULA	INPUTS (000)	VALUE
Cost/Benefit	Direct Revenues/Direct Costs	173/83	2.08
Interpretation: *This is a very good indicator!*			

Incentives/job ratio. This ratio compares the size of the incentive package to the number of jobs created. This is one of the more common indicators of a project's impact used in the public arena. Elected officials like to evaluate a project based upon the dollar of incentives paid per job created.

Table 12   INCENTIVES/JOB RATIO

	FORMULA	INPUTS (000)	VALUE
Incentives/Job	Total Incentive Package/ Number of Jobs Created	1,100/.200	5,500
Interpretation: *$5,500 per job is very low. This indicator is positive for this deal!*			

Return on investment (ROI). The ROI evaluates the amount of total private investment that is leveraged by the total public investment. It shows how much money was returned through the investment made by the public sector. Here the goal is to achieve the largest number possible.

Table 13

RETURN ON INVESTMENT

	FORMULA	INPUTS (000)	VALUE
ROI	Private Investment/Public Investment	6,700/1,100	6.09
Interpretation: *Six dollars back for every dollar put in! Great sign!*			

Incentives/wage ratio. This is a prime indicator of how much is being paid to create new jobs in the community. Here the goal is to have the lowest number possible in order to keep the costs of creating the jobs at a minimum. Projects with a ratio below one are great. Ratios below two are good. Ratios above two must be evaluated on a case-by-case basis.

Table 14

INCENTIVES/WAGE RATIO

	FORMULA	INPUTS (000)	VALUE
Incentives/Wage	Total Incentives Package/ Total Wages Paid to Employees	1,100/7,000	0.16
Interpretation: *Very, very good value. Another great sign.*			

Break-even analysis. The break-even analysis tells the community when it will begin to start making money on the project. This analysis compares the incentive package to the revenue stream and computes a time (in years) when positive cash flow will be achieved. The goal in this analysis is to achieve the lowest number possible.

Table 15

BREAK-EVEN ANALYSIS

	FORMULA	INPUTS (000)	VALUE
BEA	Total Incentives/ Net Annual Revenue	1,100/90	12.2
Interpretation: *A 3- to 5-year break-even is a little easier to swallow. However, this may make great sense at the right time for the right community.*			

FOUR COMMON MISTAKES IN CONDUCTING AN EIA

Calculating EIA is fairly straightforward and becomes easier to execute with practice. When calculating EIA, avoid these common mistakes:

- Equating cost of doing business with economic impact analysis
- Mixing different pots of money
- Confusing present and future values
- Viewing construction expenses as economic benefits

Equating cost of doing business with equal economic impact analysis. When a company comes to the community, it focuses on the cost of doing business, which is the collective taxes and fees levied by taxing jurisdictions at the site they select. However, the cost of doing business for this company is not the same as the economic impact. These are two different scenarios that must be kept separate in order to maintain accuracy.

EIA is specific to the unit of government. The costs and revenues that will be generated by the city will be different than those obtained by the county. The county's figures will differ from the state or province that again will differ from the federal government. Even though each of these units of government will be taxing the company in some manner, the economic impact on each unit will differ, sometimes considerably.

Mixing different pots of money. Remember the process of packaging the deal? You used resources from the local government, the state or province, and, where available, the federal government to package the deal. These resources helped close the deal but also must be considered in the economic impact calculations.

The EIA for a local community will address costs and revenues *for the local community*. If the deal involved funds obtained by the county, state/province, and federal government, they must either be:

- Added in as additional revenue to the local unit of government, or
- Subtracted from the incentive package if not part of the local unit's costs.

Let's take another look at Table 5:

Table 5

INCENTIVE PACKAGE

Road Improvements	$ 145,000
Sewer Plant	800,000
Workforce Training	22,000
Tax Abatement	133,000
Total Incentive Package	$1,100,000

In this table, it is highly probable that the community in the example would have received funds from the state or provincial government to help defray the cost of that sewer plant. The amount of funds received from the outside unit of government must be either subtracted from the total incentive package or added in as revenue to the community.

Another potential hot spot in Table 5 is the fact that workforce training dollars are commonly not an expense of the local unit of government. Here again, if these funds were received from another unit of government and provided directly to the company, they must be subtracted from the incentive package to calculate the EIA.

Confusing present and future values. To be accurate in determining EIA, all monies must be analyzed using the same time frame. Dollars paid today must compare to dollars received today. Calculations can be oversimplified by comparing today's dollars (e.g., road improvements paid in the first year) with tomorrow's dollars (e.g., a tax abatement received by the company over the course of the next ten years).

To maximize the accuracy of the analysis, all dollars must be brought to present-day terms in order to be accurately tabulated in the analysis.

To clarify this concept, take another look at the incentive package in Table 5. The tax abatement of $133,000 is actually a net present value determination of a ten-year abatement brought into present-day valuation. By doing the calculation in this manner, the present-day (first-year) expenses of the road and sewer plant improvements can be compared with the value of the tax abatement.

Viewing construction expenses as economic benefits. It is common practice to report construction payroll as part of the secondary economic benefits associated with a project. Some people do not report these numbers for two reasons:

1. In most cases, those construction jobs were already present and operating in the community. They were merely being moved from another project to this project during the construction period. When this happens, there is no real economic benefit since the jobs already existed.
2. For public sector improvements (e.g., road, sewer, etc.), a tax had to be generated to establish the funds that would pay for the wages and materials associated with the project. In this case, the cost and the benefit associated with it cancel out each other. The net effect for public sector improvements then becomes zero.

The characteristics of EIA are:

- A valuable benchmark for project performance
- A key decision-making aid
- A unique, value-added service that enhances the practitioner's position in the community

PAY FOR IT NOW OR PAY FOR IT LATER

The cost of an EIA varies. If the techniques in this chapter are used and calculated on an Excel spreadsheet, the cost would be negligible. However, an economist or accountant can be hired to calculate the economic impact figure. In these cases, the cost of having the analysis completed could exceed $100,000 for a large project. Regardless of the cost, it is much better to understand the impact of a company's move before the final decision is made.

EIA: WORTH THE TIME AND EFFORT

The time frame for conducting an EIA can vary considerably. If an organization has developed (or purchased) a program *and* has preloaded the variables exclusive to the project community, an EIA can be developed for a project in an afternoon.

If the practitioner is starting from scratch and developing spreadsheets from this chapter, the EIA can be put together in two to three days. If a consultant is hired to conduct this work, the time may exceed four months.

FINAL THOUGHTS

An EIA can be considered a success when a consensus in the community is achieved. A completed EIA will give the community a rallying point around which they will either accept and promote or reject a project. The EIA provides the basis upon which the community will make sound decisions for bringing a project to closure.

The methodology used in this chapter is designed to give the practitioner a quick and effective method for calculating EIA. It is much simpler to use than more exhaustive studies, yet it produces conclusive results that assist in effective decision-making at the local level. The key points to remember are:

- The input information is readily available. The few variables that are needed can be obtained and loaded into a spreadsheet long before the prospect arrives in the community.
- The math is simple. Basic addition, subtraction, multiplication, and division will yield the desired results.
- The results can be disputed. Differing assumptions during the input process, differing methods used in the calculations, and different scopes or perspectives can result in greatly divergent conclusions from studies conducted on the same project.

In conclusion, EIA provides the tool to accomplish effective project evaluation. It is a unique, value-added service that gives economic developers the ability to achieve consensus for, or if necessary against, public sector support of planned private sector investment. It can be done with as little as an afternoon of work or the investment of a significant amount of money. Regardless of what is spent at the front end, the results can be invaluable in guiding decision making in the public sector.

SOURCES

Block, A. Harvey. *Impact Analysis and Local Area Planning; An Input-Output Study.* Transaction Publishers, 1977.

Bleakley, Kenneth. *Economic Impact Analysis: Assessing a Project's Value to a Community.* American Economic Development Council, 1993.

Burchell, Robert W., et.al. *The New Practitioner's Guide to Fiscal Impact Analysis.* Center for Urban Policy, 1985.

Davis, H. Craig. *Regional Economic Impact Analysis and Project Evaluation.* Raincoast Book Distribution, 1990.

Kirkpatrick, Colin. *Sustainable Development in a Developing World: Integrating Socio-Economic and Environmental Assessment.* Edward Elgar Publishing, 1998.

Listokin, David, et.al. *Development Impact: Assessment Handbook.* Urban Land Institute, 1993.

Parkin, James. *Judging Plans and Projects: Analysis and Public Participation in the Evaluation Process.* Ashgate Publishing Company, 1993.

Schaenman, Philip. *Using and Impact Measurement System to Evaluate Land Development.* University Press of America, 1976.

WEBSITES

Bureau of Economic Analysis . . . *www.bea.doc.gov*

Census Bureau . . . . *www.census.gov*

EconData.Net . . . . *www.econdata.net*

Economic Research Service . . . . . *www.econ.ag.gov*

Government Information Locator Service
. . . . *www.usda.gov/gils*

Statistical Abstract of the United States
. . . . *www.census.gov/prod/www/*
statistical-abstract-us.html

Stat-USA . . . . *www.stat-usa.gov*

SIX MAJOR PROGRAMS

LOCI   Georgia Institute of Technology
Continuing Education
P.O. Box 93686
Atlanta, GA 30377-0686
404-385-3501
Fax: 404-894-8925
robert.lann@edi.gatech.edu

IMPLAN Minnesota IMPLAN Group
1725 Towner Drive West
Suite 140
Stillwater, MN 55082
651-439-4421
Fax: 651-439-4813
info@implan.com

REMI   Regional Economic Models, Inc.
306 Lincoln Avenue
Amherst, MA 01002
413-549-1189
413-549-1038
www.remi.com

FOCUS! Development Services
2553 Calaveras Drive
Suite 165
Valparaiso, IN 46385
219-241-2798
219-531-5633
mooney.devserv@verizon.net

Community Project Assessment System (CPAS)
(Local Municipal Economic and Fiscal Impact Customized Models)
Regional Project Assessment System (RPAS)
(Regional Economic and Review Impact Customized Models)

Applied Economics
14682 North 74th Street
Suite 100
Scottsdale, AZ 85260
480-922-9397
smurley@appliedeconomics.net
www.appliedeconomics.net

About the Author . . .

Jim Mooney, CED, has been practicing economic development for more than two decades. He has served public and private sector clients around the globe. He is currently president of Development Services (DeSCo), an economic development consulting firm specializing in financial and market analysis. Mr. Mooney can be reached at *mooney.devserv@verizon.net*.

ECONOMIC IMPACT ANALYSIS CHECKLIST ✓

PROJECT TITLE _____ PROJECT NUMBER _____

Item	Have	Need
Key Constants		
New Employees Who Will Build Homes — 20%	✓	
Value of Homes as Percentage of Income — 230%	✓	
New Employees Who Will Become Residents — 32.3%	✓	
Propensity for Local Resident Consumption — 85%	✓	
Propensity for Non-Resident Consumption — 10%	✓	
After Tax Income Available for Non-Essential Spending — 33%	✓	
Projecting Revenue		
Assessing Practices		
Tax Rates		
Investment by:		
Land		
Building		
Personal Property		
Projecting Costs		
General Fund Budget		
Population		
Incentive Package		
Census Data		
Persons per Household (pph)		

EIA WORKSHEET

PROJECT TITLE _____ **PROJECT NUMBER** _____

Category	Formula	Results
Revenue		
	Investment x Assessing Rate x Tax Rate Example: $10MM x 100% x 22/1000 = $220M	
Per Capita Costs		
	General Fund Budget/Population Example: $5,500MM / 12,225 = 450	
Project Costs		
	New Jobs x Resident % x PPH x PerCapitaCosts Example: 200 x 32.3% x 2.86 x 450 = 83M	
Gross FY Cash Flow		
	Revenue – Project Costs Example: 220M – 83M = 137M	
Net FY Cash Flow		
	Gross FY Cash Flow – Incentives Example: 137M – 800M = (663)	
Business Secondary Spending		
	COGS x Percent in Local Economy x Multiplier Example: 5,000,000 x 10% x 1.45 = 725,000	
Residential Secondary Benefits		
	Distribution of x Expendable x Propensity New Jobs Income to Consume Example: (200 x .323) x (35,000 x .33) x 0.85	
Non-Residential Secondary Benefits		
	Distribution of x Expendable x Propensity x Multiplier New Jobs Income to Consume Example: (200 x .677) x (35,000 x .33) x 0.10 x 1.45	
Total Secondary Benefits		
	Residential + Non-Residential Secondary Benefits Secondary Benefits	
Cost/Benefit Analysis		
	Direct Revenues/Project Costs Example: 220M / 83M	
Incentives/Job Ratio		
	Total Incentive Package/Jobs Created Example: 800M / 200M	
Return on Investment		
	Public Investment/Private Investment Example: 800M / 10MM	
Incentives/Wage Ratio		
	Total Incentive Package/Annual Wages Paid Example: 800M / 7MM	
Break-Even Analysis		
	Total Incentives/Annual Revenues Example: 800M / 220 M	

CHAPTER 9

THE HOST COMMITTEE AND TEAM
Preparing for the Site Visit

Jack Wimer
President, Wimer Industrial Leadership

———— ◆ ————

The prospect's visit is very important in the decision-making process, as it provides the opportunity to display what the community has to offer in terms of land, labor, and lifestyle. The site visit allows the prospect to see the dirt, talk with peers, and evaluate the quality of the labor force. Coordinating a site visit is just as important as assessing the community. Both require people and information that will take the process to the next phase of a successful location.

The people who prepare for the site visit are referred to as the **host committee**. The job of this small group of individuals is to arrange for the logistical, transportation, and information needs of a business prospect while that prospect is in the community for a site visit.

The host committee also supports the **host team**—those responsible for handling the qualified prospect upon their arrival in the community. It is as if the community has passed the written exam with the prospect being satisfied with what they have seen on paper and would now like to conduct an on-site oral exam with selected members. Since it takes hundreds of hours and sometimes thousands of dollars in attraction activities to get even one qualified prospect into the city limits, the importance of handling the hosting assignment correctly cannot be underestimated.

> **TIP:** The host committee prepares for the prospect; the host team delivers the goods.

Site visits are the blind dates of economic development. Host committees and teams know that they do not come along every day, but when they do, it is their responsibility to make sure that the community makes a good impression.

CREATING A HOST COMMITTEE AND TEAM

When doctors or paramedics reach the scene of an automobile accident, they are bound by a general rule that goes back hundreds of years in their profession: First, do no harm. Their job is to treat the patient, but in their attempts to do so, they should not make matters worse.

The host committee and team must remember that a site visit is a process of *elimination* before it becomes a process of *selection*. There are usually many sites to choose from, and the site selector's first job is to decide as quickly as possible which sites to eliminate so that they can evaluate the sites that best meet their needs. Therefore, members of the host committee or team should be people who represent a knowledgeable and positive image of the community and will do no harm.

THE HOSTESS WITH THE MOSTEST

Every community has volunteers who work behind the scenes to make sure that things get done. Oftentimes, they either do the work themselves or they manage other volunteers. In preparing for a prospect's site visit, they are called the host committee and are usually made up of six to nine individuals who may not be recognized leaders but they provide leadership and do what needs to be done. They will have lots of responsibility and try to do the most they can to help the community's economic prosperity.

Getting people involved in the host committee on a volunteer basis is usually not a problem. It is more difficult to keep people *off* this committee, since this committee's work is right in the middle of the action and also *seems* to lack heavy lifting. Getting the right people involved is crucial, and keeping the wrong people away from the host committee is at least as important.

The economic development professional and a respected community member need to approach the people who are right for the host committee. The host committee should be selected long before a prospect decides to come to town. Their tasks may be big or small, but they are all essential and necessary.

The host committee members must be diverse in their experience and knowledgeable about the community. The prospect will dictate who will participate in the visit, and the agenda will be dictated based on the visit. The first visit is usually a very confidential tour to evaluate the basic location factors; the second visit may be an evaluation of the community and second review of the sites and reassessment of labor, etc. The prospect may visit several times and bring different decision makers on each visit. Each prospect visit is different, and the host committee and agenda needs to adjust to the needs of the prospect.

TEAM EXPERTISE

The host team should be experts in their fields and should be able to answer development questions. Depending on the prospect, the site and building experts should be developers and brokers. Their participation, however, should be approved by the prospect. Many prospects do not want to meet with brokers during the first visit. Others should be prepared to showcase the sites and buildings.

THE "A" TEAM

The individual members of a host team (i.e., the individuals who will show the town to the prospect and answer most of the questions) are usually selected by the economic development official and may or may not be a part of the host committee. Often, existing business owners with employment in the top 30 percent of companies in the area make good host team members. They may not be able to commit the necessary time to be an active committee member, but they are essential to responding to the needs of a business on site visits with a prospect.

The prospect has needs, but one of those needs is not to have an entourage. Some communities make a prospect visit something akin to a parade. This is a bad idea. Three people on the actual community tour are plenty. Each host-team member has a specific mission:

- To drive and give a general tour of the community.
- To discuss any specifics, such as financing or labor quality.

TIER 1 — PROFESSIONAL EXPERTS	TIER 2 — BUSINESS EXECUTIVES	TIER 3 — AMBASSADORS

Sites and Buildings
Labor
Training Programs
Transportation
Utilities
Telecommunications
Permit Process
Financing
Incentives
	Local Employers
	    Manufacturers
	    Technology
	    Professional
	    Services
	Universities and Colleges
		Housing
		Schools
		Community Tour
		Spousal Tour

- To discuss other topics important to the prospect.

One team member should also be available to leave the group to gather information and to go ahead of the others to make changes in the plan, in case of logistical needs or an emergency.

Host team members should have these four attributes:

1. **A sense of hospitality.**
   The words "host" and "hospitality" are from the same root word. The job of the host committee is to provide for the needs of the prospect, not to take over the prospect's life and hard sell the deal into existence. Words that describe a good host-committee member are cooperative, confident (but not boisterous), knowledgeable, pleasant to be with, and a good listener. The selling part comes later.

2. **Knowledge of the community.**
   The host committee members should know —within general ranges—the population of the community, how many railroads serve the town, the mayor's name, how many police officers are on the force, or when that river flooded last and how far the flood water reached. There will be multiple questions regarding other businesses in the community and a hundred other offhanded

questions. Otherwise, the prospect won't care to make conversation. The prospect is there to *learn*. A good host can tell a prospect what he or she needs to know without going on all day about it.

3. **Knowledge of the community leaders.**
   The host committee member needs to have a good working knowledge of the local government and how it works at the official level and at the personal level. Prospects will often probe host members for information about local politics in order to find out if the community is friendly to business. Of course, the host committee should not speak for or commit to anything on behalf of city officials.

4. **Knowledge of the needs of business.**
   This is an area where host teams frequently fail. Host teams need to be able to speak the language of the business. That is why it is essential that one member of the team be related to the prospect's field. More often, an individual from a supplier or a comparable but noncompetitive company should be available to answer some of the industry-specific questions. Getting the prospect to talk about needs is very important. Being able to respond to those needs or show that they can be met is even more important.

TIP: It's easy to make assumptions about the prospect's interest

PROSPECT TYPE	DO THIS . . .	BE CAREFUL . . .
Manufacturing	Include other manufacturers	Don't think all manufacturers need unskilled assembly workers
Headquarters	Show them raw land as well as existing buildings	Don't leave them with commercial realtors
High-Technology	Show them K-12 schools as well as colleges and universities	Don't assume they just care about quality of life
Distribution	Show them housing and labor statistics	Don't think they care only about transportation services
Back Office, Call Center	Show them housing and labor statistics and day care facilities	Don't think that good telephone infrastructure will close the deal

SUCCESS STARTS WITH A PLAN

The following nine steps will give the community a sense of what kind of activities are needed to host a visiting prospect:

1. **Create a simple plan for how to handle a prospect.** Identify whether this is the first, second, or third visit. Attempt to find out what will be most important to the prospect during this visit. Use past visits as a benchmark. Write a script as if it were a play. Develop a plan from the perspective of the prospect and not from the community. Think about what would be important to the prospect. The prospect wants to first know that his or her company will be successful in the community.

2. **Define exactly what success will look like.** If the host committee and team do a good job, how will it be apparent? Success with the prospect's business will depend on a lot of factors. The host committee needs feedback mechanisms—either from actual prospects or from consultants who would stand in as prospects—to find out how they are doing. Create sample itineraries for a four-hour tour, one-day tour, and two-day tour. Also meet with existing companies to identify those that are willing to meet with prospects coming to town. Prep these companies on what a prospect might be looking for, such as questions on labor force, costs, utilities, labor unions—usually business-operation factors.

3. **Plan a budget for the host committee.** It doesn't take much money to prepare or conduct a site visit, but don't scrimp on details and style. The host committee should have some authority to spend money in areas it believes will help seal a deal. Prospects make decisions on substance first, and style may help give a competitive edge. Spend the extra dollars.

4. **Identify the available resources and what it takes to employ them.** A wise host committee makes good use of the resources of others. Also, keep in mind that getting a resource committed is only part of the job. For example, a local car dealer may loan the committee a nice large SUV for the tour, but it will need to be very clean inside and out and full of gas on the day of the prospect visit. It's the little things that count and which the committee needs to make sure take place.

5. **Evaluate the need for technology**—computers, database information about the community, projectors, special rooms for presentation, maybe even a helicopter for a tour. The healthy host committee uses technology to its advantage, but not to the point of distraction. On the low-tech side, when showing property it is good to have aerial and street maps either in binders or boards to help orient the prospect to the community. These maps should show where the sites are in relation to major highways, railroads, airport, other businesses, and the community itself. Every major business should be marked on the aerial. It's important to decide *before* the prospect comes what kind of technology will be used in the presentation effort.

6. **Evaluate the need for the prospect to experience community history, tradition, and values.** This may sound odd, but it always comes up. Should the team show the prospect just the industrial sites or should they take the prospect on the tour of the restored 100-year-old theatre where Will Rogers once appeared on stage? Both methods are effective, but blending the two in just the right proportions requires planning.

7. **Identify the sources of friction**—physical or personal—in the community that would keep the host committee from doing its job. Consider problems that exist and have a back-up plan. Tour the route with the team and inspect it for trash, broken-down cars in front yards, and things that make the community unattractive. The host committee may not be responsible for this kind of mess, but the team will bear the responsibility of explaining it to an important pros-

pect. Therefore, it becomes their business to reduce the friction and solve the problem before the team meets the prospect.

8. **Practice with the host team.** Take the plan created earlier and make a standard tour itinerary, route, and presentation for a prospect, knowing that it may need to be modified for different kinds of companies. Practice this route several times with community citizens that can offer insights for improvements.

9. **Document the economic development efforts through existing businesses.** Existing businesses will become the best recruiting agents. The host committee can help celebrate economic development accomplishments to show how businesses have thrived in the community. If the look of businesses and the community has been improved, let people know, even if the prospect hasn't visited yet.

FIVE TIPS TO HELP THE HOST COMMITTEE HANDLE THE PROSPECT

Tip #1: Prepare and rehearse well before the visit.

Prepare the community's leaders and citizens for visits from prospects. Share the vision about the community's future. Let the community know the general plan. Many prospects like to spend time alone, and they will ask a few average citizens what they think.

Prior to each visit, prepare an itinerary for every visit. Rehearse the tour with a stand-in prospect about once every two months.

Also, rehearse a 30-second script about the advantages of the community. Know what to say if stuck in an elevator with the CEO of General Motors for one minute. This pre-rehearsed message will often come in handy.

Don't allow surprises. Do dress *rehearsals*! Imagine the small glitches that could take place and prepare for them ahead of time. Have a back-up car, a back-up driver, a back-up projector bulb, etc.

Tip #2: Be knowledgeable.

The host committee's first priority is to know the facts about the community. Help the prospect understand the community better, without force-feeding information. Never guess at answers to the prospect's questions. Either know or find out. Have the data prepared on one-page fact sheets (front and back) by subject that can be given to the prospect as issues arise. Make sure the data is current, and provide direct contacts for follow-up on each subject. Go first class with printed materials. Good materials no longer have to be expensive. Today, color printers that cost under $100 can make presentations that could have required a $15,000 printer just five years ago.

Know which of the community's available buildings and sites are suitable for the prospect. Be sure the community has several products to sell.

Know the labor force—availability, skill levels, cost. Be familiar with utility rates for several sizes of industrial use. This may seem complex at first, but rate quotes from the utility company on small, medium and large users are usually enough information to satisfy the prospect's initial needs. Also, have a financial expert available to provide detailed answers to the prospect's questions.

In addition to knowing the community, the host committee should know about the prospect's industry. Industry knowledge can be gathered in short order via the Internet. When a prospect senses the economic development professional is speaking his language and understands his business, the conversations usually open up dramatically.

Tip #3: Remember that relationships are critical to success.

Try to meet prospects in person before a site visit. Business attraction is still selling, and selling is still about relationships. Try to make contact with the prospect in a nonthreatening way before he or she comes to view the community. Also, show sensitivity to the prospect's need to build relationships within the community. Don't sit in on the prospect's meetings with local businesses.

Know what to say if stuck in an elevator with the CEO of General Motors for one minute.

Networking is particularly important. Know the government or province economic development officials. The host-committee members need to be up to date on the people who are making things happen in their community.

Make friends with the consultants. Economic development consultants see three or four deals each month. Most small- to medium-sized communities see fewer than two or three deals a year. The consultants can help review the presentation and the products behind it and can help ensure they are competitive. Most economic development consultants will be willing to donate some of their time.

Know commercial real estate people. Builders and developers can help explain the cost of construction and the road blocks typically encountered. Don't drop off the prospect to meet alone with a commercial realtor, however.

Network with other developers. Even though other developers may be competition, they enjoy pleasing people. If a competing developer can't land a prospect because he is missing a critical element, he may share that prospect, with the hope that the favor will be returned some day.

Know contractors and architectural and engineering firms. Even in small towns, the contractors who build and the architects who design the structures come from somewhere. Find out where they are and get to know them.

Know the utility and railroad people. Utility and railroad companies are in the unique position of having business assets that are *very* geographically dependent. They need to develop in very specific areas and are usually very willing to help economic development efforts, with time, talent, and funding.

Tip #4: Add the special touches.

Prior to the site visit, prepare written testimonials from existing firms. Existing business people and their experiences in the community are the true measurement of how the community *really* treats businesses.

Provide the prospect with an 8-1/2- by 11-inch business card holder made of heavy plastic so the prospect can keep the cards of those persons he or she meets.

Shoot a videotape of the tour so the prospect can review it later and show it to his or her boss.

Have the room, people, audio-visual devices, etc., *ready* well before the prospect arrives. Be sure to change all light bulbs, batteries, etc., and verify that they work.

Be sure the community tour includes both the good and bad parts of town. The prospect will know instinctively if he or she is being kept from certain parts of town. Show the good and the bad and explain what is being done to make the bad parts better. Honesty with the prospect brings rewards.

Conduct the tour from a large, four-door vehicle. Show special sensitivity to the prospect's needs by allowing him or her to choose where to sit in the car. Don't assume the prospect likes the front seat. Many professional prospects like the back seat, where they can make notes in private and spread out materials.

During the tour, mention historical places and community traditions, but don't go on forever about it.

Prepare the community's offer to the prospect in writing. Most communities don't take the time to do this extra step, which is greatly appreciated by the prospect.

At the end of the visit, offer to ship all binders and literature to the prospect. This will make traveling easier.

Tip #5: Follow up effectively.

Follow up the prospect's visit by phone. Avoid making useless conversation. Instead, call with additional information. Don't expect any one communication or item to sell the community alone. Closing a deal always takes a combination of factors.

FINAL THOUGHTS

People in your community have put a lot of time and effort into convincing a corporate site selector to visit. In addition, the process is very expensive. The host committee plays a very important role to make sure that all the hard work, money, and preparation does not go to waste. Because the companies that want to relocate are acting under very tight decision-making time frames, the host committee rarely has much time to begin its efforts of putting people and material together. Host committees must have a good industrial team with knowledgeable people who are familiar with the industrial site, workforce, and utilities, and they must be ready to deliver this information succinctly, honestly, and in a moment's notice.

If, as suggested earlier, communities do think of this visit as the next step after passing the written exam, they will know that if they have prepared sufficiently, then their efforts will lead to success. They will be rewarded not only with an "A," but also with new jobs and increased tax revenues.

SOURCES

Forman, Maury, and Jim Mooney, editors. *Learning to Lead*, Kendall/Hunt Publishing Company, 1999.

——————. *The Race to Recruit*. Kendall/Hunt Publishing Company, 1996.

Kotler, Haider, and Rein. *Marketing Places*. Maxwell Macmillan Canada, Toronto.

McHenry, Howard. *Small Town America Community Development Manual*. CITYMARK, Harrisonville, Missouri.

Mississippi Department of Economic Development. "Growing," video.

About the Author . . .

Jack Wimer, President, Wimer Industrial Leadership, is a consultant and trainer who serves the economic development profession with new ideas in area development, community marketing, and prospect management. He mixes the qualities of a technology innovator, a market strategist, and a futurist to assist community leaders in making economic development a measurable reality. He has also spent countless days in small communities, assisting in the preparation necessary for site-selector visits. He has authored strategic plans for several statewide development organizations and consulted members of the U.S. House of Representatives, senators, governors, and mayors on issues relating to economic development. Mr. Wimer can be reached at *jack.wimer@compuware.com.*

TALENT IDENTIFICATION CHECKLIST ✓

PROJECT TITLE _____ **PROJECT NUMBER** _____

Community Identify who you feel are the COMMUNITY'S TOP 10 most qualified leaders, regardless of their present titles or positions.
The individuals recommended should be respected and dependable and have outstanding qualities in leadership, expertise, talent, and/or skills.

	NAME	OCCUPATION	EXPERTISE	TALENT/SKILLS
1.	_____	_____	_____	_____
2.	_____	_____	_____	_____
3.	_____	_____	_____	_____
4.	_____	_____	_____	_____
5.	_____	_____	_____	_____
6.	_____	_____	_____	_____
7.	_____	_____	_____	_____
8.	_____	_____	_____	_____
9.	_____	_____	_____	_____
10.	_____	_____	_____	_____

County Identify who you feel are the COUNTY'S TOP 10 most qualified leaders, regardless of their present titles or positions.
The individuals recommended should be respected and dependable and have outstanding qualities in leadership, expertise, talent, and/or skills.

	NAME	OCCUPATION	EXPERTISE	TALENT/SKILLS
1.	_____	_____	_____	_____
2.	_____	_____	_____	_____
3.	_____	_____	_____	_____
4.	_____	_____	_____	_____
5.	_____	_____	_____	_____
6.	_____	_____	_____	_____
7.	_____	_____	_____	_____
8.	_____	_____	_____	_____
9.	_____	_____	_____	_____
10.	_____	_____	_____	_____

From _Small Town America Community Development Manual_ (Citymark, Harrisonville, Missouri).
All materials used with permission.

CHAPTER 10

CLOSING THE DEAL
The Secrets Revealed

Leslie Parks
Consultant

Jim Mooney, CED
President, Development Services (DeSCo)

——— ◆ ———

Pssst, want to hear a secret? Economic developers are salespeople. The product is the community and the customer is the investor. It's as simple as that.

For some reason, the economic development profession shies away from acknowledging this critical fact. By doing so, economic developers deny themselves the opportunity to focus on the critical aspects of negotiating and closing deals in the community.

An economic development sale or deal requires negotiation skills similar to those used in a private sale and additional skills and strategies unique to the public arena. In order to help the practitioner acquire the necessary skills for success, this chapter will address both skills. The best advice for closing the deal is to be *prepared* in advance of the final negotiations or closing.

WHAT IS AN ECONOMIC DEVELOPMENT DEAL?

In economic development, sales are often called "deals." From the investment side of economic development, these sales usually involve a business looking to expand in its current location or relocate to a community from another region. The closing of the sale or deal results in investment and, frequently, job creation and economic wealth for the community.

Often, recruiting a business entails a competitive site-selection process that involves a number of communities. In this case, there may be more than one closing opportunity. In the first phase of the competition, businesses gather data and information about the candidate locations. Communities are asked to complete a detailed site-selection questionnaire that often includes a list of incentives. The field of candidates will be narrowed based on the questionnaire and initial due diligence. Occasionally, depending on the number of sites being considered, a community may have an opportunity to meet face to face with the business to present its case before the first cut of candidate sites is made.

In most site-selection processes, however, the community does not get an actual meeting during the initial review. The one-sided competition process can make negotiating and closing the deal more difficult for the community, as it is placed in the disadvantaged position of having to respond to requests for information without any communication with the company.

Usually, an economic development deal includes some type of assistance, such as financial incentives or concession of development rights. Communities should understand that even when closing the deal appears to be dependent on substantial incentives, they are usually not a priority for corporate location requirements. Other factors, such as workforce quality, occupancy costs, or time-to-market imperatives, are more important than incentives. Unless the community can offer the most critical location requirements, incentives will not bridge the gap. Incentives can be the tiebreaker between two communities that have the same location advantages. For these reasons, knowing what factors rank highest in a business's location decision hierarchy is an important strategic advantage and is critical to closing the deal.

THE CHALLENGES OF CLOSING A DEAL

An economic development deal has several unique characteristics that set it apart from a typical deal in the private sector. These characteristics require a strategy and skills set that are in many ways different from those used for conventional sales transactions. The following factors make closing an economic development deal unique:

- *An economic development deal has many players.*

As previously explained, a deal often begins with a competition in which several communities are contenders. In the initial stage of the inquiry, staff does not have direct communication with the company but usually deals with an intermediary such as a site-selection consultant. Another intermediary can be added if the site-selection questionnaire comes through the state's offices and that staff is involved. Dealing with the final decision maker, although one of the most important elements of successful selling, is not characteristic of an economic development deal.

Once a community has been selected as the location, the negotiation begins. The process can become more complex in terms of players and issues involved. Usually, any conditions or business terms that staff have offered during the negotiation process must be approved by a public body such as a city council, board, or a regulatory agency. Not having that decision-making authority makes the negotiation and closing process more difficult to manage. In fact, during the negotiations the number of players on the field is likely to increase and may include elected officials, other city staff, community groups, the media, and others who will try to exercise their influence. Managing these competing interests requires skill, energy, and patience, as well as a good strategy.

- *Politics is a factor.*

The lack of decision-making authority allows for another potential complication in the closing process. If the business doesn't get what it wants in terms of incentives or other concessions during the closing negotiations, it may choose to invoke the eleventh commandment of an economic development deal and go political. That is, the company may put pressure on government officials or agencies to concede to its demands. A strategy for closing the deal must include a plan for managing the political decision makers and their role in the process.

- *The prospect wants to close the deal quickly.*

An economic development deal often takes longer to complete than most sales transactions because of the politics involved. However long the public-sector side of the deal takes, the driving factor in site selection in the new economy is speed. Most companies are more interested in how quickly they can get through the development process, complete construction on a building or make improvements, and open their doors for business than coming away from a protracted negotiations process with a huge incentive package. The time-to-market cycle for most businesses is too short to allow them the luxury of spending a year finding the right location and lucrative incentives.

REASONABLE GOALS AND OBJECTIVES FOR A DEAL

In closing an economic development deal, four desired outcomes or guiding principles should be the foundation for a negotiation strategy:

- The deal concludes in a time frame that meets the business's schedule.
- The deal minimizes the financial risk to the community.
- The deal attains a reasonable return on investment for any incentives given.
- The deal brings quality jobs to the community.

Take time to analyze the community's strengths and weaknesses and to develop reasonable goals and objectives. This builds confidence that will make future deals easier to negotiate and close. Once the business relocates to the community, the economic development team will feel a tremendous sense of satisfaction and accomplishment. But remember, if this deal doesn't materialize, another one will take its place.

FOUR STEPS TO CLOSING A DEAL

After the prospect has toured the community and met key leaders and decision makers, negotiating the deal begins. The four steps to closure are:

1. Negotiating
2. Recognizing buying signals
3. Closing
4. Tieing up loose ends

Step 1:
NEGOTIATING

Some economic development professionals may think they have no negotiating power because they don't understand that they are salespeople. They also often feel very pressured to create jobs and investment so they attempt to take any deal at any price. If an investor quickly perceives this attitude, the ability of the professional economic developer to negotiate any type of performance standards is lost.

Therefore, the first step to successful negotiation in economic development is for practitioners to realize:

They do not have to take every investment opportunity that crosses their desk. Not every deal will be a good fit for the community. The company or site selector acting on the company's behalf will approach the community to see if it is a good fit for that particular business. At the same time, economic developers need to assess the company to see if it is a good fit for the community. The economic developers' potential for success will elevate exponentially when they focus their time, efforts and resources on those companies that are the best fit for their service territory.

They are responsible for making good deals for their communities. Toward this end, they must select those that make the lowest impact on infrastructure, that leverage the assets contained in the local workforce, and that generate the greatest return on investment. Great economic development professionals learn to cull and pick the highest priority projects.

They always have the option of saying "No." Economic developers must approach every deal with the mindset that they will give it their all, as long as it makes good economic sense for their community. If and when the economics of the deal fall below an acceptable threshold of return, the professional salesperson will terminate the negotiations. Sometimes this move itself is a negotiating strategy. At other times it's a statement by the professional that this deal is configured in such a way that the best option available for the community is to focus on the next opportunity.

With these points in mind, the practitioner can negotiate with the prospect using the following techniques:

- *Asking for more than is expected*
- *Bracketing*
- *Declining the first offer*
- *Flinching*
- *Concentrating on the issues*
- *Nibbling*
- *Using patterns of concession*
- *Using two reference points*

Asking for more than is expected—This positioning strategy allows room to relax the criteria later in the negotiating process if necessary. For example, the community may be willing to put in a deceleration lane on an access road if the investor creates a minimum of 35 new jobs. However, by requiring 50 new jobs in the initial discussion with the prospect, room is created to fall back to the lower requirement during the negotiation process. It is far easier to relax investment criteria later in the process than it is to increase it. Moreover, with a little luck the community may get all 50 jobs by setting this as a performance standard at the outset of the negotiations.

Bracketing—Bracketing commonly occurs when both sides make their initial moves (often referred to as "gambits") in the opening stages of negotiations. A good example of bracketing might occur in the initial discussions of a tax abatement. Assume that the community has the ability to offer up to 12 years of tax abatement for a given level of investment. When the discussion of tax abatements enters the conversation, the prospect may ask for all 12 years while the economic development professional may open with an offer of two years. Once this has occurred, the tax abatement term is bracketed between two and 12 years. The negotiations from this point forward will occur between these two extremes.

Declining the first offer—Any corporation worth its salt will create an opening gambit less than where they hope to end up in the negotiations. This is usually a test to see how sophisticated the community may be in the negotiation process. If the first offer is accepted, the investor will often hold the community in less regard than had they negotiated the best possible deal. An example of how this strategy may be used would be when a community has low-interest (or no-interest) financing available for projects that create a minimum number of jobs and/or achieve a certain level of investment. A shrewd company, realizing the community may be going through an economic downturn, may attempt to access this financing without meeting this criteria. A savvy economic developer may opt to decline their first offer and continue to work with the company to extract more investment or jobs in order to achieve a greater economic return for the community.

Flinching—To most people, flinching is often considered to be a reaction one would see in response to a pin prick. However, flinching can also be simply a stall or delayed reaction to an offer made by an investing company. Another flinching strategy is to look up at the negotiator with wide eyes. This is definitely not a tactic for everyone, because only a few can do it and not make it look fake. However, those that can do it well have found a way to convey the thought, "Did I just hear you correctly?" through a simple body movement. It's a nonverbal method of communication that suggests to the investor that the offer may be a bit hard to get through the approval process in its current form.

Concentrating on the issues—Psychologists often like to categorize people as achievers, facilitators, and power mongers. Achievers focus on results more than people while facilitators and power mongers often focus more on people than results. (Facilitators focus on "What's in it for them?" while power mongers focus on "What's in it for me?") For these last two types, the focus on the personal side of the equation can sometimes get them into trouble when dealing with personalities instead of closing the deal. Often, the personality of the counter-party becomes such an overwhelming issue that the deal falls apart for really inane reasons. Skilled professionals do what they can to eliminate, minimize, or neutralize the personal issues and focus on the results.

Nibbling—In this strategy, the performance criteria expected from the investor is developed in stages as opposed to occurring at all once. For some economic developers, this is a hard strategy to execute, because they feel they need to lay all of their cards on the table in the first or second meeting. The community information packet may include the incentive award guidelines so as to expedite the negotiation process. When this occurs, a take-it-or-leave-it situation is created. The opposite approach of extolling certain performance standards a little bit at a time eliminates the shock that may occur with presenting everything up front. Then, the company slowly develops a relationship with the economic developer while also learning what is expected when they invest or expand in the community. As the relationship develops, the ability of the investor to accept the expected performance criteria is greatly enhanced, thereby increasing the chance for successful closure of the negotiating process.

Using patterns of concession—The economic developer must understand what the fallback position may be *and* that it matters how that position is arrived at. Returning to the tax abatement example, the community has the ability to award up to 12 years, the project qualifies for a total of ten years, and the opening brackets have been set at two years (by the community) and 12 years (by the investor). The economic developer knows they are willing to concede up to ten years; however, they have to be careful how they get there.

The most successful pattern of concession is to first establish the brackets and then to concede by decreasing amounts. Using the example of the tax abatement with brackets set at two and ten years may result in the following pattern of concessions:

Succeeding Negotiating Round	Tax Abatement Years Conceded
1	4
2	2
3	1
4	0

In this strategy, each succeeding year the concession by the economic developer is cut in half. By negotiating in this manner, a clear message that the pot is running out of money is stated in an indirect manner. In that final round when no increase occurs, the investor returns to his or her office comfortable with the fact the company has received the best deal it qualifies for and they are ready to accept the terms offered by the economic developer. Although the tax abatement example was used here, these concepts can be applied to other economic development incentives.

Using two reference points—As the economic developer negotiates the deal, two reference points work well to guide the process. The first is the incentive policy developed by the community prior to the emergence of the investor, and the second is through the use of economic impact analysis.

An incentive policy is an excellent tool for managing community expectations while also helping the practitioner find out how aggressive the community will be with the use of incentives. It often requires a great deal of upfront effort to establish this policy. However,

CONCESSIONS— A FEW MISTAKES TO AVOID

Giving it all away up front	When the economic developer concedes everything up front, it sends a wrong signal to the investing company. Assume that the investor comes back to the economic developer and states that they want the full 12 years of tax abatement. In response, the economic developer says, "I'll tell you what, I know I can give you ten years, why don't we settle on that amount and call it a day?" When the investor sees such a large concession so fast, they can be led to believe that the 12-year option is still possible. This may cause them to continue to negotiate for the 12 years and become frustrated or angry when it can't be awarded.
Conceding by increasing amounts	Occasionally, the economic developer will negotiate by giving away more years in each succeeding round of negotiations. Practitioners who follow this strategy begin with the mindset that there will only be one round of negotiations. They want to award the absolute minimum amount in the early rounds yet fail to close the deal. In later rounds, their mindset changes to one of "If I give them a little more this time maybe the deal will close." This fatal mindset awards the prospect for asking for more, as each time the amount of award becomes greater. This method should always be avoided.
Conceding by equal amounts	Again, using the tax abatement example, the economic developer is holding eight years of potential tax abatement in the pocket (the difference between their opening gambit of two years and the maximum allowable award for a project of this size of ten years). If there are four rounds of negotiation, the critical mistake here would be to award two years in each round of negotiation. Think about the message this sends: the economic developer is telling the prospect that for every request, an equal response to their request will be met. No end is established by the actions of the economic developer. Therefore, the prospect always feels that more years can be obtained by asking.

once it is in place, it defines the playing field upon which negotiations will occur. The time invested in creating this policy is invaluable.

Economic impact analysis is a process by which the economic development professional is continually calculating the impact of the project and incentive package back to the community. It creates a method by which a quantitative review of the project can be used to help determine good incentive award policies and procedures. (See Chapter 8.)

Step 2:
RECOGNIZING BUYING SIGNALS

One of the unwritten skills necessary for any economic developer is the ability to read people. In negotiations, it is one of the most essential.

During discussions with the prospect, the economic developer must detect the subtle moves made by any company or site selector. These help the practitioner know if the prospect is moving in the right direction. Some of the more common encouraging signals by the prospect are:

▶ Making positive comments about the community/site
▶ Expressing sincere interest in clarification of details
▶ Offering feedback without prompting
▶ Leaning forward in meetings and discussions
▶ Moving from cool to warmer interactions with the economic developer
▶ Smiling more and more as interactions continue
▶ Undertaking a thorough (as opposed to cursory) review of written documents
▶ Expressing a desire to visit the community or site multiple times

Obviously these signals are very important behaviors an economic developer is seeking during the negotiation process. As these signals are expressed to the investor by the practitioner, a reciprocal expression received from the investor will encourage the economic developer to press forward with structuring a deal.

INCENTIVES—
A MEANS TO AN END

Economic developers may have the widest range of experience and the greatest incidence of abuse of incentives of any profession.

Although incentives are important tools to use to extract certain behaviors from investors, the abuse of these tools by economic developers has been highly discussed in public and private circles for decades. Unfortunately, in many instances the criticism levied upon the profession may be justified.

When viewed as essential assets to secure investment in the community and close deals, incentives can be presented in a positive light. When viewed as corporate welfare, incentives can be seen as a waste of public-sector assets. Once properly understood and effectively used, incentives can be instrumental in closing a deal on the best possible terms for the community.

The charts on the following page offer some valuable guidelines to help the economic developer view and use these assets correctly.

Step 3:
CLOSING

PREPARING FOR THE CLOSE

Before entering the competition of recruiting businesses and closing deals, a foundation for successfully attracting new business must be laid. Richard L. Fosmoen's chapter, "The Public Sector's Perspective," in *Managing Development through Public/Private Negotiations*, cites three major tenets that should guide public-sector staff in negotiating a deal:

First, clearly define the public sector's objectives.

Second, always know who the players are and keep them involved.

Third, keep the negotiations as simple as possible.

The chart on page 168 expands on those three basic tenets and recommends additional tools and resources that should be in place before a community enters the competition.

INCENTIVES . . .

ARE

- **Negotiating tools.** The economic developer can move the community into greater economic return by using incentives with prospects. The incentive provides the leverage that the community needs to position for success with investment negotiations.

- **Deal-closing tools.** Incentives are used at the end of the negotiation process, not the beginning.

- **Performance rewards.** Incentives are excellent tools for extracting compliance with the master plan and zoning ordinances, achieving investment levels, and creating jobs.

- **Win/win opportunities.** When incentives are used correctly, the community creates a win for themselves by facilitating investment and job creation. They also create a win for the prospect by helping to offset or defray some of the expansion costs. Both sides win when successful incentive utilization occurs.

ARE *NOT*

- *Giveaways.* The community cannot give away what it does not have. Incentives leverage investment cash flows to help close the deal. In most cases that cash flow is generated from the new investment created by the project when the deal closes.

- *Entitlements.* No community is obliged to give away incentives. The option to offer or retain them is the community's discretion.

- *Deal openers.* Don't offer incentives in marketing letters. At the early stages of decision making, the company is looking at access to market, cost of doing business, and quality of life. After a number of communities are screened through these filters, the community will have an opportunity to close the deal. Incentives can be used effectively during the closing process.

CORPORATE INCENTIVES

One-Stop Shopping
- Expedited Permitting
- Expedited Site Plan Review
- Readiness to Assist

Infrastructure Improvements
- Local Development Fund
- Tax Increment Financing
- Special Assessment

Lowered Operating Costs
- Tax Abatements
- Utility Inducements
- Foreign Trade Zones
- PILOTS (Payment in lieu of taxes)

Land Preparation
- Adjustments to Zoning
- Land Banking
  - Discounted Land
  - Land Banking
  - Land Leases

Lowering Debt Service
- Industrial Revenue Bonds
- Loan Guarantees
- Deferred Payment Mortgages
- Interst Rate Buy-downs

Construction Assistance
- Pre-permitting
- Compatible Scheduling
- Contractor Selection
- Non-strike Agreements

WORKFORCE INCENTIVES
- Pre-employment Screening
- Workforce Investment Boards (WIB)
- Targeted Job Credits (Welfare to Work)
- Tech-transfer Funds
- Guaranteed Graduates

EMPLOYEE RELOCATION INCENTIVES
- Community Presentations
- Preapproved Mortgages
- Spousal Employment
- Temporary Housing
- Temporary Transportation
- Child Acclimation Assistance
- Discounted Home Furnishings
- Moving Cost Reimbursements
- Weekend School Programs

THINGS TO DO BEFORE CLOSING THE DEAL	
Build consensus.	Complete an economic development plan that all stakeholders in the community, city administration, and elected officials have had the opportunity to buy into and have a clear role. If the community has adopted a unified vision and strategy for accomplishing its economic development goals and objectives, the chances of the deal closing smoothly and quickly are greater. This consensus can help minimize the chances of the political card being used during negotiations and can limit the number of players on the negotiating team. There are no guarantees, however.
Make sure that all elected officials and city administrators understand their role in the business recruitment process and deal negotiations.	Completing a community assessment and establishing clear economic development goals and objectives will help keep business recruitment efforts focused and also help define the roles for city decision-makers. It's not uncommon for well-meaning stakeholders in the community to think they are experts on business attraction—specifically, what types of businesses the community needs. To a certain extent, it is desirable to have key stakeholders act as agents for attracting and supporting new businesses. The goal is to avoid chasing businesses that aren't a good fit for the community. If elected officials and other business leaders need to be involved, consider establishing a high-level advisory board or ambassador group that can assist with formal meetings at the front end. The challenge will be to keep the negotiations team separate from this high profile group.
Develop clear criteria and a community policy for incentives that all decision-makers support.	An incentive policy, developed and approved by the public body, will clearly define goals and objectives. There can be flexibility to accommodate each deal, but thresholds or triggers should be defined. A policy that includes performance expectations and clawbacks is reasonable, as long as they are stated early and consistently in the negotiations and not during the last stage or closing of the deal. "The other shoe falling" phenomenon would greatly damage the credibility of the community and the chances of closing the deal.

MAXIMIZING THE CHANCES OF CLOSING THE DEAL

On the following page is a "Top Dos and Don'ts for Closing a Deal" chart. While none of the recommendations are foolproof, they are effective for laying a foundation for a balanced economic development program and maximizing the chances of successfully closing the deal.

Step 4:
TIEING UP LOOSE ENDS

The buyer has reviewed the product and liked it. The terms of the sale have been set. The economic developer has watched the buying signals, and the prospect and community have shaken hands on the deal. Now it's time to go out for a pizza and celebrate, right? Not quite.

At this point of the negotiations, the best practitioners earn their paychecks. As the deal progresses, successful economic developers keep detailed notes in their project files. These notes define the deal and the performance expectations of both the investor and the community. At some point, these notes need to be consolidated into a concise memo and shared with the decision-makers.

There are two types of written correspondence before the closing is executed. The first is the Memorandum of Understanding (MOU), and the second is the Letter of Intent (LOI). Each serves a specific function throughout the negotiating process.

The MOU, often called a work in progress, is a brief memorandum summarizing verbal discussions held between the two parties to confirm what has been stated. Often, there are multiple versions of the MOU, so make sure that the most recent MOU is being used in the negotiations.

THE TOP DOs AND DON'Ts FOR CLOSING A DEAL

1. Conduct due diligence.
Research the prospect well in advance. Once the negotiations are under way, it's too late to start gathering intelligence about them. Corporate due diligence should include a company's industry sector profile that details its customers, suppliers, business cycles, location requirements, etc. (See Chapter 7.) A comprehensive due diligence effort includes:
- *What the company's mission and core values are.*
- *Who the senior executive are and where they live.*
- *Where the employees live.*
- *The most important location factors for the company.*

2. Always maintain the confidentiality of the client company.
Never be the source of the leak. Site-selection competitions often don't allow communities to meet face-to-face with representatives of the company during the initial stage of the inquiry. Typically, the community doesn't even know who the company is, and, once it is known, there is usually a request for confidentiality. Even though the company's identity seldom remains confidential, staff should never leak it—especially to the press—and should take every precaution to ensure that confidentiality. Violating confidentiality can create distrust on the part of the business and damage the community's credibility, both of which can complicate a closing of the deal.

3. Make sure all stakeholders are in sync.
Everyone on the team—including staff, city administration, and elected officials—needs to understand and accept his or her role in the negotiations. This task will be made easier if an economic development agenda or strategy has been developed with the participation and support of the stakeholders. Staff should meet with them in advance and clearly delineate their roles and responsibilities. If possible, they should be coached on what their appropriate response would be if the business representatives choose to circumvent staff during the negotiations process. Getting these officials to agree to a back-seat role during the negotiations is a challenge, because everyone wants to be a deal maker. Keeping elected officials briefed on a regular basis in a closed session will help.

4. Make sure the deal is facilitated by the economic development professional. Diffuse the "political" card.
If staff is successful in Point No. 3, the political option should be diffused. The deal breaker or negotiations stalemate will most likely occur over incentives. Therefore, as part of the negotiations strategy, all stakeholders should agree in advance what the maximum incentives will be.

5. Don't use additional incentives to close the deal.
The open checkbook option is easy to fall back on when negotiations stall and the deal looks shaky. Keep to the agreed cap; otherwise, once the bidding war starts, it can take on a momentum of its own that is difficult to stop. One deal for a high-tech corporate headquarters started at $9 million in public assistance and ended up costing $33 million because there was no approved incentives policy, no agreement on a cap, and no one wanted to risk losing the deal. Although it will be a difficult position to hold, know what the bottom line is for concessions in a deal and stick to it during negotiations.

6. When the deal is completed, make sure *everyone* gets kudos.
Once the public body has approved the deal, a celebration is in order. Everyone who worked on the deal deserves a special acknowledgment for his or her efforts. If there is a public ceremony for a ground-breaking or building opening, make sure that all of the elected officials and staff are invited and acknowledged. This effort goes a long way towards ensuring that the next deal goes smoothly and is just as successful.

7. Never think the deal is closed until the company moves into the building.
Be prepared for surprises. There will be many starts and stops during the site-selection competition and negotiations. Business cycles and plans change frequently and rapidly. The community must be patient, flexible, and willing to accommodate the business's timeline. It's pointless to try to control the process, but the community should always be responsive and avoid being the cause of any delays.

In less intensive negotiations, these memorandums are little more than confirmatory correspondence between the economic development office and the prospect. However, it has become common practice to have the MOU reviewed (and sometimes drafted) by the municipal attorney to ensure legal compliance during the negotiation process. Typically, but not always, the MOU addresses performance levels to be achieved by both parties to the deal.

The LOI involves the base understanding achieved by the final MOU, and it incorporates what types of actions each party may take in the event of nonperformance. These actions are often referred to as "clawbacks." Clawbacks allow the community to rescind certain incentives if the company does not provide the amount of investment nor job creation established during the negotiations. They also allow the company an option for seeking recourse on the community if they do not perform as promised. An attorney usually creates this document. It is lengthy and detailed but essential for all of the largest deals.

Once the deal is in writing and signed by all concerned, the sale can be considered approved by both sides. However, as mentioned earlier, the deal is never fully closed until the company moves into the building.

FINAL THOUGHTS

Effective economic developers learn early on that the product they are selling is their community, the customer is the investor, and the sale is closed through successful negotiation and effective use of incentives. Investment decisions move along a continuum involving negotiation, looking for buying signals, closing, and then reducing the deal to writing. The process is similar in ways to selling furniture and automobiles, but it also requires skills specific to economic development.

The payoff, however, is larger than most other sales. In economic development, the close of the sale means economic expansion, job creation, improvements in the standard of living, and strengthening the economic fabric of the community.

The greatest salespeople should be in this profession. They must be trained, informed, and, most importantly, prepared to negotiate, compromise, and win economic opportunities for their communities.

SOURCES

Dawson, Roger. *Secrets of Power Negotiating for Salespeople*. Career Press, 1999.

"15th Annual 2000 Corporate Survey," *Area Development*, December 2000.

Hopkins, Tom. *Sales Closing for Dummies*. Hungry Minds, 1998.

Karrass, Chester. *The Negotiating Game*. 1992.

Kirlin, John J., and Rachel L. Levitt, editors. *Managing Development through Public/Private Negotiations*. The Urban Land Institute and the American Bar Association, 1986.

Lyne, Jack. "'99's Top Deals: Case Studies in Fast-Track Strategies," *Site Selection*, May 1999.

Webster, Bryce. *The Power of Consultative Selling*. Prentice Hall, 1987.

About the Authors . . .

Leslie Parks was Director of Economic Development for the City of San Jose before leaving in 2001 to become a private economic development consultant. While in San Jose she was responsible for business recruitment and retention. As a private consultant she develops competitive marketing assessments for communities. Coming from Silicon Valley, she has special expertise in the high technology sector and new business models for integrating economic development and workforce development. Ms. Parks can be reached at *lparks2000@earthlink.net*.

Jim Mooney, CED, has been practicing economic development for more than two decades. He has served public and private sector clients around the globe. He is currently president of Development Services (DeSCo), an economic development consulting firm specializing in financial and market analysis. Mr. Mooney can be reached at *mooney.devserv@verizon.net*.

PROJECT TITLE _____ **PROJECT NUMBER** _____

The art of attracting a company to a community and closing the deal has many of the same attributes as selling a car or other major investment item. There are the facts and figures, the emotions of the buyer, and the relationship built between the seller and buyer during the process. Ultimately, success rests on the ability of the seller to fully understand who the actual decision-makers are and on what basis the decision is being made.

The site-selection process will vary depending on the type of operation and on the rationale for needing a new company location. Since many of these decisions are kept in strict confidentiality until the final location is selected, the community must anticipate client needs and make an educated guess on who are the true decision-makers.

Headquarters Operations

Key decision drivers include quality of life, access to company facilities and key markets, local airport and support services for corporate jets, "reasonable" operating costs, favorable business environment, and matching community and company cultures.

Items to check for:

☐ Executive needs analysis is completed and successful familiarization trips are provided for top executives and their spouses under strict confidentiality
☐ All available facilities and greenfield sites are reviewed and compared to specified needs of the client
☐ Business environment needs defined and evaluated
☐ All aspects of local quality of life defined and evaluated
☐ Executive assimilation process into community along with their community involvement expectations are discussed
☐ Applicable incentives are defined
☐ Timing on start-up is reviewed

Back Offices/Call Centers

Key drivers include cost, ability to attract and compete for local labor, and start-up time.

Items to check for:

☐ Cost analysis for construction and ongoing costs is accurate
☐ Labor resources and competitors are reviewed within commute zone of each top facility candidate
☐ All available facilities and greenfield sites are reviewed and compared to specified needs of the client
☐ Access and capacity of telecommunications for each site are reviewed
☐ Air access and cost to key company facilities are reviewed
☐ Training and education resources are reviewed against specific client needs
☐ Applicable incentives are defined
☐ Timing on start-up is reviewed

_____

* _Prepared by John M. Rhodes, President, Moran, Stahl & Boyer,_ **www.msbconsulting.com.**

PROJECT TITLE _____ PROJECT NUMBER _____

Manufacturing Operations

Key decision drivers include cost, supply chain logistics, availability of specialized skills, and start-up time.

Items to check for:

- ☐ Cost analysis for construction and ongoing costs is accurate (taxes, labor, energy, water, sewer, logistics, materials, etc.)
- ☐ All available facilities and greenfield sites are reviewed and compared to specified needs of the client
- ☐ Access and capacity of utilities for each site are reviewed
- ☐ Training and education resources are reviewed against specific client needs
- ☐ Applicable incentives are defined
- ☐ Timing on start-up is reviewed

Distribution Operations

Key decision drivers are cost, optimization of logistics, and start-up time.

Items to check for:

- ☐ Cost analysis for construction and ongoing costs is accurate
- ☐ All available facilities and greenfield sites are reviewed and compared to specified needs of the client
- ☐ Applicable incentives are defined
- ☐ Timing on start-up is reviewed

R&D Operations

Key decision drivers include access to university with target R&D programs, quality of life, reasonable access to other company facilities and markets, favorable operating costs, local technician talent, presence of key market competitors, access to venture capital, and facilities that meet needs of R&D function.

Items to check for:

- ☐ Cost analysis for construction and ongoing costs is accurate
- ☐ All available facilities and greenfield sites are reviewed and compared to specified needs of the client
- ☐ University R&D programs are reviewed
- ☐ Utility access and capacity for each site are reviewed
- ☐ Training and education resources for technical staff are reviewed
- ☐ Cost and direct destinations for air access are reviewed
- ☐ Technical labor resources are reviewed
- ☐ Presence of industry competitors is evaluated
- ☐ Applicable incentives are defined
- ☐ Venture capital options are reviewed
- ☐ Timing on start-up is reviewed

Note: *R&D operations are frequently co-located with company headquarters or manufacturing operations, which requires the criteria for each type of operation to be integrated into the overall location evaluation process.*

CHAPTER 11

PROJECT REVIEW
Searching for Reasons

Rick L. Weddle
President, Greater Phoenix Economic Council

——— ◆ ———

It has often been said that economic development is too simple for most people to understand. For some crazy reason, people seem to think that large or important problems or issues must necessarily have complex or complicated answers. When it comes to basic economic development processes, that concept is simply untrue. When it comes to the economic development site location process, we tend to complicate matters by attempting to explain why development occurs and where companies tend to locate by using and sometimes abusing almost every analytical process except the most important one. That is customer feedback or, simply put, just asking the customer why. That is what the project review process is all about: finding out the real reasons why companies locate where they do.

Unfortunately, the process of learning why companies do what they do and translating that information into actionable knowledge is not as easy as it sounds. It does require organization, discipline, and a little hard work on the part of the economic development practitioner. Consequently, a systematic and organized approach to securing and assessing customer feedback is recommended. Such a structured approach will be referred to in this chapter as a **project review**.

The following questions should be kept in mind in the project review process:

- *What is a formal economic development project review process?*
- *Why is customer feedback from the review process so important?*
- *What are the different types of reviews that should be conducted?*
- *What can be learned from a systematic review process?*
- *How should an effective project review process be organized?*
- *What do you do with, and how do you use, the project review findings?*

If all this seems too obvious and logical, then you're getting the point. Effective project reviews are simply the process of getting inside the customer's thought processes to identify and understand the rationale for their decision making. Then it is about putting the information or knowledge gained to use, either in improving your handling of future projects or correcting disadvantages so as to be more competitive the next time around. Let's take a look at what a project review is and what it is not.

As a customer feedback mechanism, the project review process is helpful with securing important market information so you can better understand what exactly it means to you and your community. It is, therefore, a key learning process essential to planning and implementing effective economic development programs and activities. A good project review process will provide you with three key insights:

This chapter originally appeared in *The Race to Recruit: Strategies for Successful Business Attraction*, Maury Forman and Jim Mooney, editors (Dubuque, IA: Kendall/Hunt Publishing Co., 1996). Reprinted with permission of the author.

> *Effective project reviews are simply the process of
> getting inside the customer's thought processes to identify
> and understand the rationale for their decision making.*

Market Intelligence—a systematic project review process covering all projects in aggregate will generate essential information regarding customer preferences, site selection and elimination factors, and the relative desirability of your various product offerings, community resources, and attributes.

Project-Specific Knowledge—critical insight into your community's competitive posture can be gained by conducting detailed reviews of specific projects. You can learn a great deal about the relative competitiveness of both how you manage the process and what you have to sell.

Competitor Information—project reviews, both company-specific and in aggregate, will reveal important competitor information. From the review, you should be able to clearly document just who your top competitors are by project type and how they compare to your community's offerings. Moreover, you can see how their recruitment process compares to what you are doing.

It is also important to remember what a project review is not. It should not be considered as a mechanism for fixing or assigning blame or fault when a project goes wrong or the community fails to attract a particular company location. Unfortunately, this is often the chief reason a project-specific review is undertaken. We've all seen examples of a project that goes wrong and places an elected official or the economic development staff under fire. There is a tendency in economic development to blame the economic development staff for failures that, more often than not, are due to fundamental competitive disadvantages that are beyond the ability of anyone to control or impact over the near-term. Of course, if there is a staff failure or management

process problem, it should and will be uncovered in a valid project review process. The problem is that when finger pointing, fault finding or blame shifting is the principal reason for undertaking a project review, then blame tends to be laid, regardless of the real reasons, at the feet of the economic development or sales staff. Attempts to document community competitive disadvantages after you are already under fire make you look defensive and appear as lame excuses at best. The only way to avoid such negative situations is to put a formal project review process with standardized procedures in place well in advance of recruitment losses or trigger incidents. In fact, a formal review process can minimize and, in some cases, prevent finger pointing and fault finding because everyone knows a formal structured process is likely to reveal and disclose the real underlying reasons for recruitment failures.

When things go well and you have just landed a new facility location, remember that the project review process is not merely a public relations tool or mechanism to give credit or glory to those who helped make the project a success. To be sure, giving credit and rewarding those who have helped is an important aspect of the process. It is not, however, the primary reason and should not overshadow the real purpose of learning how to improve the process and do better the next time around.

WHY CUSTOMER FEEDBACK IS IMPORTANT

Remember that your "next best customer" will, for the most part, have a profile just like your "last best customer." Sadly, many economic development practitioners don't get this point. They are too busy trying to manipulate detailed and sophisticated targeting models (based on a consultant's analysis of generalized industry operating requirements compared to a cursory review of your community's resources and attributes) to take the time to stop, look, and listen to their marketplace. The best source of economic development intelligence and near-term targeting information is right there before your eyes. It is direct customer feedback. It is the best source of market intelligence for two simple reasons. First of all, it is the straight truth from the customer—unfiltered and unaltered. It may, in fact, be the only real truths you will hear, because almost everyone but the customer has a vested interest in the local development process and necessarily speaks from that perspective.

Secondly, it is readily accessible and there for the taking. It lies in your files, records, recollections, conversations, and direct marketing experiences with previous and current customers or clients. It lies in the findings, conclusions, and opinions of those firms that have already considered your community and either located a facility or eliminated your community from further consideration. It is a gold mine of information. But like a gold mine, the value lies beneath the surface. In order to benefit, you must work to extract it. You must find a way to dig out—or mine—this valuable source of market data and information.

IMPORTANT FINDINGS FROM THE PROJECT REVIEW PROCESS

Let's turn now to look at just what type of valuable information or key findings you may expect from a formal structured project review process. As already noted, project reviews generally take two forms. They are:

- Ongoing systematic reviews of all projects in aggregate
- Project-specific reviews conducted on a case-by-case basis

The direct information to be gained through these two separate types of project review processes is similar but different. An ongoing review process will yield more generalized information that is highly useful in guiding the targeting of your program and the focus of your marketing efforts. Collected in aggregate form, such information is easily compared to note trends and common practices. Verification of customer trends and site location practices can help you to segment general target industry groupings and concentrate your marketing resources where they will yield the best results.

On the other hand, project-specific reviews do not generate comparative data. Rather, they provide accurate customer feedback regarding specific and detailed elements of the site location process. Company-specific project reviews will give you a clear and valid picture of the relative competitiveness of both your community's product offerings and your economic development management processes. Such detailed information is very valuable in formulating strategies and action plans needed to address specific competitiveness and/or program management issues and concerns.

CONDUCTING ECONOMIC DEVELOPMENT PROJECT REVIEWS

As noted above, two types of project review processes are recommended. A comprehensive economic development program should have an organized process in place to conduct both ongoing aggregate project reviews and the more detailed company-specific project reviews. Failing to organize such simple customer feedback mechanisms is like trying to fly blind when you don't have to. Conversely, operationalizing the process of surveying your customer base lets you operate with real time market information and may create a distinct competitive advantage for your

Customer feedback, no matter how valid or accurate, does you no good while sitting in a pile on your desk. To be valuable, it must be utilized effectively.

community and your program. Let's take a look at what it takes to begin such an important customer feedback program.

ESTABLISHING AN ONGOING PROJECT REVIEW PROGRAM

The economic development process is rarely managed so as to collect important market intelligence needed to effectively guide current and future program efforts. In planning marketing programs we tend to follow published information about target firms and decision-maker practices. We also tend to make quite a few assumptions that may or may not prove to be accurate. In the sales management process, we are usually too busy trying to get on to the next deal to take the time to put meaningful data collection and analysis programs in place. One way to avoid this situation is to establish a regular procedure for reviewing all projects, both successful and unsuccessful. It is recommended that this procedure involve a formal structured customer or client survey conducted at least twice annually.

Depending on the number of projects involved, the survey can be conducted either by telephone or by mail. Although more time consuming, the telephone survey is more highly recommended. Mail surveys may be better suited for surveying a large audience. The telephone survey is much better suited for a smaller audience, because it is more accurate and provides you with a controlled response rate. Direct telephone contact also enables you to probe for customer feedback in a more open-ended manner. Whether you use the mail or telephone approach, the process involves developing a standardized customer feedback questionnaire, rigorously surveying as many customers as possible, compiling the data in an understandable format, and then putting the information gained to good use.

PROJECT REVIEW QUESTIONNAIRE DESIGN

Considerable attention and thought needs to be given to the design of the project review questionnaire. A word of caution is due here: Many economic developers attempt to collect too much detailed information. Consequently, clients or customers are reluctant to answer such detailed questionnaires. Moreover, once the information is acquired in such detail, meaningful analysis is quite complicated and is often shelved until there is "more time to do the job right." Customer feedback, no matter how valid or accurate, does you no good while sitting in a pile on your desk. To be valuable, it must be utilized effectively.

A straightforward questionnaire that involves very simple but essential customer feedback points is all you need to yield valuable market intelligence. To this end, open-ended questions often are the most effective. While each development program should customize the list of questions for their own particular market needs and requirements, questions will typically be grouped in four specific areas:

- *Why was our community initially considered?*
- *Why was our community eliminated?*
- *Why was the successful community selected?*
- *What could have been done to change the site-selection decision?*

WHY WAS OUR COMMUNITY INITIALLY CONSIDERED?

While this may seem elementary, few if any economic developers routinely ask this question to customers or clients. Even fewer fully understand exactly why their community is considered in the marketplace by various types of clients. Most economic developers have a good understanding of site selection factors and the relative importance these factors hold in company location decisions. What many don't understand is that their particular community is often considered for reasons that may not appear on such standardized surveys.

For example, the December 1995 issue of *Area Development Magazine* published the tenth annual survey of site selection factors. This survey indicated that labor cost was the number one rated factor in final company site location decisions. Few experienced practitioners would dispute this finding. Even so, the chief reason a particular company initially considered your community for a project location will rarely be simply "labor cost."

More often than not, the initial reason for consideration may be more closely linked to more obvious factors as:

- Available building that appeared to meet initial requirements.
- All communities of a certain size in a particular market area or along a particular transportation corridor.

This doesn't mean that labor costs or other key location factors aren't important. It means that companies do things for a wide variety of reasons that often don't show up on published surveys or reports. It also means that while labor costs are vitally important in being eventually chosen as the winning location, it may not be the most important reason that companies consider your community in the first place. It follows that you can't be selected as a winning site if you aren't considered in the first place. The key with this line of questioning is to better understand what you can do to be considered initially. You want to find ways of becoming "top of mind" and, therefore, short-listed for initial consideration.

WHY WAS OUR COMMUNITY ELIMINATED FROM CONSIDERATION?

This question goes to the foundation of your community's overall competitive posture. In other words, what are the principal barriers to your success in locating new business and industry? Once again, you will be likely to find that the reasons you are frequently eliminated may or may not track directly with published information regarding site selection factors or objective assessments of your community's strengths and weaknesses. Since reasons for elimination may include both product and process issues, you should probe for open-ended answers here. Let the customer open up and speak to you entirely from the customer's point of view. This can be particularly insight-

ful. Responses to this question cover a wide range of issues but could reveal:

- The available building didn't really fit (especially if that was the only reason you were being considered in the first place). Perhaps it was the right size and cost but didn't meet the company's requirement for image or wasn't in good enough condition and would require extensive repair.
- The company was concerned about your community's ability to meet their labor availability requirements within their desired or intended cost range. For example:
  - Adequate information was not submitted to enable the company to fully assess the cost.
  - Factors that looked good on paper did not meet expectations or compare favorably with competing locations after more detailed analysis.

WHY WAS THE SUCCESSFUL COMMUNITY SELECTED?

You may be surprised to learn that the reason the successful community was selected may not be directly tied to why communities were considered in the first place or why your community was eliminated. It is not that these factors aren't related, but rather that the process of site elimination and selection varies greatly from company to company and involves a great many variables, all weighed to fit the particular company's requirements. Frequently, in response to this question you will be provided with a generalized answer that blends a number of variables together leading to a bottom line operating cost conclusion. Even so, you can find out important strategic information if you probe for open-ended responses. You may be surprised to learn answers such as some of the following:

- The successful community had an available building that closely met the company's requirements and gave them a considerable time and capital cost advantage.
- A recently approved incentive package in the successful community's state provided a substantial operating cost advantage.

- The winning community's recruitment approach tipped the balance in some unique or unanticipated way.

Note the consistent references to "available buildings" in each of the above question areas. I have long felt that an available building inventory is highly underrated on most site location factor surveys. To be sure, on balance, it is only one of many factors. However, my experience suggests that as many as 85 percent of business/industry clients begin their search by looking for an available building. So when it comes to being considered by such clients, an available building is perhaps the most important factor. This is the kind of significant customer feedback you need to be gathering from customers in your community.

It follows that if you are staying close to your customer—and your competitors—you shouldn't find yourself surprised by who is frequently beating you on recruitment deals. The key here is to probe for new trends and stay tuned to market changes that will affect future location projects. Be sure to listen and learn.

WHAT COULD HAVE BEEN DONE TO CHANGE THE SITE SELECTION OUTCOME?

This question will help you learn if, in fact, anything could have been done to change the location decision outcome. In the vast majority of instances you will be told that either there was nothing you could have done to change the outcome or the things that could have been changed were beyond your ability to impact within the project decision time frame. Even so, you should probe with open-ended questions to learn all you can about exactly what would have made a difference. Sometimes you will be surprised. Always you will end up better informed and better focused on what you could do better next time.

DESIGNATING SURVEY RESPONSIBILITY AND DECIDING WHO TO SURVEY

For consistency purposes, it is recommended that survey responsibility be designated to either one person, a group, task force, or committee that can carry through on a regular schedule. The key here is to provide both consistency and credibility, especially if the survey is being conducted by telephone. You may want to assign the responsibility for managing the process to someone in an administrative position that is not directly involved in the sales management or client handling process. This, of course, depends entirely on the size of your staff and human resource capacity.

Deciding who to survey is equally important. A comprehensive survey process will survey all customers or clients on both successful and unsuccessful projects. This will be needed to generate balanced information that will be of real use in guiding future program direction.

The survey effort should be directed to the principal individual with whom the economic development effort had direct contact. This individual is not only a key member of the site location team, but also the person in the best position to critique your efforts and your community's relative competitive posture. If he or she is unavailable or unwilling to participate, attempt to get the feedback from someone else directly involved in the location process. Direct involvement is essential, because, as you will find out, published reasons for considering and/or eliminating communities and selecting the eventual winner are usually not the only reasons. In many instances, they are not even the most important reasons. You have to cut through the public relations spin and try to find the underlying rationale.

A comprehensive survey will include all customers or clients on both successful and unsuccessful projects.

The timing for an ongoing survey process will have a direct impact on the accuracy of the information gained. Experience suggests that survey efforts conducted immediately following an unsuccessful project rarely have the accuracy or candor of later surveys. The principal reason for this is that the company may think you are still in the sales mode and are still trying to impact the project outcome. Also, all elements of the final location may not be complete and the company's focus is on wrapping up and getting the deal done, not on helping you understand what went wrong or what you could have done better. Survey experience indicates that the optimum timing for conducting surveys is six to nine months after the final decision was made. That is long enough for most of the project location work to be fully under way and quick enough so that memories remain valid.

Often you will find that, after such an interval, the lead member of the site selection team will be very candid and quite helpful in responding to your questions. This is especially true if you approach the questioning as a part of a structured process and assure that the information provided will be reported only in aggregate form, thus providing a measure of confidentiality. It is important to note that nobody will be candid about telling you where you failed or where your community is non-competitive if they think their name will end up in the newspaper. It is not good for them, you, or anyone for that to happen. If it does happen, don't expect to do any repeat business with the firm anytime soon.

COMPANY-SPECIFIC
PROJECT REVIEWS

Company-specific reviews differ from ongoing reviews in a number of ways. First, they are almost always conducted individually and soon after the project decision is made, rather than at some future time when a group of firms may be surveyed. Secondly, they are typically conducted for the express purpose of either learning what went wrong (and how it can be corrected or avoided next time) or what went right (and how it can be improved upon in the future). And finally, company-specific project reviews are sometimes conducted in an effort to conduct a cost-benefit analysis of a particular project. Or in other words, did the community provide too much, too little or just the right amount to the company, in terms of financial incentives? Such an assessment can prove helpful in selling the project to the community.

POLICIES AND PROCEDURES
FOR CONDUCTING
PROJECT REVIEWS

Since company-specific project reviews are frequently conducted at the end of an unsuccessful project, it is important to establish a standard set of policies and procedures or guidelines within which the project review will be conducted. Project review procedures should govern when and on what type of projects a full review will be conducted, who should be involved in the process, how the facts of the project will be compiled and verified, and how the findings or results will be reported or communicated to the public. Debating and adopting such procedures in advance of an actual project review will assure an orderly and productive process.

THE PROJECT REVIEW TEAM

In order to establish credibility of the project review process, the project review team should involve both those involved in the particular project and also those stakeholder groups who, although not directly involved, have a direct stake or interest in the economic development process. Representatives of those involved in the process typically include members and representatives of the recruitment team. Other stakeholder groups that may be included in the process are elected officials, public sector staff, economic development agency board of directors, organized labor, and citizen or neighborhood groups directly impacted or affected by the project.

Remember that involvement of stakeholders in the project review process is not just to secure their input and oversight of the process. If conducted correctly, the project review process will develop strategic information about the community's relative competitive posture. It is, therefore, an extremely important community leadership educational tool.

WRITTEN CHRONOLOGY OF EVENTS

Project review processes must be correctly focused or the review team may tend to ramble from issue to issue. An important starting point for focusing discussion and review is the chronology of events associated with the project under review. Remember that, after the fact, it is sometimes difficult for laypersons to understand why certain action steps were or were not taken. Putting events into chronological order will help to make sense of the process. It will also help to guide discussion along the project decision timeline so as to better understand the process from the customer or client's point of view.

COMPANY PARTICIPATION AND INVOLVEMENT

If possible, involve the company in the review process. It adds credibility to the overall effort and helps focus and guide discussion. If the recruitment effort was unsuccessful, be prepared for the company to decline to openly participate. In these instances you may try to talk to the company privately to explain the process and solicit its indirect involvement and participation.

If the recruitment process was successful, you will be more likely to secure company participation. This is especially true if the company needs your help in selling certain aspects of the project to the community. Such matters may include resolving zoning issues, coordinating transportation improvements, accomplishing utility line extensions, monitoring financial incentive compliance, and assimilating management into the community. In these instances, company participation will be likely. Their candor, especially on negative matters, may be severely limited.

PROJECT REVIEW MEETINGS

As soon as the chronology of events has been prepared, send it to the recruitment team members for review and comment. Make certain you have all the events and dates correct before sitting down to review the project. It can be quite embarrassing and damaging to your credibility if substantive corrections to the chronology have to be made or noted in the midst of the initial review meeting. It is recommended that a community leader who is supportive of the economic development program be secured to chair the project review meeting. While it is essential that the review be conducted at an arm's length from the recruitment team, it is equally important that it be conducted in a friendly environment, if at all possible.

WRITTEN SUMMARY OF FINDINGS

The project review process will culminate with the preparation of a written summary of findings. In most instances this report will be in summary form, omitting many of the details covered through the general assessment process. The summary should, however, cover and describe the following informational points and key findings:

- ▶ The purpose of the project review.
- ▶ A listing of those involved in preparing the project review.
- ▶ A description of the economic development project including the various roles and relationships of different recruitment team members in the project.
- ▶ A summary of the key factors involved in the site location process.
- ▶ A brief summary or overview of the chronology of events.
- ▶ Key reasons the community was eliminated (on unsuccessful projects).
- ▶ Key reasons the community was selected (on successful projects).
- ▶ A cost-benefit analysis of the project (on successful projects) that examines the level of direct financial incentives provided in comparison to the direct and indirect financial return to the community.

A summary of action steps (if appropriate) is recommended. The action step summary should identify and address any product or process disadvantages and the appropriate actions, both near- and long-term, needed to improve the community's competitive posture.

> *The communications plan is essential in those instances where you have been unsuccessful in recruiting a large showcase project.*

MANAGING COMMUNICATIONS

The project review process is not complete until the results, findings and conclusions are communicated to key stakeholder groups. It is, therefore, important that you develop a specific communications strategy and plan. The plan should address both internal and external, or public, audiences. Remember that an important aspect of the project review process is community education, hence the significance of a solid communications plan.

The communications plan is essential in those instances where you have been unsuccessful in recruiting a large showcase project. This is true regardless of whether the failure is due to either a community resource disadvantage or a specific failure/limitation in the economic development management process. In either instance, you want to do more that just respond to the criticism regarding the problem or failure. You want to turn the project review into a learning exercise and try to focus on either what the community needs to do over the long-term to correct the resource disadvantage or on what you are doing immediately to correct the management problem and make sure it doesn't happen again.

Remember that the public and the media find it difficult to follow long, detailed explanations. But a project review report is just that—a long and detailed explanation of a situation for which most people will seek a simple explanation. They will want to know why you won or lost, who gets the credit or blame, and what is going to be done next. Therefore, your communications plan should attempt to focus on one or two compelling issues or message points that further your overall communications objective. Your communications objective should link to the reason the report was prepared and focus, if possible, on future action.

Your communications plan should be prepared in conjunction with the project review team's work so that consensus will exist with regard to both the message and the delivery of the message. In other words, you need to make sure, to the extent possible, that everyone on the project review team is in general agreement and supportive of the overall communications message.

FINAL THOUGHTS

Now that you have collected all this information, what are you going to do with it? That depends entirely on what you have learned. Don't assume that everyone will see the project review findings and immediately understand their implications or even know what to do with the information gained. It is important that you establish direct communication links to both community leadership and economic development marketing and sales staff.

Community leaders need to be regularly apprised of the ongoing information flow from the project review process. In doing so, you will be helping to educate leadership regarding the need to constantly improve your community's competitive posture. You will be creating an awareness that the economic development program success is, in large part, dependent upon the community's ability to provide what prospective companies require from the marketplace. This education process should focus on segmenting the information into two areas: what can and cannot be changed. For example, while it is impossible to alter the distance to key markets, you might succeed in increasing market presence and economic development success by building a speculative building tailored to a particular industry segments requirements. Just as you can't directly impact the cost of labor, you can provide specialized training programs, on-the-job training subsidies, and a host of other program initiatives that may serve to improve relative competitiveness. Again, the key is not just what you learn from the process, but what you do with what you learn.

The most important near-term use of information gained from the project review process may be in the areas of industry targeting, marketing program focus, and sales management. Comparing the customer feedback to other industry targeting data should provide important insight into how general industry groups can be better segmented and thus understood. Identifying the reasons yours and other communities are initially considered can help fine-tune marketing programs to reach target firms with the correct images and messages. Understanding why and how you frequently are eliminated from further consideration will help you revise your sales management processes to remain alive in the site location process. Again, getting close to your customers and understanding their decision processes more fully will pay real dividends over time.

About the Author . . .

Rick L. Weddle joined Greater Phoenix Economic Council (GPEC) as President and CEO in July 1997. Since that time, the public/private partnership has assisted 124 companies with expansions and/or relocations to Greater Phoenix and created more than 19,500 jobs with an average salary of $36,958 (July 1997 through December 2001). These companies have generated more than $1.4 billion in capital investment and an estimated $184 million in annual state, county, and community revenues. Mr. Weddle is also the Chairman of the University of Phoenix Advisory Council and the Dean's Advisory Council at Arizona State University. In September 2002, he will become the first Chairman of the Board of International Economic Development Council, an organization formed by the merging of AEDC and the Council for Urban and Economic Development (CUED). Mr. Weddle can be reached through *rweddle@gpec.org*.

PROJECT REVIEW QUESTIONNAIRE

PROJECT TITLE _____ PROJECT NUMBER _____

WHY WAS OUR COMMUNITY INITIALLY CONSIDERED?

_____
_____
_____
_____
_____

WHY WAS OUR COMMUNITY ELIMINATED?

_____
_____
_____
_____
_____

WHY WAS THE SUCCESSFUL COMMUNITY SELECTED?

_____
_____
_____
_____
_____

WHAT COULD HAVE BEEN DONE TO CHANGE THE SITE SELECTION DECISION?

_____
_____
_____
_____
_____

PROJECT TITLE _____ PROJECT NUMBER _____

PROJECT TEAM:

Name	Organization	Key Role
_____	_____	_____
_____	_____	_____
_____	_____	_____
_____	_____	_____

KEY FACTORS INVOLVED IN SITE SELECTION / REJECTION:

a) _____
_____

b) _____
_____

c) _____
_____

d) _____
_____

e) _____
_____

CHRONOLOGY:

Date	Activity
_____	Project initiated by our organization
_____	_____
_____	_____
_____	_____
_____	Project closed as successful/unsuccessful

COST BENEFIT ANALYSIS:

$_____ Private investment
$_____ Incentives
$_____ Ratio

Washington State Office of Trade and Economic Development Resources

The Washington State Office of Trade and Economic Development offers a variety of resources to educate communities on successful economic development strategies. Some of the more popular publications include:

Building Your Hometown's Future
A strategic planning manual for community revitalization groups. Published 1994

The Race to Recruit: Strategies for Successful Business Attraction
A guidebook of strategies for business attraction with chapters written by various site selectors and practitioners. Book includes ready to use check lists for practitioners on different attraction techniques. Published 1996

Washington Entrepreneurs Guide: How to Start and Manage a Business in Washington
This guide focuses on information that will be useful to those people starting a business in Washington State. In addition to chapters that deal with all aspects of entrepreneurial activity, the book also includes a business resource directory. Published 1997

How to Create Jobs Now and Beyond 2000: A Step by Step Guide to Creating Jobs in the 21st Century
An instruction manual of creating jobs in the new millennium that outlines measures economic development professionals and volunteers can take to enhance the quality of life in their communities. Published 1998

Infrastructure Assistance Directory
An on-line database of Infrastructure Assistance Programs provided by the Infrastructure Assistance Coordinating Council. Visit the on-line directory at: www.infrafunding.wa.gov.

Infrastructure Financing for Small Communities in Washington State
The methods and sources of resources available for infrastructure financing can be confusing, complicated and costly. This manual is intended to help communities make the best decisions possible for their citizens. An extensive list of loan and grant programs is provided as part of the appendix, as well as worksheets to practice calculations and organize community information. Published 1999
   View this publication in HTML on the Web infrastructuremanual/default.htm (please note that the appendices are not available in HTML). View/download this publication in Adobe Acrobat infrastructure.pdf (please note the Adobe version is 956KB and may take several minutes to view/download) Download Adobe® Acrobat Reader® http://www.adobe.com/products/acrobat/readstep2.html here for free.

Learning to Lead: A Primer on Economic Development Strategies
Provides a general overview of the major issues related to economic development. The intent of the book is to help decision-makers make informed choices regarding their community strategies. Published: 1999
   View/download this publication in Adobe Acrobat learning_to_lead.pdf (please note the Adobe version is 2055KB and may take several minutes to view/download) Download Adobe® Acrobat Reader® http://www.adobe.com/products/acrobat/readstep2.html here for free.

Old Growth Diversification Fund Program 2001 Annual Report
The 2001 annual report describes the use of the Old Growth Diversification Fund and how it leveraged funds for Washington communities. View/download this publication in Adobe Acrobat old_growth_report.pdf.

Organizing a Successful Downtown Revitalization Program Using the Main Street Approach
This 85-page booklet contains answers to many frequently asked questions by communities beginning a downtown revitalization program. Includes step-by-step instructions for goal setting and action plan development as well as sample budgets, by-laws, and roles and responsibilities for board and committee members. Published 2000

View/dowload this publication in Adobe Acrobat) ../downtown/manual_color.pdf (please note, this publication may take up to two minutes to open).

Tips for Writing Grant Proposals
This handbook offers practical tips for community organizations and local governments as they seek help with community economic development projects. Published 1996

View/download this publication in Adobe Acrobat grant_tips.pdf (please note the Adobe version is 203KB and may take a minute to view/download) Download Adobe® Acrobat Reader® http://www.adobe.com/products/acrobat/readstep2.html here for free.

A Workbook for Project Development
This workbook outlines the steps needed to develop an economic development project.

Keeping Business Happy, Healthy, and Local: A Business Retention and Expansion Primer, 2nd Edition
This publications lays out a strategy to help economic development practitioners identify the needs and concerns of existing business and develop plans and programs to assist them, thereby ensuring their economic health. Published 2002

Community Wisdom
A light hearted yet educational look at economic development offering 75 tips, ideas and thoughts that practitioners should be aware of. Published 2002

Ordering Information
Please contact the Office of Trade and Economic Development via:
email: cac@cted.wa.gov
mailto:cac@cted.wa.gov
Include the publication title, your name, address, and phone number. Please note, there may be a charge for publications or some publications may be sold out or out of print.